A Multidisciplinary Handbook of
Child and Adolescent
Mental Health
for Front-line Professionals

of related interest

Supporting the Mental Health of Children in Care
Evidence-Based Practice
Edited by Jeune Guishard-Pine OBE, Gail Coleman-Oluwabusola and Suzanne McCall
Foreword by Jenny Pearce OBE
ISBN 978 1 84905 668 7
eISBN 978 1 78450 172 3

Introducing Mental Health, Second Edition
A Practical Guide
Caroline Kinsella and Connor Kinsella
ISBN 978 1 84905 596 3
eISBN 978 1 78450 050 4

A Practical Guide to Mental Health Problems in Children with Autistic Spectrum Disorder
It's not just their autism!
Khalid Karim, Alvina Ali and Michelle O'Reilly
ISBN 978 1 84905 323 5
eISBN 978 0 85700 697 4

Responding to Self-Harm in Children and Adolescents
A Professional's Guide to Identification, Intervention and Support
Steven Walker
ISBN 978 1 84905 172 9
eISBN 978 0 85700 306 5

Reflective Practice in Mental Health
Advanced Psychosocial Practice with Children, Adolescents and Adults
Edited by Martin Webber and Jack Nathan
ISBN 978 1 84905 029 6
eISBN 978 0 85700 396 6

Understanding Attachment and Attachment Disorders
Theory, Evidence and Practice
Vivien Prior and Danya Glaser
ISBN 978 1 84310 245 8
eISBN 978 1 84642 546 2
Part of the Child and Adolescent Mental Health series

A Multidisciplinary Handbook of
Child and Adolescent Mental Health
for Front-line Professionals
Third Edition

Nisha Dogra, Andrew Parkin,
Fiona Warner-Gale and Clay Frake

Jessica Kingsley *Publishers*
London and Philadelphia

First published in 2018
by Jessica Kingsley Publishers
73 Collier Street
London N1 9BE, UK
and
400 Market Street, Suite 400
Philadelphia, PA 19106, USA

www.jkp.com

Library of Congress Cataloging in Publication Data
Names: Dogra, Nisha, 1963- author. | Parkin, Andrew (Child and adolescent
    psychiatrist), author. | Warner-Gale, Fiona, author. | Frake, Clay, author.
Title: A multidisciplinary handbook of child and adolescent mental health for
    front-line professionals / Nisha Dogra, Andrew Parkin, Fiona Warner-Gale
    and Clay Frake.
Description: Third edition. | London ; Philadelphia : Jessica Kingsley
    Publishers, 2017. | Preceded by A multidisciplinary handbook of child and
    adolescent mental health for front-line professionals / Nisha Dogra ...
    [et al.]. 2nd ed. c2009. | Includes bibliographical references and index.
Identifiers: LCCN 2017022484 | ISBN 9781785920523
Subjects: | MESH: Mental Health | Child | Adolescent | Mental Health Services
    | Psychology, Adolescent | Psychology, Child
Classification: LCC RJ499.3 | NLM WS 105.5.M3 | DDC 618.92/89--dc23 LC
record available at https://lccn.loc.gov/2017022484

British Library Cataloguing in Publication Data
A CIP catalogue record for this book is available from the British Library

ISBN 978 1 78592 052 3
eISBN 978 1 78450 309 3

Printed and bound in Great Britain

Contents

CHAPTER 1

Defining Mental Health

Definitions of mental health

There is no one definition of mental health in children and young people. It is considered to be an over-arching concept about the quality of well-being in people's lives. It is generally agreed that is influenced by a number of factors, but only one of these is ill-health. There is a range of terminology used when talking about and defining mental health in children, which can include mental well-being, emotional well-being, and psychological well-being, as well as mental health. Some people tend to steer away from using the term 'mental health' as it is still considered to have stigmatising connotations, and can sometimes be thought to imply negativity or the notion of illness. In order to take account of this, some definitions place an emphasis on positive outcomes, or on the absence of negative conditions.

The World Health Organization (WHO) definition (2014) seems to be aligned to the concept of mental health as a dynamic state, within which the individual can develop their own potential, and build positive relationships with others, defining mental health as:

> Positive mental health is essential if children are to flourish and lead rich and fulfilling lives. It provides a solid foundation for all aspects of development. Many things can contribute to a child or young person being mentally well. These aspects are relevant to all children and young people, not just those with difficulties or vulnerabilities, and include physical health and well-being, nutrition and exercise, as well as family, relationships, education, leisure time and social life, as well as a sense of confidence and self-esteem. Understanding what a mentally healthy child looks like can help professionals to sustain it and to focus on areas that can be strengthened: it can also help to identify areas where there may be difficulties and to think about interventions that might help.

There are a few commonly used definitions that are used to describe mental health in children and young people in ways that most of us can recognise. The Health Advisory Service (1995, p.5) suggested the following definition of mental health:

- a capacity to enter into and sustain mutually satisfying personal relationships

- continuing progression of psychological development

- an ability to play and learn so that attainments are appropriate for age and intellectual level

- a developing moral sense of right and wrong

- the degree of psychological distress or maladaptive behaviour is appropriate to the age of the child and the context within which they live.

This definition implies that there is an ideal state of mental health that all strive to reach. Another similar and also commonly used definition (Mental Health Foundation 1999) suggests that children who are emotionally healthy will have the ability to:

- develop psychologically, emotionally, creatively, intellectually and spiritually

- initiate, develop and sustain mutually satisfying personal relationships

- face problems and setbacks, resolve them and learn from them in ways appropriate for the child's age

- be confident and assertive

- use and enjoy solitude

- become aware of others and empathise with them

- play and learn

- develop a sense of right and wrong.

Again, this definition may be criticised for presenting an idealised and simplified view of mental health. It also perhaps fails to acknowledge the diversity of human responses to different experiences and the diversity of human individuality and ability. However, both definitions focus on trying to define what mentally healthy young people should be able to do should they so wish and, in that way, they begin to provide some clarity about when young people are not mentally healthy. The second definition makes no mention of developmental issues. These play a central part in young people's mental health, so it is important to take them into consideration.

Mental health is to some extent a culturally bound concept, and these definitions are clearly set out from Western perspectives. Despite this, they provide a common starting point from which young people's mental health can be considered. It is important to remember that good mental health is not a static state, good mental health is dependent on several factors and a change in these factors may lead to changes in mental health status.

Mental health as a continuum

It is important to emphasise that there is a continuum between mental well-being and mental disorder or mental illness. At one end of the spectrum is complete mental health and at the other severe mental disorder. The continuum between the range of 'normal' human experience and mental disorder (with the possible exception of psychosis) means that the cut-off between what is normal and abnormal can be hard to define. Mental health problems can emerge along the continuum and may or may not culminate in a diagnosis of mental illness or disorder.

It is not just the presence of symptoms that defines a disorder but also its impact on the individual's functioning. For example, feelings of anxiety before big events are perceived as a normal response and something that most people experience. However, in some individuals the levels of anxiety may prevent functioning and therefore warrant attention. In others, the symptoms may be severe but manageable and therefore not seen as limiting. Similarly, a phobia of spiders may have little impact on an individual, whereas a phobia of needles may be less easily ignored.

Using the notion of a continuum, there are behaviours that in certain contexts may indicate mental illness. These can include erratic behaviour, mood lability (changeable mood), agitation, disinhibition, paranoia, incoherent speech, unusual or inappropriate repetitive actions, hearing voices, and holding fixed irrational beliefs that are not culturally contextual. However, it is important to note that these behaviours may also be indicative of other problems that are not associated with mental health, such as confusional states due to infection or intoxication.

Further concepts around 'well-being' and mental health have suggested that it is important to view the mental health continuum as a 'health continuum'. Being able to do this means that we must add an extra axis, which takes into account the well-being of the individual within their own abilities and whether or not they are subject to distress. For example, a young person could have a diagnosed mental health disorder or illness, yet be achieving good mental health, i.e. accessing help, enjoying a good quality of life and being free from distress (Jorm *et al.* 1997). This can be viewed within a four-quadrant diagram where a young person can move from one quadrant to another dependant on the current life situation and state of well-being.

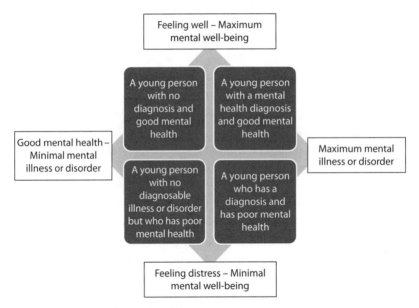

Figure 1.1 States of mental well-being

It must be recognised that there can be an inability or unwillingness by some young people, parents and professionals to recognise that distress is a component of human experience and not necessarily a mental health problem. If this is recognised, it can be appropriately addressed rather than labelled as a mental health problem and passed on to specialists for management. It is also important to empower individuals to take responsibility for their own health, including mental health, in appropriate ways. That requires greater openness and willingness to talk about mental health. It means making mental health everyone's business. All professionals working with young people have a responsibility to consider young people's psychological health as well as to pay attention to their physical health.

Stigma surrounding mental health

Evidence has shown us that emerging mental health problems are very common in children and young people, affecting at least one in every four each year. At any given time, one in 10 children and young people have a *diagnosable* mental health problem (Green *et al.* 2005). However, only 40 per cent of these receive professional help (CMO 2012). Evidence indicates that children and young people, in general, tend to show low levels of help-seeking in relation to their mental health and only around 40 per cent of parents would admit to anyone that they had a child with a mental health problem (Time to Change 2012). In particular, this avoidance of help-seeking is more of an issue amongst boys and young men than it is in girls. It is often because of the stigma attached to being identified as having a mental health problem that many young people avoid asking for help until the point that their problems become a very real crisis for them.

> Young people are afraid to admit to having a mental health problem through fear and shame. Many young people end up suffering in silence until something drastic happens. (Young Person, Time to Change, 2012)

The extent of stigma is widespread, far-reaching and can affect people throughout their lifespan. In a report published by Time to Change (2014), 9 out 10 people interviewed, reported that they had experienced some form of stigma in relation to their mental health problems (Time to Change 2014). Stigma is described as having a severe impact on the confidence and ability of those needing help. In fact, some people who have experienced stigma and discrimination because of their mental health problems have described the experience as equal to, if not worse than, the mental health problem itself (Pescosolido *et al.* 2007; Young Minds 2011).

The severe and pervasive effects of the stigma of mental health are known to impact on both individuals and families, and can result in intense feelings of shame, isolation and social exclusion (Wahl 1999). There is an increasing body of knowledge that has explored the impact of stigma in children and young people who may have mental health needs. It has been acknowledged that there is potential for the effect of stigma to be so insidious that it can significantly reduce access to children's mental health services; it can create fear, marginalisation and low self-esteem in children, and diminish the effectiveness of help and interventions. Stigma can have such a significant effect that there is a potential for mental health problems to increase in severity.

Many of the terms used to describe people with mental health problems are derogatory. Individuals with mental illness are often perceived to be unpredictable (volatile, emotional, unstable, off-the-wall), aggressive (violent, crazy) or having 'something missing'. There is little differentiation between mental health problems and formal mental illness within the general public. Terms may be loosely used and poorly understood. There is also a discrepancy between lay and professional use of widely used terms such as depression, panic and stress.

The stigma related to mental health has been described as a global concern (WHO 2014), and it affects people with mental health problems worldwide, in many different ways. It is said to be highly prevalent and has persisted over time. In fact, studies undertaken by the Indiana University, Bloomington (2015) have suggested that the disparity in outcomes for people with serious mental illness are, in part, due to the cultural norms, attitudes and behaviours towards people with mental illness across societies.

There are at least three main reasons for stigmatisation, which is a complex area:

- a fear of people with mental health problems because of perceived aggression and unpredictability; there can also be fears that individuals with mental illness have criminal intentions

- concerns that there can be a fine line between 'normal' experience and mental health problems: it is often easier to see mental health problems as belonging to others (i.e. 'them-and-us') as this allows individuals not to have to consider the vulnerability we all have to experiencing mental health problems – a fear of the unknown and an unwillingness to be open about mental illness can perpetuate prejudice

- conflicting cultural/religious beliefs about the causes of behaviour (e.g. djinns or possession).

The stigmatisation process incorporates three elements that happen within individuals, groups and society as a way of communicating the negative effects of stigma: problems of knowledge (ignorance), problems with attitudes (prejudice) and problems with behaviour (discrimination) (Thornicroft *et al.* 2009).

- *Knowledge* relates to poor understanding and ignorance about mental health and well-being and how it can affect people and potentially themselves.

- *Prejudice* relates to negative, emotive pre-judgements and attitudes about mental health.

- *Discrimination* can be defined as the poor or less favourable treatment of people, including a reduction in access to life chances, opportunities and resources, which can arise as a result of stigma. Discrimination may be applied to people with mental health problems on the basis of belief, perceptions and alleged or other attributed characteristics, rather than actual ones.

Children and young people have shared their experiences, thoughts and ideas about stigma and how to change the way that people view mental health for the better. They feel that stigma should be tackled early on, and across the generations and organisations. They can see that the key places to talk about mental health are in schools and colleges, and that messages can be communicated through social media, digital methods and by hearing real stories about mental health and recovery.

Children, young people and their families want to be at the centre of approaches to tackle stigma and they want to learn new skills and gain confidence to talk about mental health. However, they say it is the responsibility of us all to help to make change happen (Warner-Gale, Walker and Tuffrey 2016).

Ways in which stigma can be addressed are described in Chapter 16.

Exercise 1.1: Reflective questions

1. How comfortable are you talking about mental health and mental health problems?

2. What terms do you use to describe mental health problems or individuals experiencing mental health problems?

3. What is your own understanding and experience of mental health and mental health problems?

4. Do you think there are areas of your practice in which you could do more to help de-stigmatise mental health problems? If not, what are you already doing to ensure that you provide equitable services (whatever area you are in) to all young people you come into contact with?

5. If you think you could do more to de-stigmatise mental health, how do you think you might be able to do this?

References

Chief Medical Officer (2012) 'Our Children Deserve Better: Prevention Pays.' In *Mental Health Problems in Children and Young People.* London: Department of Health.

Green, H., McGinnity, A., Meltzer, H., Ford, T. and Goodman, R. (2005) *Mental Health of Children and Young People in Great Britain, 2004.* London: Office of National Statistics.

Health Advisory Service Report (1995) *Together We Stand: The Commissioning, Role and Management of Child and Adolescent Mental Health Services.* London: HMSO.

Jorm, A.F., Korten, A.E., Jacomb, P.A., Christensen, H., Rodgers, B. and Pollitt, P. (1997) '"Mental health literacy": A survey of the public's ability to recognise mental disorders and their beliefs about the effectiveness of treatment.' *Medical Journal of Australia 166,* 4, 182–186.

Mental Health Foundation (1999) *Bright Futures: Promoting Children and Young People's Mental Health.* London: Mental Health Foundation.

Pescosolido, B.A., Perry, B.L., Martin, J.K., McLeod, J.D. and Jensen, P.S. (2007) 'Stigmatizing Attitudes and Beliefs about Treatment and Psychiatric Medications for Children with Mental Illness.' *Psychiatric Services 58,* 5, 613–618.

Indiana University, Bloomingtom (2015) 'Stigma in a global context – mental health study.' Available at www.indiana.edu/~sgcmhs/index.html, accessed on 6 June 2017.

Time to Change (2012) *Children and Young People's Programme Development: Summary of Research and Insights.* London: Time to Change. Available at http://www.time-to-change.org.uk/sites/default/files/TTC%20CYP%20Report%20FINAL.pdf, accessed on 6 June 2017.

Time to Change (2014) *National Attitudes Report 2013.* London: Time to Change.

Thornicroft, G., Rose, D., Law, A., Evans-Lacko, S. *et al.* (2009) *Moving People Evaluation Protocols: Evaluation of the National Anti-Stigma Programme in England 2008–2011.* Unpublished report, Institute of Psychiatry, London.

Wahl, O.F. (1999) 'Mental health consumers' experience of stigma.' *Schizophrenia Bulletin 25*, 467–478.

Warner-Gale, F., Walker, L., and Tuffrey, A. (2016) 'Working in Partnership with Children and Young People to Tackle Mental Health Stigma: Together We can Change Minds.' In T. McDougall (ed.) *Children and Young People's Mental Health: Essentials for Nurses and Other Professionals.* London: Routledge.

World Health Organization (2014). *Mental Health: A State of Wellbeing.* Available at www.who.int/features/factfiles/mental_health/en, accessed on 6 June 2017.

Young Minds (2011) *Stigma – A Review of Evidence.* Available at www.childhub.org/en/system/tdf/library/attachments/stigma-review.pdf?file=1&type=node&id=24940, accessed on 17 July 2017.

Further reading

Bella-Awusah, T., Adedokun, B., Dogra, N., and Omigbodun, O. (2014) 'The impact of a mental health teaching programme on rural and urban secondary school students' perceptions of mental illness in southwest Nigeria.' *Journal of Child and Adolescent Mental Health 26*, 3, 207–215,

Gale, F. (2008) 'Tackling the Stigma of Mental Health in Vulnerable Children and Young People.' In P. Vostanis (ed.) *Mental Health Interventions and Services for Vulnerable Children and Young People.* London: Jessica Kingsley Publishers.

McDougall, T. (ed.) (2016) *Children and Young People's Mental Health: Essentials for Nurses and Other Professionals.* London, Routledge.

Time to Change (2014) *Making a drama out of a crisis.* Available at www.time-to-change.org.uk/sites/default/files/Making_a_drama_out_of_a_crisis.pdf, accessed on 17 July 2017.

Vostanis, P. (ed.) (2007) *Mental Health Interventions and Services for Vulnerable Children and Young People.* London: Jessica Kingsley Publishers.

CHAPTER 2

Meeting the Mental Health Needs of Young People

How common are mental health problems in young people?

It is now recognised that many mental health problems can begin in childhood. Given the number of epidemiological studies (surveys that are usually based in the community and aim to identify the number of individuals experiencing specific problems), it can be somewhat difficult to understand why there are still such variable rates of recorded prevalence (that is the number of cases) of mental health problems in young people. Generally, studies use one of two approaches. The first is to use the classification and diagnostic manuals that exist – the Diagnostic and Statistical Manual of Mental Disorders (American Psychiatric Association 2013) and the International Classification of Diseases (World Health Organization 2016) – wherein a disorder is classed as present if the diagnostic criteria are met as defined by these manuals. The second approach is to ask about general symptomatology and describe 'caseness' (that is, that the person being asked has enough symptoms to be defined as a clinical case) if a certain threshold is reached irrespective of what the diagnosis is on a classificatory system. However, many emerging mental health problems in children and young people occur further down the continuum of mental health, and it is now recognised that there are significant benefits from intervening early, as in many cases children can be prevented from developing more serious mental health concerns.

Studies will give different results depending on the measures used and the cultural context in which they are used. The Child Behaviour

Checklist (CBCL: Achenbach and Edelbrock 1983) is a widely-used measure and has been developed to be completed by parents, young people and teachers. It defines caseness by a checklist, which is then scored. Thus, for example, a prevalence study using the CBCL in Vietnam found that Vietnamese young people had lower CBCL scores than standard US norms (McKelvey *et al.* 1999).

In the UK and many other countries, the Strengths and Difficulties Questionnaire (SDQ) is also widely used for screening emotional and behavioural problems in children and young people (Goodman *et al.* 2000). It can be used in clinical assessment, evaluating progress and outcomes, epidemiology and research. Many children and young people's mental health services use the tool as part of their initial assessment.

The SDQ includes questions about 25 attributes, some from a positive and others from a negative perspective. The 25 items are divided between five scales of five items each. The five scales enable the generalising of scores for conduct, hyperactivity, emotional problems, peer problems, and pro-social behaviour; all but the last are summed to generate a total difficulties score. There are three versions: one for self-reporting in ages 11–17, and two for the parent or teacher to complete, related to ages 4–10 and 11–17.

The total SDQ scores can be classified according to established norms (cut-offs), which define the level of 'caseness', i.e. whether or not the score would fall into the realms of producing a possible clinical diagnosis for the child. The scores are then grouped within three domains – normal, borderline and abnormal. The scores can also be used to demonstrate which areas the children's needs might be related to. Scores falling into the abnormal score band would be considered likely to identify probable 'cases' for mental health disorders. Goodman (1997) undertook several studies using the SDQ and found that approximately 10 per cent of a community sample, i.e. those not perceived as having a mental health need, would fall into the abnormal band, with a further 10 per cent falling into the borderline band. It has been suggested that prediction of mental health disorder is more reliable when employing multi-informants (Goodman *et al.* 2000).

This may reflect a true difference in the prevalence of disorders or it may reflect different cultural conceptualisation of what constitutes a disorder or a problem. The design of the measure may also be culturally contextual.

The World Happiness Report cites research that found over half of children who have a mental health problem will experience mental ill health as adults. Furthermore, it also suggests that mental health problems such as depression can be more disabling than physical problems such as arthritis or asthma (Helliwell, Layard and Sach 2016). Worldwide, approximately 10–20 per cent of children and adolescents experience mental health disorders and a large number of these young people remain untreated as services to support them simply do not exist (WHO 2005). Other figures given by WHO support the view that young people's mental health is an important issue: for example, 17 million young people aged 5–17 in Latin America and the Caribbean are affected by disorders severe enough to require treatment; 10 per cent of schoolchildren in Alexandria, Egypt, suffer from depression, and anxiety in final-year schoolchildren is 17 per cent. In the US, a youth survey estimated that 13 per cent of children aged 8–15 have a diagnosable mental disorder (Centers for Disease Control and Prevention 2012). A survey in Great Britain (Office for National Statistics 2005, 2015) found rates of 10 per cent in 5–15-year-olds of similar mental health disorders. It also determined that boys are more likely to have a mental health problem and that prevalence increased with age. This gender difference is consistent with findings from other countries. More recently, in 2009 and 2014, mental ill health prevalence was compared across two cross-sectional samples of children aged 11–13 in England. It was found that there were similar levels of mental ill health (19.7% compared with 19.0%) in both cohorts (Fink *et al.* 2015). However, this study found that there had been an increase in emotional problems in girls, and a decrease in boys presenting a risk of developing mental health problems over the time period.

Recently, however, there has been an indication that mental health problems in young people are on the rise – a Global Burden of Disease study, which compared both physical and mental health problems worldwide from 1990 to 2010, found that the prevalence of mental health difficulties, more particularly anxiety and depression, has increased over this period in developing countries, with the largest increase typically occurring in adolescents and young people (Murray and Lopez 2013).

Generally, the cross-cultural comparison of prevalence rates tends to show that there are great similarities in the characteristics of psychopathology manifested in different settings, although rates of symptomatology vary (Bird 1996). Prevalence rates of child mental health problems are generally between 15 and 20 per cent. The diagnostic measure studies are less comparable than the ones using CBCL as they have a greater potential for different interpretations. However, it is still difficult to say whether the divergent rates reflect different rates in different cultures or contexts or differing data collection methods.

There can also be different rates within the same country, for instance, between different environments. The prevalence rates for inner-city areas are generally higher than for rural areas. The prevalence rates using diagnostic measures range from 12.4 per cent (in France) to 51.3 per cent (in Germany) but are consistently above 10 per cent. Even studies that have different prevalence figures consistently show that boys have greater rates of 'externalising' problems (i.e. problems that are expressed through behaviour that impacts on the external environment, such as aggression, non-compliance, and so on) and girls of 'internalising' problems (i.e. behaviours that reflect a turning inwards, such as depression, anxiety and deliberate self-harm) (Bird 1996). Prepubertal girls have fewer problems than boys of the same age, but the rates of problems in girls increase with age. Rates are also consistently higher in poorer deprived areas. Rates also vary between reports by parents and self-reports by young people.

Models of Children and Young People's Service Provision described over two decades ago in the Health Advisory Service (HAS) Report (1995) were of a four-tiered model of service provision in the UK, and it is still a widely-accepted framework for configuring services. Although there is some variation in the way the framework has been developed and applied across the country, it has created a common language for describing and commissioning services, and planning young people's mental health services from prevention through to the management of mental health problems.

More recently, however, there has been a move towards mapping the concepts of universal (tier one or primary care), targeted (tier two) and specialist services (tiers three and four) onto the tiered model. These terms are used across children's services more widely. Within this model, an emphasis is being placed on early intervention, the importance of which has been well rehearsed in research. These terms have now largely replaced the tiered levels of provision when talking about which organisations are best placed to provide support across the pathway.

The direction of travel for services in the UK, is to move away from the tiered model of provision towards a more integrated, needs-based service model (which addresses in part the concept of universal, targeted and specialist services), in order to address provision of children's mental health services more strategically through a pathway approach. This move has been advocated in recent policy in England (Department of Health/NHS England 2015).

There are a number of emerging models of service provision developing in the UK, including the tiered model, which are set out below.

The four-tiered model

Within this model, most children and young people with mental health problems will be seen at tiers one and two of provision. However, it is important to bear in mind that neither services nor people fall neatly into tiers. For example, many practitioners work in both tier two and tier three services. Similarly, a child or young person may move up through the tiers if their presentation becomes more complex. However, in reality, some children require services from a number (or even all) of the tiers at the same time.

The tiered model is not intended as a rigid template but more as a conceptual framework for ensuring that a comprehensive range of services are commissioned and available to meet *all* the mental health needs of children and young people in an area, with clear referral routes between tiers.

Tier one

Children and young people's mental health services at tier one are provided by practitioners working with children in universal services on a day-to-day basis, who are not mental health specialists. Tier one practitioners are able to offer general advice and treatment for less severe problems. They contribute towards mental health promotion, identify problems early in the child or young person's development, can offer some support and can refer to more specialist services, if mental health needs are more complex or severe.

This tier includes agencies that offer first-line services to the public and with whom they make direct contact. It encompasses education, social services, health and voluntary agencies. This level is beyond that of the support available within the family and the community and involves outside agencies in the management of the young person's problems. They are services (sometimes also referred to as mainstream or primary care services) that are provided to, or are routinely available to, all children and their families. Universal services are designed to meet the sorts of needs that all children have. They include early years provision, mainstream schools and youth services for example, as well as health services provided by GPs, midwives, health visitors and school nurses.

At tier one there may also be specific services that provide support aimed at particular groups of children, but often from within universal (or mainstream) services. Tier one can also include services provided directly to individual children who have been identified as having additional needs, such as those provided via schools to children with special educational needs. Targeted services may be provided within this tier that also include services aimed at groups of children and their families with more complex needs, such as targeted parenting support. Recent guidance in England, 'Future in Mind' (Department of Health/ NHS England 2015), suggests that embedding targeted services within universal settings can ensure more rapid support without the delay of formal referral, and enable front-line practitioners to seek help and advice. Developing networks across universal and specialist professionals can strengthen inter-professional relationships and trust.

Tier two

Mental health practitioners at tier two level tend to be working in teams in community and universal settings (although many may also work as part of tier three services).

Tier two practitioners offer consultation to families and other practitioners. They are also key in identifying more severe or complex needs requiring further assessment and/or specialist intervention (which may lead to treatment at a different tier), and providing training to practitioners at tier one level.

They can be from a variety of multidisciplinary backgrounds with some specialist knowledge of child and adolescent mental health. Tier two could include those universal level staff in health, social services, education, specialist voluntary agencies or nongovernmental organisations who have specialist training or responsibilities relating to mental health.

Tier three

This is usually a specialist multidisciplinary team or service working in a community mental health clinic or a specialist children's mental health outpatient service, providing a specialised service for children and young people with more severe, complex and persistent disorders. It can sometimes comprise professionals who also work at tier two.

Team members are likely to include child and adolescent psychiatrists, social workers, clinical psychologists, community psychiatric nurses, cognitive behaviour therapists, family therapists, child psychotherapists, occupational therapists, and art, music and drama therapists.

Tier three can also include more detailed multidisciplinary assessments of individuals over a longer period of time than is usual for tier two. This includes day resource assessment and management facilities, which use the input from all members of a multidisciplinary team to provide different perspectives. They usually see young people who have been seen by tier two/three staff in an outpatient clinic context.

Tier four

This is defined as very specialised mental health interventions and care provided by health, social and education services for relatively few, but very troubled, young people who have the most complex psychological and psychiatric problems. It includes highly specialised outpatient services, and inpatient services, as well as some regional and national centres that provide specific interventions. These can include secure forensic adolescent units, eating disorders units, specialist neuro-psychiatric teams, and other specialist teams (e.g. for children who have been sexually abused), usually serving more than one district or region.

It must be noted that some young people may need access to inpatient care for their mental health needs without the involvement of other agencies. The healthcare staff, though, will need to liaise with education services to ensure that the young person's educational needs are met.

The stepped-care model

The stepped-care model is recommended by the National Institute for Health and Clinical Excellence (NICE 2011) and can help to organise the provision of services and to help people with common mental health disorders, their families, carers and healthcare professionals to choose the most effective interventions (British Psychological Society 2012). In the stepped-care model, the least intensive intervention that is appropriate for a young person is typically provided first, and people can step up or down the pathway according to their changing needs and in response to treatment. Implementation of the stepped-care model aims to enable children and young people to achieve their full potential by reducing the impact of mental health and emotional problems through improved provision of coordinated care across child health, social care and specialist children and young people's mental health services.

The THRIVE model

In recent years, there has been a coherence developed about what an ideal children's and young people's mental health service might look like, with an increased focus on work in schools and promotion of community and individual resilience.

The THRIVE model (Figure 2.1) (Timely, Helpful, Respectful, Innovative, Values-based, Efficient) (Wolpert *et al.* 2014) proposes to address some of the issues outlined above and is aligned to emerging thinking on payment systems, quality improvement and performance management. The model outlines groups of children and young people and the sort of support they may need and tries to draw a clearer distinction between treatment on the one hand and support on the other. Rather than an escalator model of increasing severity or complexity, the model suggests 'resource-homogenous groups' (although it is understood that there will be variations in needs within each group) who share a conceptual framework as to their current needs and choices.

The THRIVE model (Figure 2.1) presents four clusters for young people with mental health issues and their families, as part of the wider group of young people who are supported to thrive by a variety of prevention and promotion initiatives in the community. The diagram to the left describes the input that is offered for each group and the diagram to the right describes the state of being of people in that group. It has been developed using language informed by consultation with young people and parents with experience of mental health services.

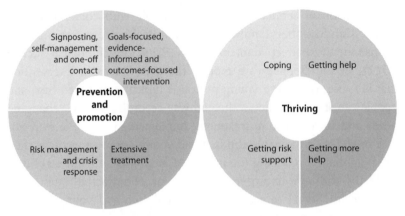

Figure 2.1 The THRIVE model: Four conceptual clusters of care

Each of the four groupings is distinct in terms of:

- needs and/or choices of the individuals within each group
- skill mix required to meet these needs
- dominant metaphor used to describe needs (well-being, ill health, support)
- resources required to meet the needs and/or choices of people in that group
- the groups are not distinguished by severity of need or type of problem.

The middle designation of 'thriving' is included to indicate the wider community needs of the population supported by prevention and promotion initiatives.

Hub model

The hub model was developed in response to the need for a new local infrastructure for services and support for children, young people and families – from early intervention to social care (4Children 2016). The idea of the hub model is to have new and expanded 'hubs' at the heart of every community for support and advice, bringing together and coordinating services, from midwives and health visitors to childcare and support for young people, building early intervention in at the core, and including support for families with complex needs, safeguarding, child protection and social care.

In summary, the approach would:

- create local Children and Family Hubs

- further embed these at the heart of their communities, bringing together local support and resources in a joined-up way

- continue to develop the strength of providing universal as well as targeted services, building Early Intervention and offering support as their core business as well as providing support for families with complex needs

- support children as they grow up, from 0–19 years.

Hub services can be rather diverse in order to accommodate and respond to local need.

The management of young people's mental health problems in universal services (Primary Care)

For many young people, especially preschool children, attendance at the general practitioner's (GP or family doctor) surgery is very common. On average, around 90 per cent of preschool children are taken to their GP in one year. This figure is still high among older children, around 65 per cent per year. The majority of young people see their doctor for physical health problems; only a small proportion (2–5%) present with some form of mental health problem (emotional or behavioural difficulties). However, research has shown that up to a quarter of children attending primary care have mental health problems and although these children are regular attendees, they mainly present with physical rather than mental health symptoms (Sayal and Taylor 2004). These rates are higher than those found in the general community. A range of mental health problems are seen in universal services. These problems can include behavioural problems, hyperactivity and anxiety, all of which can cause major concerns for parents. There can also be a number of young people who present with physical symptoms (such as headaches, nausea, abdominal pain), who have associated mental health problems (around a quarter of those presenting with physical problems). These presentations are sometimes called psychosomatic presentations – that is, physical symptoms are presented but the underlying problem is psychological.

Although these figures relate to known presentations, it is acknowledged that many more problems are present in the general population that are either not recognised or not presented. Professionals in universal services are well positioned to recognise and to provide assessment and treatment for emerging mental health problems in young people, whilst identifying those who require intervention from specialist child and adolescent mental health services (CAMHS). They are also well placed to develop and contribute to mental health promotion and preventive strategies concerning young people's mental health, which is covered in Chapter 16.

Who are universal services professionals?

Universal services includes any professional who works with young people and is likely to come across their mental health problems first – that is, they are working in the front line with young people and their families. However, it must be noted that there have been some significant changes within universal services, due to cutbacks and changes in service structure in England. Figure 2.2 illustrates the range of professionals this can include.

The lists of professionals in Figure 2.2 are not comprehensive, but provide an overview of the range and magnitude of professionals working with young people who may encounter and identify mental health problems. Compiling such lists within the local area can be the first step in acknowledging that children's mental health is a universal concern and is therefore 'everyone's business'. Many of the professionals in universal services are able to provide intervention to young people with mental health problems, but staff or their employing organisation may not acknowledge this. It is not always necessary to refer every young person with a mental health problem to CAMHS. Those that are less disturbed or have their problems identified early may be most appropriately seen and dealt with by universal services.

Voluntary sector/other community professionals/non governmental organisations (local and others) including:

• bereavement services
• domestic violence projects
• Victim Support and the police
• minority ethnic group projects
• local support groups
• youth workers
• local religious or community leaders

Health professionals

• general practitioner/ family doctor
• health visitors (including specialist health visitors)
• school nurses
• practice nurses
• district nurses
• midwives
• hospital staff (especially accident and emergency)
• community paediatricians and school doctors

Universal Services

Social services

• social workers
• specialist nursery workers
• fostering and adoption staff
• residential social workers
• child protection staff
• youth offending teams
• specialist social work teams, i.e. those working in post-abuse services

Education professionals

• preschool staff
• teachers; special educational needs coordinators (SENCOs)
• educational psychologists
• education welfare officers
• pastoral staff
• behaviour support staff
• counsellors

Figure 2.2 Universal services professionals – who are they?

Interventions in universal services

Information, support and advice

Universal services professionals are in a prime position to provide families with information, support and advice regarding young people's mental health problems and also to implement preventive measures. Simple practices can be useful, such as a range of quality leaflets available for parents regarding specific problems or disorders, or being able to direct people to places where they may obtain information (e.g. local groups or libraries). It is also helpful to have some knowledge of local services available to families; often voluntary action groups, social services or CAMHS may have readily available directories.

Screening and assessment

The key to identification of those young people who require assessment and treatment by specialist CAMHS lies in universal services. These professionals should know what information they need to make an informed decision regarding a young person's mental health. This enables them to manage the problem at a universal level or to refer to specialist services as appropriate.

Background information

- name of young person
- consent of parent or person with parental responsibility* (i.e. person who is legally recognised as having a responsibility towards the young person), or consent of young person if applicable
- date of birth
- gender
- general practitioner's name
- home address
- the name and address of parents (if different from above)
- ethnic background
- language spoken
- family structure
- is the child in foster care or other substitute care arrangement?
- school – frequency of attendance, whether excluded
- any assessment under the Education Act
- social services involvement (whether there are ongoing child protection investigations/criminal proceedings)
- are there family proceedings for custody/contact or residence in cases of parental separation and divorce?
- other professional involvement (such as private counsellors)

Description of concern in detail

Describe what is happening when and how – getting examples of specific incidents/events may overcome problems of generalisation and jargon in description of behaviour.

- When did it start? (onset)
- How long has it been going on? (duration)
- How often does it happen? (frequency)
- Is it getting worse/remaining the same/getting better?
- What action has been taken to address the concerns by parents and professionals? What has worked so far?
- Are there ongoing medical investigations?
- How is the concern affecting the young person?

Other issues

- physical health
- education
- social relationships
- activities
- effect on others, i.e. family and significant others
- young person's interests and special talents

Parental responsibility is defined to include all the rights, powers, authority and duties of parents in relation to a child and his or her property.

Figure 2.3 Assessment of child mental health problems at universal services level

Many CAMHS offer consultation and training to universal services professionals on child mental health or have key individuals available for the purpose of supporting universal services professionals in their decision-making process. Which professionals can refer to CAMHS is dependent on local arrangements. In some areas only specified professionals can refer directly to CAMHS, whilst other services operate more 'open-door' criteria. When requesting advice on making written referrals to CAMHS in the UK, it is helpful to provide the background information as shown in Figure 2.3. Some services have developed referral forms to help referrers provide the necessary information.

It is important first to obtain valid consent consistent with the referring agency's policy (usually from the parents or legal guardian unless the child is able to consent). However, in some instances consultation can be offered about specific concerns without the need to reveal the identity of the young person or their family.

Direct interventions by universal services professionals

There is a wide range of intervention approaches that universal services professionals can use with young people and their families. It is important to work collaboratively with other agencies, in order to arrange effective programmes of care at an appropriate level.

Interventions can range from preventive work to assessment and treatment of some problems in a variety of settings. Some universal services professionals have developed particular skills in working with young people and families on mental health problems, for example use of behavioural techniques, parenting programmes or development of social skills groups in schools. These are discussed further in Chapter 14.

Exercise 2.1: Personal strengths and skills

Consider what personal strengths and skills you have for working with young people and their families. Then consider which of these skills would benefit from further development and how this would help you fulfil your professional responsibilities. Consider writing these out and perhaps discussing them with colleagues.

Support for universal services professionals

In the UK, CAMHS have enhanced their support provisions for professionals in universal services. Many CAMHS have existing liaison and consultation schemes, provided by specialist mental health staff, which offer advice on cases where professionals may be considering a referral to CAMHS. A specific role was developed in the UK, called the 'primary child mental health worker', to work at the interface between universal/targeted services and specialist CAMHS. The role has been steadily evolving and may be known by different titles in different services, but essentially these workers have the specific function of strengthening and supporting child and adolescent mental health provision within universal services through direct work with professionals, liaison with staff, consultation, and training.

Exercise 2.2: You and CAMHS

Before reading about specialist CAMHS, consider the following questions:

»   What is your understanding of what a specialist children and young people's mental health service does?

»   What is your understanding of the different (clinical) professionals that work within a specialist service?

»   What are the benefits of universal services staff and specialist children's mental health services being aware of each other's role?

»   How might you develop links with your local children's mental health services?

Specialist child and adolescent mental health services in the UK (CAMHS)

Specialist CAMHS focus on the needs of children and young people. They are comprised of multidisciplinary teams that work together to bring different perspectives and skills to ensure a wide range of assessments and treatments can be provided. The standard composition is:

- A child psychiatrist – a medical practitioner who has undertaken specialist training in psychiatry and child psychiatry. The specialist role of the psychiatrist is in assessment, diagnostic skills (including differentiation between physical and psychiatric and psychological presentations of health problems), prescribing medications, and (at time of writing) exercising powers under the mental health legislation.

- Clinical nurse specialists or community psychiatric nurses (CPNs) – these nurses have specialist mental health training, and their role is to assess and provide therapeutic interventions including community support for young people with mental health problems and their families.

- Psychologists – specialist skills are in psychometric testing (measuring cognitive ability) and sociometric testing (exploring personality profiles). Their training provides them with grounding in a wide range of psychological and social theories with a greater understanding of behavioural theories and treatments including cognitive behaviour therapy.

- Occupational therapists – their role can be very varied as they come into child mental health with different levels of experience. Their specialist skill is the assessment and treatment of mental health problems using an activity-based approach.

- Primary child mental health workers who work at the interface between specialist and targeted or universal services, and provide support, advice, and training to professionals in these levels of service; they also sometimes work directly with children and young people, providing short, focused, evidence-based interventions.

The team may also have other specialist therapists, such as family therapists, music therapists and play therapists, but that can be very variable dependent on local resources.

Social workers used to be an integral part of the old-style child guidance clinics, but increasingly they have been less directly involved as an integral part of CAMHS in the UK. Although psychologists are mentioned above as generally being part of the multidisciplinary team, sometimes they operate alongside it, rather than within it. Some members of the team may also have undertaken further training in particular therapies, such as cognitive behaviour therapy, family therapy and psychotherapy.

The services offered are correspondingly very variable but it is increasingly recognised that many young people referred to specialist CAMHS could actually be managed in the universal services context.

Outpatient teams generally discuss referrals at a team allocation meeting and prioritise them depending on need. Some specialist teams will also operate triage clinics where all appropriate referrals are assessed before prioritisation.

Many areas in the UK have now developed a single referral point for all children's mental health services (this is sometimes called a Single Point of Access or SPA). Some CAMHS have enabled open access and self-referral for children and families, or access via universal services to specialist services, using a pathway approach. However, some services have continued to have a point of entry at tier two, which acts as a filter to the more specialist services. The rationale behind this is that tier-two staff (working either at tier two or three level) can assess the situation before referral to more intensive assessment or therapies.

In most areas, there is usually a specific way to access the service should a child or young person be in crisis and need immediate assessment and support. Some specialist CAMHS have developed specific Crisis Teams that respond quickly to assess the young person and determine the intervention needed – some have Home Treatment Teams who will work alongside the young person and their family to support them through their difficult time. The East of England Clinical Network has developed a toolkit for CAMHS that are developing crisis services (ADS/East of England Clinical Network 2017).

It is important to become familiar with the particular model that is operated within your local area, to know the best way to help children and families access help and support.

Inpatient units exist to provide care for young people who cannot best be managed in the community. This not only depends on the severity of their mental health problems but also on the resources or skills that the community (including their family) has for supporting them. Inpatient facilities often face the dilemma of having to respond to acutely ill young people as well as those with less acute but equally debilitating problems in one unit. The needs of these two groups of young people may be very different and it can be difficult to ensure that both are met. Whilst most professionals would agree with guidelines that young people should be admitted to units specifically for young people whenever possible, in practice young people are still often admitted to less than ideal facilities.

CAMHS may also have training responsibilities for the various disciplines that work within them.

CAMHS in developing countries

As the mental health needs of young people gain more prominence, developing countries are beginning to consider service development and training. Usually this will be in the context of training those who are already in contact with young people (e.g. community and primary care staff). Besides the HAS model, WHO (2001) quotes some projects in the Middle East that have built on supporting primary care staff to deliver basic mental health services to increase access. There is, however, a recognition that primary care staff need to be adequately trained and supervised for this to work effectively. It is useful for service planners to review other models and consider which model best suits the context for which they are planning services. Development of these services may not currently be a high priority but can include:

- identifying the local priorities of child and adolescent mental health problems

- assessing the effectiveness of interventions and building in effective audits to monitor the standards of service provision

- training to enhance or develop skills of primary healthcare professionals

- research and/or needs analysis and defining the remit of a child and adolescent mental health service in the context of local need

- integrating new services with existing ones and utilising existing resources effectively

- involving the local staff and community in the development of services.

Local staff should particularly be involved in all aspects of development as, ultimately, they will be the ones left with the responsibility of ensuring that successful pilot programmes are translated into long-term changes and policy. Dogra *et al.* (2005) and Omigbodun *et al.* (2007) describe training programmes in India and Nigeria respectively and demonstrate some of the issues discussed above.

Exercise 2.3: Mapping local services

Draw up a list of local resources that you are aware of that address the mental health problems of young people, and services for parents to enable them to parent and support young people. To your list add the problem or issue that the resource addresses, and how to contact them.

When you read Part 4 it may be useful to repeat this exercise and identify resources to address the problems that you are commonly faced with.

References

Achenbach, T.M. and Edelbrock, C. (1983) *Manual for the Child Behavior Checklist and Revised Child Behavior Profile.* Burlington, VT: University of Vermont.

ADS/East of England Clinical Network (2017) *East of England Mental Health Crisis Care Toolkit – Children and Young People.* Cambridge: East of England NHS Clinical Network. Available at https://cypiapt.com/2017/02/13/crisis-toolkit, accessed on 14 June 2017.

American Psychiatric Association (2013) *Diagnostic and Statistical Manual of Mental Disorders (5th edition).* Arlington, VA: American Psychiatric Association.

Bird, H. (1996) 'Epidemiology of childhood disorders in a cross-cultural context.' *Journal of Child Psychology and Psychiatry 37,* 1, 35–49.

British Psychological Society (2012) *Consultation on Child and Adolescent Mental Health Services – A Service Model.* London: British Psychological Society.

Centers for Disease Control and Prevention (2012) *National Health and Nutrition Examination Survey (NHANES).* Available at www.cdc.gov/nchs/nhanes/index.htm, accessed on 14 June 2017.

Department of Health/NHS England (2015). *Future in Mind. Promoting, protecting and improving our children and young people's mental health and well-being.* London: Department of Health.

Dogra, N., Frake, C., Bretherton, K., Dwivedi, K. and Sharma, I. (2005) 'Training CAMHS professionals in developing countries: An Indian case study.' *Child and Adolescent Mental Health 10,* 2, 74–79.

4Children (2016) *All Parliamentary Group on Children's Centres. Family Hubs: The Future of Children's Centres – Strengthening family relationships to improve Life Chances for everyone.* London: 4Children. Available at http://cdn.basw.co.uk/upload/basw_82938-8.pdf, accessed on 14 June 2017.

Fink, E., Praveethata P., Sharpe, H., Holley. S., Deighton, J. and Wolpert, M. (2015) 'Mental health difficulties in early adolescence: A comparison of two cross-sectional studies in England from 2009–2014.' *Journal of Adolescent Health 56,* 502–507. Available at www.jahonline.org/article/S1054-139X(15)00064-6/pdf, accessed on 14 June 2017.

Goodman, R. (1997) 'The Strengths and Difficulties Questionnaire: A research note.' *Journal of Child Psychology and Psychiatry 38.* 581–586.

Goodman, R., Ford, F., Simmons, H., Gatward, R. and Meltzer, H. (2000) 'Using the Strengths and Difficulties Questionnaire (SDQ) to screen for child psychiatric disorders in a community sample.' *British Journal of Psychiatry 177,* 534–539.

Health Advisory Service Report (1995) *Together We Stand: The Commissioning, Role and Management of Child and Adolescent Mental Health Services.* London: Her Majesty's Stationary Office.

Helliwell, J., Layard, R., and Sach, J. (2016) *World Happiness Report 2016, Update (Vol.1).* New York: Sustainable Development Solutions Network. Available at www.worldhappiness.report/wp-content/uploads/sites/2/2016/03/HR-V1_web.pdf, accessed on 14 June 2017.

McKelvey, R.S., Davies, L.C., Sang, D.L., Pickering, K.R. and Tu, H.C. (1999) 'Problems and competencies reported by parents of Vietnamese children in Hanoi.' *Journal of the American Academy of Child and Adolescent Psychiatry 38,* 6, 731–737.

Murray, C.J. and Lopez. A.D. (2013) 'Measuring the Global Burden of Disease.' *The New England Journal of Medicine 369,* 448–457.

NICE (National Institute for Health and Clinical Excellence) (2011) *Common mental health problems: Pathways to care.* Clinical guideline [CG23].

Office for National Statistics (2005) *The Mental Health of Children and Young People in Great Britain.* Basingstoke: Palgrave McMillan.

Office of National Statistics (2015) *Insights into Children's Mental Health and Well-Being.* London: ONS.

Omigbodun, O., Bella, T., Dogra, N. and Simoyan, O. (2007) 'Training health professionals for child and adolescent mental health care in Nigeria: A qualitative analysis.' *Child and Adolescent Mental Health 12,* 3, 132–137.

Sayal, K. and Taylor, E (2004) 'Detection of child mental health disorders by general practitioners.' *British Journal of General Practice 54,* 348–52.

Wolpert, M., Harris.R., Jones, M., Hodges, S., Fuggle, P., James, R. *et al.* (2014) *THRIVE: The AFC-Tavistock Model for CAMHS.* CAMHS Press. Available at www.annafreud.org/service-improvement/service-improvement-resources/thrive, accessed on 14 June 2017.

World Health Organization (2001) *World Health Day. Mental Health: Stop Exclusion – Dare to Care.* Geneva: World Health Organization. Available at www.who.int/world-health-day/previous/2001/files/whd2001_dare_to_care_en.pdf, accessed on 14 June 2017.

World Health Organization (2005) *Atlas: Child and Adolescent Mental Health Resources: Global Concerns, Implications for the Future.* Geneva: World Health Organization. Available at http://apps.who.int/iris/bitstream/10665/43307/1/9241563044_eng.pdf?ua=1, accessed on 14 June 2017.

World Health Organization (2016) *The International Classification of Diseases, ICD-10 Classification of Mental and Behavioural Disorders 10th Revision.* Geneva: World Health Organization.

CHAPTER 3

Assessing the Mental Health of Young People

This chapter describes the approaches commonly taken by mental health practitioners who work with children, adolescents and families. Whilst awareness of these approaches can be helpful to the front-line professional, please bear in mind that a full mental health assessment should be undertaken following appropriate training (see Chapter 17) and with supervision. This chapter is not a substitute for training.

Interviewing young people

Introduction

A successful interview depends on the professional thinking very carefully about appropriate engagement with the young person and family. It is important to outline the proposed structure or plan of the interview, ground rules regarding confidentiality, and explain what is going to happen to dispel any fears, myths or uncertainties. It can be helpful to be explicit that it will usually involve talking together and going home at the end of the meeting, as young people may fear they will be separated from their families. Young people and their parents need information about what the service does after introductions have been made. Clarifying the expectations of everyone present assists the assessment process. If the family has concerns or anxieties about seeing you, these need to be addressed. There also needs to be consideration of whether the family is seen together or the young person is seen individually. It can also be very useful to identify whether the family has accessed the internet to find out more about the symptoms or behaviours that may be presented. This applies to both parents and young people as they are likely to access different internet resources.

The interview

The setting

It is sometimes difficult to control where the meeting takes place. However, try to make the venue as welcoming as possible with comfortable and appropriately arranged seating. Toys or games for younger children can often help to break down the barriers of a formal interview. A board and wipe-off markers (or something similar) may be useful so that young people can share their thoughts and feelings knowing that they can wipe things away before they leave the session. If you meet young people regularly in a variety of settings it is useful to carry some of these items with you, as they are not always readily available in clinics or indeed the young person's home.

Try to ensure you sit at the same level as the young person and that you are not towering above them. It is best to sit by the side of the young person rather than opposite them, which can be very intimidating and appear confrontational. Avoid having tables in the seating area unless you need them for activities.

Allow enough time to listen to the concerns and minimise distractions or interruptions. Remaining in control of the interview shows that there is a structure and focus to the process, which can help reduce anxieties and contain the situation.

Length and format of the session

Some preparatory work before the meeting is essential. It is sometimes hard to estimate how long the meeting will take, but having some timescale will help to put both the young person and yourself at ease. Young people are able to sense if you are rushed or do not seem relaxed, which might give the impression that you are uninterested or distracted. An average assessment interview in a community setting is likely to be between 30 and 45 minutes and between 60 and 90 minutes in a CAMHS setting. In either setting, it may take more than one session to complete the assessment.

Often, when asked about their expectations, young people will share their anxieties that they would be interrogated. If possible try to tell them what will happen if you plan to meet again. It can be useful to send them a user-friendly leaflet that describes what will happen during the meeting before they come to see you, and to explain what the ongoing support plan will be, where appropriate.

Setting boundaries

Clarify what is happening, how you are going to work together, what you want them to do and what the 'rules' of the meeting are. Some young people may wish to add a few rules of their own, for example permission to take a five minute break when the session is getting difficult for them. Also ensure that the young person is aware that they are able to interrupt to clarify any concerns throughout, and make sure you give them plenty of opportunities to talk about their concerns and views. Explain that they will receive feedback at the end of the meeting and that you will outline the next steps for them and agree a plan together. If a young person is verbally abusive, it can be helpful to be clear about what is acceptable behaviour. Professionals should not tolerate abuse but need to be aware that sometimes this is a reflection of illness or distress and in such cases needs sensitive handling.

Use of language

Tailor your language to the young person's level of comprehension and ability. Use clear explanations that can be easily understood. Listen to how the young person speaks and use language that matches theirs. Watch for signs that they have understood you. If they seem to have misunderstood, then look for another way of explaining. Drawings, cartoons or diagrams can be useful ways of engaging young people.

Using interpreters

Ensure that you check with an adult who knows the young person what the best way of approaching a meeting with a young person who uses languages (including Signing) other than English might be. Establish which language they feel most comfortable with. If you are not certain that a young person or their family can clearly understand the questions due to language or other communication differences, use an interpreter or interpreting services if possible. This will add considerably to the time needed to conduct the interview. You should meet with the interpreter before the interview to brief them on the nature of the information you are seeking and afterwards to clarify any issues of understanding, including their view on non-verbal communication and, if possible, the cultural context of the discussion.

It is generally not good practice to ask a young person or any other member of the family to interpret for their parents. This could put the young person in an awkward or even a dangerous position.

Interpreting is highly skilled work and given the nuances of language and meaning inherent in a mental health assessment, asking a member of the family to take on this role will compromise the quality of the assessment. In practice this sometimes cannot be avoided in a pressing situation, but in such cases an alternative should be put in place for the next appointment.

Cultural considerations

Beware of applying stereotypes and making assumptions about individuals and their cultures. A suitable definition of culture is that from the Association of American Medical Colleges (AAMC):

> Culture is defined by each person in relationship to the group or groups with whom he or she identifies. An individual's cultural identity may be based on heritage as well as individual circumstances and personal choice. Cultural identity may be affected by such factors as race, ethnicity, age, language, country of origin, acculturation, sexual orientation, gender, socioeconomic status, religious/spiritual beliefs, physical abilities and occupation, among others. These factors may impact behaviours such as communication styles, diet preferences, health beliefs, family roles, lifestyle, rituals and decision-making processes. All of these beliefs and practices, in turn, can influence how patients and heath care professionals perceive health and illness, and how they interact with one another. (AAMC 1999, p.25)

Our justification for using this definition is that it is a patient-centred definition and can be applied to clinical situations. It suggests that individuals draw upon a range of resources and that, through the interplay of external and internal meanings, they construct a sense of identity and unique culture. It is also useful because it recognises that both patients and professionals bring a complex individual self to the consultation. This definition also allows for children and their parents to understand the origins of their culture independently. It is probably more effective to have a principle-based approach to ensure that cultural issues are taken on board for all families for several reasons. Taking this approach:

- prevents facts relevant to one individual being assumed to be relevant to others that may appear to be from a similar background

- should prevent stereotyping of the young person or their family

- enables the provider to provide quality care irrespective of which factor diversity may be related to

- works with the central philosophy that young people and their families all bring perspectives which need to be taken into account.

In working with diverse groups, staff need to consider the following points:

- They need to reflect on their own biases and prejudices to ensure that these do not consciously or subconsciously justify lesser quality care for some patients.

- As many factors influence the individual's understanding of mental health and mental health services, at the outset of any assessment the patient's understanding of what they think is going to happen should be checked. Their explanation or understanding for how things are may be very useful for the interventions that are planned.

- Do not be afraid of asking if you are not sure – you just need to ensure you ask respectfully, without judgement.

- Do not be intimidated into avoiding difficult questions just because someone is from a visibly different background.

- Don't assume that because someone superficially looks as though they may be from a similar background this means they view the world in a similar way.

- Do not assume that because the last person from a particular background believed that mental illness is caused by spirits so will the next patient from a similar background.

- If there are a number of treatment options, do not assume which option the individual will choose. Discuss all the options and ensure the patient and/or family are able to make an informed choice. Different people will need different levels of explanations and time. Working with interpreters can increase the time needed.

- Ensure that you do get the patient's perspective. At times of distress and stress, family members may speak for the patient and make choices that they would make for themselves rather than think about what the patient might truly want.

It should be emphasised that currently there is no strong evidence that one type of approach is more effective than another. However, recent research with mental health adult patients revealed their preference for approaches which were consistent with the definition of diversity used above.

Seeing young people without their parents

During assessment and any subsequent work with any young person and their family, consider spending time individually with the young person. Interviewing a young person individually is usually possible from age four onwards. It can be a valuable source of information, as it will inform decisions about the young person's needs and distinguish the best way to meet them. The decision regarding whether to interview the young person or not will be guided by the young person's developmental level and confidence.

Adolescents should always be offered the opportunity to be seen individually, in order for professionals to understand their views of the difficulties and the impact they have on their life. Some professionals prefer to see the adolescent first before seeing the parents or the rest of the family as this can help in engaging with them.

The nature of the young person's problem and the expectations that the family has will often influence the decision; for example, a young person with anxiety problems may not be willing to be seen alone, especially at first.

Giving feedback

Ask the young person if they agree to you giving feedback to their parents, taking into account issues of confidentiality (see Chapter 8). Explain why you have undertaken certain tasks or activities and ensure that you explain any homework tasks to both the young person and their parents. It can sometimes be useful to provide clear written instructions to engage them in tasks between appointments and to summarise meetings.

Principles of interviewing young people

The key to interviewing young people is listening – not just hearing what they say but also how they say it and how they express themselves. Young people can be very perceptive and if they think they are not being actively listened to, they may withdraw or not bother to continue. Listening sensitively and attentively to a young person not only ensures a better quality interview but also helps with gaining the young person's trust and building a relationship. Follow the young person's cues and listen to what they feel is important for them, while trying to understand the meaning. Be clear about your understanding of what the young person is saying. This can be achieved by using reflection – reframing in your own words what you think they are trying to say and checking it out with them, or just repeating back what they have said. It can sometimes be helpful to use drawings or toys to help affirm your understanding.

Try to give feelings expressed by the young person a name: acknowledging their feelings with words will help to build their confidence and a language with which to define their feelings. Help young people to understand that they may experience a range of different feelings and that they may not always be mutually exclusive; for example, someone being angry with you does not always mean they do not care about you. You may need to make a statement such as: 'Sometimes, people who have been through what you have been through feel quite scared. I wonder if that's something you have felt.' In this way, young people have the permission to share feelings they may feel confused or guilty about.

Think about how you listen to people; are you interested in what they have to say or do you find yourself more interested in your own questions or responses? Think about whether you are able to listen to others or whether you often interrupt. Pay attention to whether you feel comfortable in letting the young person lead the discussion for a while or whether you feel you have to steer it. Recognise your strengths and weaknesses, and get comfortable with them before the interview as they can affect your relationship with the young person. Young people can often spot your uncertainties or anxieties a mile off!

Be careful not to recount your own worries; this can often make the young person feel anxious and unheard. It can be useful to recount stories that relate to someone else's problems to help normalise an issue, but this needs to be done carefully. Young people like to feel they are being taken seriously, therefore it is not useful to use their comments as a joke or light relief; but that does not mean humour should not be used when appropriate. It is undermining of the young person to dismiss, belittle or trivialise their experiences by making statements such as 'pull yourself together' or 'it's not the end of the world'.

Avoid being judgemental and critical of young people and their families but ensure you meet your professional responsibilities. Convey warmth and sincerity and have an open and approachable manner whilst maintaining professional standards at all times. Be aware of the young person's cultural and social contexts as this may clarify some of the issues.

Interviewing appropriate to the young person's age and stage of development

BIRTH TO 3 YEARS

The child is largely dependent on their parents and will not have fully developed language skills. Most interviews should be conducted with adults, but it is important to have the child present so you can observe the child's interactions and abilities.

3 TO 4 YEARS

Children will have a vocabulary of around 1000–1500 words and should be able to comprehend and answer some questions. At this stage, they will understand rewards and praise, and be able to take turns. They may be able to understand some emotions, such as sad, happy or angry, but will need some explanation of more complex emotions.

This age group usually enjoys simple games or drawings. Assessment of development is usually more successful if framed as a game rather than a formal procedure. Creative use of pictures that relate to emotions is useful to elicit feelings from this age group.

4 TO 5 YEARS

Children's language now extends to them being able to talk about meanings of words and they are able to follow directions that have more than one part. Their imagination can provide valuable insights into their worlds by allowing them to tell you a story about themselves. Remember, though, that some stories may be rather extravagant and their concept of time unclear. The use of dolls or puppets can be fruitful, as the children may shy away from drawing or want you to do it. The activities should be led by the child, but actively engaged in by the professional.

6 TO 8 YEARS

At this stage children will be able to give you direct accounts of parts of their own history. Children may be enthusiastic about taking part but may become easily bored. However, children may have difficulty in understanding, acknowledging or discussing the presenting problem.

The child will often settle down to prepared worksheets and will be able to comprehend techniques such as 'mood scales' or be able to complete sentences, such as 'One thing that makes me happy is…' or 'A good thing about me is…'. Give plenty of praise and reward completion of activities with short episodes of 'fun play' before moving on to the next task. Techniques like 'family circles' are useful, where the child puts himself or herself in a circle in the middle of a page and then in a series of evenly spaced circles will place family or friends, dependent on their significance to them.

9 TO 10 YEARS

During this stage, children respond to being given some responsibility and are able to recognise right and wrong and their feelings of guilt. They will also process information and use it in different situations or to plan ahead.

Techniques that look at consequences and benefits to their behaviours can be useful. The use of 'feelings jugs' is a good technique for this age group. The child has a worksheet with a series of empty jugs, which are labelled with an emotion, and they can colour them in to the level they feel they are at.

11 TO 13 YEARS

Young people in this age group begin to take on some adult values, whilst sometimes behaving as a child. They may vary immensely in the way they behave. They may be cooperative and communicative at one end of the spectrum and express themselves through anger at the other. At this age some young people will be organised and have a sense of ownership regarding issues relating to themselves. However, some may appear introspective, sulky or withdrawn, especially in communication with adults.

Techniques that are valuable at this stage can range from diary-keeping to poetry and stories, and problem-solving. A useful way of looking at problem-solving can be using comic strips where the young person can define a range of outcomes to different scenarios. Another useful technique is drawing a 'mountain range' in relation to the ups and downs of a problem or again using mood scales.

14 YEARS AND OVER

From this age, young people begin to take more responsibility and to think about the future. They may express concerns or worries about school, friendships and relationships and are able to see things from other people's perspectives.

It can be difficult initially to engage young people in this age group; however, presenting them with a range of choices will encourage them to take responsibility and direct the interview to some extent. Activities that look at making changes or coping with situations can be beneficial; for example, looking at an issue or problem in the past, present and future and identifying achievable outcomes with the young person.

CASE STUDY: Tim

Tim is a 15-year-old boy with a three-month history of low mood (feeling sad), poor concentration, poor sleep, tiredness, lack of interest in playing football (he had been on his school team), with deterioration of his schoolwork. His parents felt he was also irritable and argumentative, which he had not been previously. They were also concerned about his ideas of hopelessness, although he had not considered self-harm.

Tim refuses to accept a referral to CAMHS.

What strategies would you employ to engage Tim?

Interviewing families

Families are made up of individuals – an obvious truth, but it is this fact that makes interviewing a family so challenging and sometimes leaves the professional and the family overwhelmed. However, it is this same diversity of individuals that makes the family interview such a potentially rich source of information. Family interviews can also provide perspectives that are unobtainable elsewhere, as the family together is so much more than the sum of its parts. It is probably safe to assume that there are at least as many agendas as there are people in the room. In this section, we are considering a context when a family is seen together for the purpose of an assessment or family meeting to explore family issues rather than a formal family therapy session. The issues outlined are applicable in several situations, although the techniques will not be applicable to meetings such as case conferences, which have a specific and statutory function.

Preparation

A lot of work can be done before the meeting to maximise the use of the time with the family. A good place to start is to consider what different members of the family might want or expect from the meeting. Young people often feel anxious about the meeting and unsure of its purpose. The possibility of seeking help outside of the family may even have been used as a threat by parents in an attempt to improve the situation. Young people, especially adolescents, may perceive a family meeting variously as a punishment, an opportunity for revenge on their parents or simply an excruciatingly embarrassing experience. Siblings of the referred young person may feel puzzled or upset about their inclusion when they feel their sibling has the problem.

Parents may attend a meeting with a strong hypothesis about the nature of the problem and may find it hard to divert from this agenda. A common experience is parents who feel their child has a particular problem, such as attention deficit hyperactivity disorder. They may perceive exploration of other possible explanations of difficult behaviour as a challenge to that hypothesis. This can prove very tricky for primary care staff who might then feel unable to assert any opinion and feel under pressure to refer on. Other common agendas for parents include the wish to be listened to and to get practical advice and help.

Many parents can feel they have failed as carers if their child has developed mental health problems and so experience an undermining of their skills and authority. The route to an assessment and previous experiences with other agencies often shape the expectations of the family. Considering the nature and source of the information might generate some ideas on these influences.

The professional might also find it useful to reflect on their own position before the meeting and consider how their agency influences the nature of the meeting and how the family members perceive the professional. The family might see the professional as being so far removed from their own experience that it creates an unhelpful barrier between them, and the opposite can also apply. This does not mean that professionals need to identify with families, but that they should have an awareness of the possible assumptions made about them by the family. The professional in turn will need to be aware of the assumptions they are making about the family based on the information *they* have.

Convening a family meeting

The professional may be faced with the decision about who to invite to a family meeting and to some extent this will depend on the way the professional is used to working. One way is to invite the household and go from there. Another approach is to issue an open invitation to whoever the family feel might be helpful, although the extra element of uncertainty may add to the professional's anxiety about being overwhelmed. Whatever approach is chosen, studies of parents' experiences of family meetings show that they value being consulted on this issue and that it goes some way to dispel feelings of failure and disempowerment, making collaboration more likely.

Getting fathers to attend can be difficult and may be indicative of differing gender perceptions of the value of getting professional help, differences of views on the severity of the problem, levels of commitment to the emotional well-being of the family, or insecurity of employment. The time of day for the meeting has been shown to be helpful in improving attendance of fathers and school-age siblings.

Professionals may consider working with a colleague when meeting a family if they feel they may be overwhelmed by the amount of information generated in a family meeting. This has the added benefit of introducing another perspective and hence another layer of information. However, this needs careful planning to get the most benefit; for example, one professional may concentrate on the parental perspective and the other on the children. Alternatively, the plan might be for one to take a less central role and take an overview of what happens in the meeting (i.e. how things are said, how individuals respond, who says what, who takes a lead, who struggles to get heard, and so on), and for the other to concentrate on the content.

Conducting a family meeting

The issues raised earlier with respect to interviewing young people need equal consideration when undertaking a family meeting. A meeting with a family should start with introductions, explanations of roles and a clarification of the purpose of the meeting. The understanding of the purpose of the meeting is likely to vary between family members and the professional.

It may be that different family members feel constrained about what they say in front of each other. The reasons for this can include: parents not feeling it is appropriate to discuss adult issues in the presence of the children; hitherto undisclosed parentage issues; and fear of violence. It is worth considering meeting different combinations of family members, such as parents only, children only, and individual members. If this is your intention, making this clear at the beginning of the initial session can take the pressure off family members disclosing potentially risky material inappropriately. Surveys of parents who have had family meetings suggest that the opportunity to speak openly without the children is often appreciated.

Types of question

It is not possible to ask a question without its meaning being interpreted at many different levels, and this process is magnified when interviewing a family. For example, a series of questions about a child's behaviour might be seen by a parent as a criticism of their parenting skills and at the same time by the child as the professional taking sides with the parent. At first glance, this realisation might paralyse the professional, but it is helpful to note patterns of questions and answers that might occur in a session. One example is a temptation the professional experiences to direct questions at the most receptive member of the family, which marginalises the more ambivalent, hostile or quiet members and limits the perspectives. It might also negate most of the benefits of interviewing the family together. One way round this might be to spend some time asking all of the family members the same question in turn. This may appear to be a cumbersome process, but it conveys the value placed on everyone's opinion and can provide a greater depth of information compared with a series of questions to the most involved parent.

Another type of question that can be usefully employed in family meetings is to ask family members to answer from the perspective of another. For example, asking an adolescent girl to speculate on why her father gets so angry when she stays out overnight not only provides information for the professional but also for different members of the family. This technique, if used carefully, can also be used to include family members who are opting out of the conversation by asking the others to think about the situation from their perspective. It highlights a principle of families: that if something happens to one individual, it impacts on others.

Concluding family meetings

Taking into account the different views and perspectives of the family can be time consuming and it is advisable not to try to cover too much in one meeting. The varied agendas and expectations of the family as outlined earlier mean that they will take away different impressions from the interview. They may feel that someone else's view has been given a better hearing than their own. A useful technique is to put aside some time at the end of the meeting to ask each member of the family if there is something important that has not been raised. While there may not be sufficient time to explore any of these issues in any depth, they will have been raised and can be revisited at further meetings.

It is a considerable task to gather together all of the information from a family meeting, especially if you are working alone. Checking your understanding of what has been said during the meeting by asking the family at the end of the meeting can be a good way to summarise and clarify any points of information. It also helps clarify whether younger members of the family have understood what has happened and what the plan is to deal with the issues.

Exercise 3.1: Potential difficulties when interviewing young people

How would you manage each of the following scenarios?

» The young person has difficulty in separating from the parents.

» The parents are anxious about the interview.

» The young person is the one who makes the decisions in the family.

» The young person refuses to cooperate.

» The young person or their parents are hostile, rude or aggressive.

CASE STUDY: Samuel

Samuel is eight years old and has been missing a lot of school recently due to illness. Accompanied by his mother, he frequently consults his GP who can find nothing wrong with him. As a primary health worker, you have arranged a meeting with Sam and his parents with the aim of devising some strategies to help him to get back into school on a more regular basis. The day before the scheduled meeting Sam's mother telephones to ask if they all need to attend.

How would you respond?

The meeting goes ahead and you start by asking about the problem. Sam's mother describes her worries and she becomes tearful. At the same time, you notice that Sam is sinking lower and lower in his chair and his father is looking detached.

What could you do to engage a) Sam and b) his father in the session?

A mental health assessment

A standard mental health assessment plan is outlined below. Depending on the information already available, some parts may require greater inquiry than others. Some areas may need revisiting if new evidence comes to light or the problem identified does not resolve with appropriate intervention. Primary care professionals are unlikely to undertake detailed or formal mental health assessments.

The assessment is included here for primary care staff to be aware of what the assessment comprises so that they can adequately prepare young people and families they refer to CAMHS.

History taking
Presenting problem

- Establish the history of the presenting problem: onset, duration, severity, and associated factors, situations that improve or exacerbate the situation.

- For whom is it a problem and what are associated issues?

- What have the family and child already tried to make things better?

Family history

- Who is in the family? Is there contact with absent parents?

- Young people's perceptions of the family including their perceptions of any family behaviours, problems or breakdown.

- Parents' own experiences of being parented. Support within the family and extended family. Roles and relationships within the family.

- Communication within the family. Issues of domestic violence.

- Family history of mental health problems.

Personal history

- Prenatal, perinatal and postnatal history (i.e. details of the pregnancy and birth).

- Development history – were milestones reached within expected time range?

- School career, including how they separated from parents, settled into the school routine, relationships with peers and teachers and educational achievements.

- Social interests and hobbies. Social and peer relationships.

- Experiences of bullying or discrimination, including cyber-bullying.

- Sexuality and related issues as appropriate.

It is important to ask children and young people about their use of internet and social media as these are increasingly relevant factors in some presentations.

Past psychiatric and medical history
When asking about previous episodes ask about what interventions were used and if these were successful. Ask about reasons for the interventions being useful or not. Record use of any prescribed or non-prescribed medication and allergies.

Substance use
Include any contact with the police or legal services and medical and social consequences of use.

Contact with other agencies
These might include social services, education, voluntary agencies and other health agencies.

Aspects of the young person before the onset of the problem
An example of this might be temperament; history of achievements. A useful question here can be to ask how the young person would use three wishes. This can help identify the young person's priorities.

Formal mental state examination
A formal mental state examination is an essential part of a specialist assessment, but any professional should be able to record the presentation accurately, although they may not have the training to interpret it. Details of observed behaviour are an essential part of the assessment.

A child psychiatrist should make the mental state examination. Avoid making pejorative or unnecessary personal comments about the young person. State what evidence you have to support your conclusions – record the behaviours rather than just your interpretation of them. The following should be noted:

General observations

- Appearance and behaviour.

- How the young person engaged with the professional.

- Levels of cooperation, concentration, anxiety and nervousness.

- Speech.

- Tone, rhythm, pace and volume; clarity, syntax and structure.

Mood

- Objective (observed by professional, including apparent general mood state and its range, depth and reactivity).

- Subjective (young person's perceptions of their mood).

Disorders of perceptions

- Hallucinations and other perceptual abnormalities – auditory (including whether there are any voices giving commands, or making derogatory or persecutory comments), visual, somatic (i.e. internal bodily sensations), tactile (skin), olfactory (smell) or gustatory (taste).

- Disorder of thought form.

- Speed of thought, linking of ideas.

- Disorder of thought content.

- Overvalued ideas, ideas of reference (i.e. that other things or people refer to them).

- Delusions (fixed beliefs made on false premises that are not culturally contextual) – these may be grandiose, paranoid (persecutory), nihilistic, self-derogatory or religious. There may be delusions of passivity (believing that the mind or body is controlled in some way).

- Obsessions (uncontrollable and intrusive thoughts, impulses or images that recur and cause significant distress and anxiety).

Cognition

- Orientation in time, place and person; memory and concentration.

- Language and comprehension; visuospatial skills.

- Judgement and reasoning.

- Safety of self and others.

It is essential that professionals at all levels ask young people about thoughts of harm to self or others, including suicidal and homicidal ideation. Asking about such thoughts does not make a young person more likely to act on them. Indeed, asking may do the opposite, as a professional raising the issue will reduce the young person's sense of isolation, and permit planning around how to manage the risk. Young people are often relieved at having been able to share what has been a considerable burden. There is greater risk in not asking than asking. This can be approached by asking about any times that they might have felt down on themselves or thought 'What's the point?' before moving on to asking about them wishing they weren't alive and thoughts they have had of ending their life or harming themselves. If they report having had these experiences, then it is important to ascertain when and where these have occurred, degree of intent, urge, or planning, and whether they have begun to act on any of these thoughts. It would also be helpful to know who else they have shared these thoughts with, what support they have had, and what their motivations have been for not following through and for staying alive or not self-harming. These questions then naturally lead to the beginning of a formulation of a safety plan and thoughts as to who can support the young person with this plan.

Psychometric assessment

Screening and other psychometric instruments can be useful in indicating the possibility of a disorder; however, they should not and cannot replace a thorough assessment.

Formulation

The mental health assessment is followed by a formulation, which integrates all the information, making sense of the problem or diagnosis, and highlighting relevant predisposing, precipitating and perpetuating factors in a way that enables a management plan to be devised. A good formulation sets out to answer the questions: Why this person? Why this presentation? And why now?

Assessing young people with problem substance use

Young people access specialist services through front-line professionals in primary care settings, and these professionals are best placed to identify problems. Screening tools are available, such as the substances and choices scale (SACS) (Christie *et al.* 2007). A professional concerned about a young person's substance use should be open to discussing the issue with the young person. There is strong evidence that this enables young people to access services. Initially, this assessment needs to clarify a young person's substance use so that accurate and up-to-date information and advice can be given if needed. A young person with problem substance use requires a comprehensive assessment by a professional who has the appropriate skills.

RAFFT screening questionnaire to screen for substance use

R Do you ever take drugs to **R**elax, feel better about yourself or fit in?

A Do you ever drink or take drugs while you are **A**lone?

F Do any of your closest **F**riends drink or use drugs?

F Does a close **F**amily member have a problem with alcohol or drugs?

T Have you ever got into **T**rouble from drinking or taking drugs?

If the young person or his/her parents respond 'yes' to any of the above screening questions it may be useful to consider specialist services and also consider if the responses raise any child protection concerns.

(described by Liepman *et al.* 1998)

As well as identifying mental health needs, assessment should identify pattern and history of substance use, adverse consequences for the young person, risk factors to perpetuating use, beliefs held by the young person, and resources and strengths that can be called on to support the young person's aims in addressing the problem use.

Making a diagnosis

Unless they have the appropriate professional background and training, professionals should refrain from making a diagnosis as families may then find it difficult to relinquish the diagnosis even if specialist assessment proves otherwise. It is more helpful to discuss with the family the reasons for a referral to specialist services.

References

Association of American Medical Colleges (1999) *Report II. Contemporary Issues in Medicine: Communication in Medicine. Medical School Objectives Project.* Washington, DC: Association of American Medical Colleges.

Christie, G., Marsh, R., Sheridan, J., Wheeler, A. *et al.* (2007) 'The Substances and Choices Scale (SACS) – The development and testing of a new alcohol and other drug screening and outcome measurement instrument for young people.' *Addiction 102,* 9, 1390.

Liepman, M.R., Keller, D.M., Botelho, R.J., Monroe, A.D. and Sloane, M.A. (1998) 'Understanding and preventing substance abuse by adolescents: A guide for primary care clinicians.' *Primary Care: Clinics in Office Practice 25,* 1, 137–162.

Further reading

Angold, A. (2002) 'Diagnostic Interviews with Parents and Children.' In M. Rutter and E. Taylor (eds) *Child and Adolescent Psychiatry: Modern Approaches (4th edition).* Oxford: Blackwell Scientific.

British Medical Association (2001) *Consent, Rights and Choices in Health Care for Children and Young People.* London: BMJ Books.

Burnham, J. (1996) *Family Therapy: First Steps Towards a Systematic Approach.* London: Routledge.

www.sacsinfo.com/docs/SACSUserManualNoPrint.pdf, accessed on 18 July 2008.

Department of Health (2009) *Seeking Consent: Working With Children.* London: Department of Health. Available at www.gov.uk/government/publications/reference-guide-to-consent-for-examination-or-treatment-second-edition, accessed on 3 July 2017.

Dogra, N. (2007) 'Cultural Diversity Issues.' In P. Vostanis (ed.) *Mental Health Interventions and Services for Vulnerable Children and Young People.* London: Jessica Kingsley Publishers.

Graham, P. (1993) *Child Psychiatry: A Developmental Approach (2nd edition).* New York: Oxford University Press.

Hobday, A. and Ollier, K. (1998) *Creative Therapy: Activities with Children and Adolescents.* Leicester: BPS Books.

Hobday, A. and Ollier, K. (1999) *Creative Therapy 2: Working with Parents.* Leicester: BPS Books.

Kendall, R.E. (1998) 'Diagnosis and Classification.' In R.E. Kendall and A.K. Zeally (eds) *Companion to Psychiatric Studies (4th edition).* Edinburgh: Churchill Livingstone.

Maguire, G.P. (1998) 'The psychiatric interviews.' In R.E. Kendall and A.K. Zeally (eds) *Companion to Psychiatric Studies (4th edition).* Edinburgh: Churchill Livingstone.

McCrum, S. and Hughes, L. (1998) *Interviewing Children (2nd edition).* London: Save the Children.

Pearce, J. (1994) 'Consent to treatment during childhood. The assessment of competence and avoidance of conflict.' *British Journal of Psychiatry 165,* 713–716.

Rutter, M. and Taylor, E. (2002) 'Clinical Assessment and Diagnostic Formulation.' In M. Rutter and E. Taylor (eds) *Child and Adolescent Psychiatry: Modern Approaches (4th edition).* Oxford: Blackwell Scientific.

Swadi, H. (2000) 'Substance misuse in adolescents.' *Advances in Psychiatric Treatment 6,* 201–210.

Worden, M. (1998) *Family Therapy Basics.* Pacific Grove, CA: Brooks/Cole.

CHAPTER 4

Child and Adolescent Development

Psychological development in childhood

An understanding of psychological development underpins concepts in mental health throughout the lifespan as well as being crucial to understanding developmental delay. Psychological development begins at birth, or even before, and continues through to old age. As with physical development, there are periods of particularly rapid psychological development in childhood and adolescence; these periods are the focus of this section. Physical and psychological development are closely related throughout – from the coordination of motor and perceptual function in early childhood with increased exploration of the world and the child's developing identity in relation to that, to the changes at puberty and the physical and psychological sequelae of that. Psychological development is outlined in this chapter and then we briefly review developmental delay because children with developmental delay have increased likelihood of developing mental health problems.

Bronfenbrenner's (1979) model of layered contexts is a fairly widely used model to explain how different areas of the child's life influence development. The model also helps explain how the interaction between the different levels may relate to the factors that may lead to mental health problems discussed in Chapter 6. The layers are the microsystem, mesosystem, exosystem and the macrosystem. The first layer (microsystem) is at the level of the relationships in which the child is actively involved, for example, with parents, siblings and peers. These interactions inevitably depend on context and the child's characteristics (or personality). The mesosystem describes how the different components of the microsystem come together.

The exosystem is the wider local community such as the neighbourhood. The macrosystem is usually more remote, but may still be a major social influence, for example, through socioeconomic policy on child rearing, education and health policies and wider social and cultural contexts. It is worth noting that different factors may be important at various stages of the child's life. Some adverse family factors may be mitigated by external factors that come into play as children get older (e.g. peer support).

Psychological development consists of cognitive, emotional, social, and moral development, which will be considered in turn. Children also gradually develop a concept that everyone, including themselves, has a mental state. This is known as 'theory of mind' and is described first as it is relevant to all aspects of psychological development. Table 4.1 summarises the theories of development described in this section.

Ages given throughout this chapter serve as indicators of when skills may develop, but these ages should not be taken as fixed and indeed there is often overlap.

Table 4.1 Comparison of developmental theories in childhood

Age	Eriksen	Piaget	Vygotsky	Theory of Mind	Kohlberg
0–1	Trust vs. mistrust	Sensori-motor	Pre-intellectual speech		Punishment and reward orientations
1–2	Automomy vs. shame and doubt				
2–3		Pre-operational	Practical intelligence	Capable of deception	
3–4	Initiative vs. guilt			Distinguish thoughts/ objects/perceptions/ knowledge	
4–5			Use of external symbols	Pass false belief tests: people hold different beliefs	
5–6	Industry vs. inferiority				
6–7				Distinguish fantasy/ reality more reliably	

cont.

Age	Eriksen	Piaget	Vygotsky	Theory of Mind	Kohlberg
7–8		Concrete operational	Internal dialogue	Understand different interpretations: link thoughts	Good child and authority orientations
8–9				Understand inference	
9–10					
10–11				Understand basic nature of other cognitive processes	
11–12	Identity vs. confusion	Formal operational			Social contact and ethical principle orientations
12–13					
13–14					
14+				Distinguishing problem solving/hypothesis testing	

Theory of mind

'Theory of mind' is the understanding that oneself and others have mental states; that is recognising that other people also have thoughts, feelings, beliefs, intentions, and knowledge, and might have a different perspective to one's own and might be able to pretend or hide aspects of their mental state. This ability is in part developed by eliciting clues from other people's social behaviour. From a very young age, this includes paying attention to people and copying them. Specific steps during development are described below:

- From the age of two or three years a child begins to learn that it is possible to deceive others – cognitive deception (misrepresenting or hiding information).

- By the age of four years a child recognises that thoughts about an object are distinct from the object itself and that thoughts, perceptions and knowledge are different from each other.

Similarly, the differentiation of experienced and expressed emotion emerges at the same age.

- It is not until a year later that they begin to understand that others may hold different beliefs (i.e. pass 'false belief tasks'). Preschool children rarely acknowledge their own or others' thinking, even when given clues about this. Children may be unable to distinguish fantasy from reality until beyond six years.

- Around this age, children also begin to recognise that other people may have likes/dislikes and emotion states that differ from their own. They can name basic emotions in others, such as 'happy', 'sad', and 'angry'. They also learn what might influence other people's emotion states; for instance, 'mum will be angry if I hit my brother'. They will have learnt by now that people's actions may be influenced by what they want.

- Their theory of mind will have developed sufficiently by this stage to engage in imaginative play by themselves or with others as other characters, enabling more sophisticated play, for instance enacting scenes from their experience, such as purchasing goods in a pretend shop, or visiting the doctor.

- It is not until the age of seven or eight years that children recognise that one thought may trigger another ('stream of consciousness'), that this is only partially controllable, and that events/places/memories may trigger thoughts ('cognitive cueing'). Around this age children recognise that different interpretations may be placed on the same event or phrase (e.g. they begin to understand more sophisticated jokes, such as those involving puns).

- By the age of eight years, children have developed a basic understanding of inference – that another thought or desire may lie behind a statement or action (e.g. looking longingly at a box of chocolates when they want to eat one, or saying, 'That looks like a fun toy', meaning they want to play with the toy).

- It is not until after ten years of age that children develop an understanding of the basic nature of other cognitive processes, such as different types of memory, reasoning, attention and comprehension. Development of the ability to distinguish between different cognitive processes continues through adolescence and into adulthood.

The use of words by adults that refer to thinking and feeling enhances the development of theory of mind. Adults and other children can help to promote the development of theory of mind through ordinary interactions and play by tuning in to the child's interests and behaviour in order to comment on the child's possible intentions. For instance, with the box of chocolates example above, commenting, 'Oh, so you'd like a chocolate…', or explaining why someone else might be upset or might hold a different belief to them can extend understanding of their own and other people's mental processes. Other ways in which this is commonly achieved include role play, exploring the possible thoughts, feeling, intentions, and desires of characters in books, and making links between a child's past experience and what is currently happening for other people (e.g. 'Do you remember feeling sad like that when you lost your teddy?').

Cognitive development

Cognitions may be simply described as 'mental processes'. These include understanding, believing, calculating, knowing, creating, reasoning, generating ideas, inferring, conceptualising, fantasising and dreaming, as well as coordinating motor function and perception. Three theories on cognitive development have greatly influenced this area: Piagetian theory, information processing theory and Vygotskian theory.

Piagetian theory

Piaget (1950) described four phases of development that are universal, and that develop at much the same rate irrespective of environmental and cultural influences. His theory influenced educational practice internationally. The phases result from the interaction between the maturation of the central nervous system, physical experience, social interaction, and a psychological homeostatic mechanism. The last allows equilibration, which is the incorporation of new experiences into previously held concepts. Piaget suggested that cognitive development depends on a process of adaptation (or equilibration), which involves two steps: assimilation – relating new information to previous understanding; and accommodation – changing one's prior understanding of an issue or concept as a result of new information. This may involve changing a pre-existing belief or schema, or developing a new one. As people often struggle to change their beliefs, this can be the more challenging step of adaptation.

Adaptation is the process of finding a point of balance (or equilibrium) between assimilating new information and changing pre-existing schema into which this new information would not otherwise fit. Repeatedly readjusting this equilibrium to achieve a homeostasis is what drives learning.

The four phases of development from birth to early adolescence described by Piaget require increasing conceptual skills, and not everyone reaches the same potential within each phase. They are based on observations and experiments he conducted, and have since been tested and replicated in other studies.

Phase 1: Sensorimotor (birth–2 years)

In this phase, children begin to associate and integrate perceptions and motor actions; for example, awareness of the motor function involved in the movement of the arm while seeing the arm move and /or receiving information about the position of that arm in space (proprioception) promotes understanding that 'this arm is part of my body and can be controlled by me'. They understand that objects still exist, even when they can no longer see them. The development of such concepts is assisted across cultures by games such as 'peek-a-boo'.

Phase 2: Preoperational (2–7 years)

From late toddlerhood through to the early preschool years, children enter this phase, in which they can make mental representations of objects and imagine the actions associated with them. Their view of the world is egocentric, meaning they see themselves as having a greater influence on events than they have in reality, and vice versa.

Phase 3: Concrete operational (7–11 years)

In the next phase, from middle to late childhood, thoughts are logical and coordinated. The child remains 'concrete' in his or her thinking, meaning that he or she is limited to tangible and fixed concepts. The development of concepts such as 'preservation of volume' can be demonstrated at this age; for example, a child who has developed this will recognise that water poured from a tall thin jug into a short wide jug remains the same in volume. A younger child witnessing the same demonstration would state that there is more water in the tall thin glass because the level is higher.

Phase 4: Formal operational (11 years and onwards)

From about 11 years old, children enter the fourth phase, in which they are able to think in abstract terms. In this phase, children can begin to apply concepts that are beyond their direct experience, and make prepositional statements that follow a logical argument and test out their own hypotheses, such as about the physical properties of objects.

Information processing theory

There have been several proponents of information processing, based on the work of Miller, Galanter and Pribram (1960). Information processing is a cognitive function whereby information is recognised, coded, stored, and retrieved. Very young children use very basic processes, with the development of deliberate strategic approaches in later childhood. The mind functions as a set of parallel 'units' working contemporaneously, with each unit representing a small item of information. Each unit may represent, for instance, one characteristic of a familiar object (e.g. texture of a blanket). Several units relating to one object may be located in different parts of the brain. These units of information may relate directly to each other without the need for a centralised control. Thus, the mind constantly re-evaluates and collates information. Children use increasingly sophisticated and involved processes as they mature.

Vygotskian theory

Vygotsky (1978) described the dependence of cognitive development (including thinking, memory and attention) upon external factors, such as the social environment, which includes the context of guiding adults who 'scaffold' the child's development. This approach recognises the close links between cognitive, social, and language development. Cognitive development depends on the child making active use of social interactions and internalising these. Thus, 'internal' (cognitive) development depends on 'external' (social) interaction, not the other way around – in contrast with the ideas of Piaget and information processing theory.

Four phases are identified:

1. Infants and toddlers (up to two years) use vocal activity as a means of social contact and emotional expression: this is known as 'pre-intellectual speech' and 'preverbal thought'.

2. The second phase is the development of 'practical intelligence', with loose links between use of language and problem solving.

3. Later, children start to use symbols external to themselves to assist internal problem solving, for example talking oneself through problems, finger counting.

4. These are finally internalised, as language is then used in internal dialogue to develop thought and to reflect (though external tools are still used for difficult problems, as of course is the case for many adults!).

Vygotsky concluded that cognitive development depends on the social environment and context of guiding adults or older peers. Specifically, a child's cognitive development is enhanced by encouraging the child to complete tasks with assistance that would be beyond the child's potential to complete without that assistance. Consider those skills already acquired to be the child's actual developmental level ('What I can do'), whilst the next level of skills would be the child's current potential developmental level that could be achieved with assistance ('What I can do with help'), which Vygotsky referred to as the Zone of Proximal Developmental. Skill levels above this may be beyond the child's current potential, even with assistance ('What I can't do'). Adults and older peers often create situations that support the child to work within his/her Zone of Proximal Development, a process called 'Scaffolding'. An example in developing a cognitive skill in a child's Zone of Proximal Development is supporting a child to complete a jigsaw by re-orienting an unplaced jigsaw piece so that the child can see anew for him or herself where the piece goes. In this example, the child's sense of self-competence and an understanding of collaboration (social cognition) are also enhanced.

Emotional development

The preschool years are a period of particularly rapid emotional development, as they are for many aspects of psychological development. Emotional development is a complex area, which is best described by detailing the tasks that a child needs to accomplish.

The tasks of emotional development include:

- recognising the significance of emotions and differentiating between emotion states (i.e. combination of feelings, associated behaviours and level of arousal) in self and others

- learning to contain emotions and the socio-culturally appropriate and acceptable expression of emotions (the regulation of emotions); and, as a result,

- distinguishing between emotions experienced and emotions expressed, both in self and in others (related to theory of mind, described above) understanding the impact of emotions on behaviour and relationships (the regulatory capacity of emotions).

Development of differentiation of emotions

Differentiating between emotions has a biological significance in terms of survival. Learning proceeds from birth (and possibly before), is difficult to assess in preverbal ages, and is more reliably demonstrated for 'complex' emotions in later childhood. The ages at which a reliable understanding of each emotion is achieved are given in Table 4.2.

Table 4.2 Emotions consistently identified with children by age

Emotion	Age from which each emotion is included (years)
Happy	5+
Sad	
Afraid	
Angry	
Shy	
Proud	
Worried	7+
Grateful	
Excited	
Surprised	
Jealous	
Guilty	
Disappointed	10+
Curious	
Relieved	
Disgusted	
Ashamed	14+
Shocked	
Embarrassed	
Depressed	

(after work by Harris *et al.* 1987)

The expression, concealment and sharing of emotion

Learning to contain and appropriately express emotion is learnt from parents and peers both by direct intervention (e.g. parental management of tantrums) and vicariously (e.g. observation of adults' and peers' emotional responses to a situation). Learning to regulate emotions in this way is a lifelong process, but is of paramount importance throughout childhood and adolescence.

At a preschool age, the development of learning when and how to hide feelings probably occurs simultaneously with an understanding that others can also do this. This is partly dependent on the development of theory of mind, and is akin to the understanding of cognitive deception. As well as being regulated, emotions are regulatory. They may influence interpretation of events, potential responses to events or situations, and behaviour of the individual and others. Notable steps in emotional development are:

- from birth to 18 months – emotional state can be determined by behavioural responses (e.g. parents can distinguish specific cries and vocalisations, which they understand to convey different needs)

- from 18 to 24 months – expression of first words describing emotions

- at around two years – increase in the use of pretend play to express feelings and frequent expression of anger or frustration through tantrums

- by three years – competence at talking with parents, siblings, and peers about feelings (this varies with parents' use of words to describe emotions); frequent use of play or humour, gesture and facial expression to express emotion.

The ability to share emotions (i.e. the mutual expression and registration of feelings) in early childhood facilitates the resolution of difficult emotions, which leads to enhanced understanding and regulation of emotions, which leads to ability to provide constructive responses to conflict, and predicts increased cooperation in later childhood and possibly adulthood.

The ability to share emotions with peers about third parties (e.g. disgust) is apparent by the age of five years and predicts acceptance by friends and peers, which in turn predicts the self-regulation of 'difficult' emotions such as anger, anxiety and fear. This interaction between social and emotional development continues throughout childhood. By the age of ten years there is increased sharing between friends of socially undesirable feelings in a socially acceptable manner. As children develop they increasingly share emotional experiences and memories with a same-gender friend (or small group of friends), deriving relief from being 'understood' and enhancing the friendship. A child is more likely than an adult to understand the emotional expression of a peer of the same stage of development, which may explain the potency of therapeutic groups.

Social development

Social development is interdependent with other aspects of development. There are two broad ways of describing social development. One is by plotting the tasks of social development throughout the lifespan, which Eriksen (1965) first described. The other is by examining the details of social interaction (see 'Social skills' below), and how this influences peer relationships. The nature of attachment influences social development, the relationships that young people have with peers and adults, and how this subsequently develops in adult life. Attachment and attachment disorders are described in Chapters 6 and 9.

Eriksen's 'eight stages of man'

Eriksen (1965) described the 'Eight Stages of Man', a model for socio-emotional development in humans. Longitudinal cohort studies of up to 80 years have demonstrated the validity of these concepts in 'Western society'. Moving on to each stage is not dependent on complete resolution of tasks and conflicts in previous stages. The stages relevant to childhood are:

Basic trust vs. mistrust (first year of life)

The child will develop trust in the world if his/her needs are predictably met. Otherwise, the child may develop a perception of the world as a hostile and unpredictable place. Gross deprivation at this stage may lead to emotional detachment in childhood and throughout life, with difficulties forming deep and lasting relationships in adulthood.

Autonomy vs. shame and doubt (1–3 years)

The child acquires confidence in his/her own ability as opposed to self-doubt. The child begins to recognise his/her own will and ability to be independent, and may feel guilty if he/she does not conform to expected behaviours. This stage is about learning to balance one's own wishes against those of others. Failing to exert oneself may lead to reduced confidence and initiative, but failure to take into account others' wishes may make it difficult to integrate into society fully.

Initiative vs. guilt (3–5 years)

The child acquires more social skills and assumes greater responsibility for themself. A sense of time begins to develop. The child builds on the tasks accomplished in the previous stage. Successful resolution at this stage results in a confident and outgoing child. Others may develop fears or problems with nightmares as they struggle to resolve the conflict between their own needs and others.

Industry vs. inferiority (5–11 years)

The challenge here is to achieve and overcome feelings of failure. The child will be industrious in schoolwork, sport and social relationships. If these are not achieved, then the child may feel a sense of failure and inferiority. He/she may also become isolated from the peer group.

Identity vs. confusion (11+ years)

In this stage, the child acquires a firm sense of who he/she is (separate from the family), what he/she wants from life and where he/she is going. This is further discussed in the adolescent development section later in this chapter.

The three remaining stages for completeness are: intimacy vs. isolation (young adulthood), generativity vs. stagnation (middle adulthood), and integrity vs. despair (old age).

Social skills

Essential social skills include eye contact, turn taking, listening, interaction in play, learning appropriate behaviour and physical contact. These influence popularity, peer relationships and friendships. To respond appropriately to another child's social behaviour, a child needs to follow six steps:

1. encode that behaviour

2. interpret it

3. search for appropriate responses

4. evaluate and select a response

5. enact the response

6. monitor the outcome.

This is similar to the steps described in information processing described in the Cognitive Development section earlier in this chapter. The successful development of peer relationships is partly dependent on these skills.

The development of these skills can be enhanced by talking the child through a particular scenario that has just occurred or interrupting and 'pausing' an interaction between the child and a peer or adult in order to assist them in describing a step that the child has missed. Use of a peer group (either in the child's natural setting or in a therapy setting) is a potent way of enhancing social skill acquisition.

Peer relationships and play

Peer relationships vary in quality and size, and their nature shows in development throughout childhood. Both popularity and friendships depend upon behavioural and emotional interactions, which in childhood are commonly exercised through play.

Children are initially closely monitored and moderated by parents or other adults. Infants and toddlers will hold on to an attachment figure while looking at (i.e. being interested in) peers. Adults 'scaffold' (see Vygotsky above) early infant–infant interaction. From two to four years, skills increase with age, largely through play. Initially mainly rough-and-tumble, this develops into pretend role play (socio-dramatic play). Play develops from toddlerhood to school age in four identifiable stages:

- solitary play (child plays by self)

- parallel play (child plays alongside others, may mimic, etc.)

- associative play (child plays with others, but without organised structure)

- cooperative play (child plays with others with routine, acceptance of rules, and 'productively').

Peer group size increases with age, which, as with other aspects of psychosocial development, occurs earlier in girls than boys. The quality of interactions changes throughout childhood as identifiable groups of friends develop.

Popularity

Popularity is relatively stable over time and can be measured by ascertaining the perceptions children have of each other in their peer groups. Five groups can be distinguished on this basis and are shown in Figure 4.1.

Popularity is influenced by characteristics of both the group as a whole, and the individual child. These characteristics include physical attractiveness, obesity, handicap and temperament. Social withdrawal may have an interactive causal association with dislike of a child by the peer group.

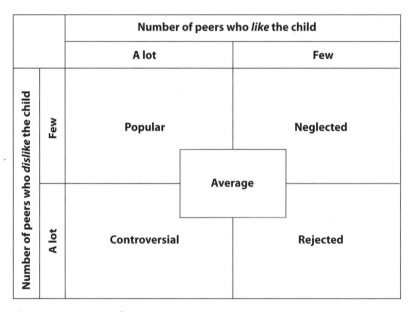

Figure 4.1 Peer popularity

The use of the six steps of social skills differs between the five groups. For instance, popular children follow through the six steps. Neglected children encode and interpret, but may go no further. Rejected children 'crash in' at stage 5, often with an inappropriate response of which peers are intolerant. Controversial children often follow through, but are erratic in their responses. They are often bullies or victims of bullying.

Friendships

Friendships develop from toddlerhood. Their development has three identifiable stages:

1. reward–cost basis (usually up to 8 years) – for example, with shared activities, live nearby

2. normative (entered at 9–10 years) with shared values, rules and sanctions

3. empathic (entered at 11–12 years) with increased understanding between friends, self-disclosure and shared interests.

CASE STUDY: Sunil

Sunil is an eight-year-old child who lives with his parents. The extended family is very close, with most family members living nearby. Sunil developed a very close relationship with his paternal grandparents, visiting them daily. When he was seven years old, both grandparents died in a road accident.

Sunil's parents found this extremely difficult to cope with, and his mother in particular found it very difficult to talk about her in-laws, or to have any photographs or memories of them around the house. Sunil attended the cremation and found it confusing. It became very clear to him that every time he brought up the subject of his grandparents and their death, his mother either burst into tears, became angry, or changed the subject. Therefore, Sunil stopped talking about them, finding this to be helpful to his mother. At school, teachers noted that he was more isolated and distant, and that the quality of his schoolwork deteriorated. This continued for a number of weeks, but whenever his teacher asked him whether there was any problem, he would deny it.

Eventually, Sunil's parents took him to see his GP because he was becoming increasingly irritable and aggressive towards them. When seen on his own, Sunil told the GP that he was very sad that his grandparents were not alive, and he wondered whether he had been responsible for their death. A referral was made to the local child and family psychiatric service and the whole family was seen. It became clear that Sunil's parents had felt unable to help Sunil with his grief because of the difficulty that they were having with their own. Sunil's parents agreed to a referral to a bereavement counselling agency for bereavement counselling in their own right, and Sunil was seen individually on six occasions, every two weeks. During that time, Sunil was able to clarify a number of his misperceptions and explore his own grief. This led to a resolution of many of his symptoms of irritability, poor concentration and physical aggression. Through their attendance at the bereavement counselling service, Sunil's parents also managed to move on through this grieving process and the family was able to grieve together.

- What concerns did Sunil have, and what are the related developmental issues?

- What is the role of a specialist CAMHS in a presentation like this?

Friendships from early childhood predict the quality of friendships in later childhood and adulthood. Low peer acceptance also predicts early school dropout and, more controversially, higher rates of juvenile and adult crime. Friendships from middle childhood onwards are mostly formed on a mutually voluntary basis. Children benefit in different ways from friendships and have differing expectations of them. Companionship is a common characteristic, with increased provision of emotional support and intimacy with increased age.

Moral development

Relatively less has been written on moral development. Most work in this area is based on Kohlberg's model.

Kohlberg's model

Kohlberg (1973) applied Piaget's theories to develop a framework for moral development. This theory more accurately describes the development of moral reasoning rather than moral behaviour. Although this theory is based on cognitive development, moral development is very closely interwoven with social development. Kohlberg described three levels of moral development:

Level I Pre-conventional morality

Stage 1: punishment orientation (child obeys rules to avoid punishment)

Stage 2: reward orientation (child conforms to expectations to have rewards)

Level II Conventional morality

Stage 3: good child orientation (child conforms to avoid disapproval of others)

Stage 4: authority orientation (child upholds laws and rules to avoid censure of authorities)

Level III Post-conventional morality

Stage 5: social contact orientation (child's actions are guided by principles commonly agreed on as essential to public welfare; principles are upheld to retain respect of peers)

Stage 6: ethical principle orientation (child's actions are guided by self-chosen ethical principles that usually value justice, dignity and equality; principles are upheld to retain self-respect).

It is important to distinguish between the development of moral concepts and changes in behaviour. The two are usually interdependent, but both should be assessed.

Adolescent development

Adolescence is loosely defined as a period of transition from puberty (around 10–14 years of age) to late teens or early twenties. Psycho-biologically, adolescence can be seen as associated with a process of maturation and changes in brain structure that only occur at this stage of life and that are most likely prompted by the hormonal changes of puberty, which continue into the early-to-mid-twenties. It is, however, culturally and historically variable. In Western societies, adolescence is generally seen as a time of transition from childhood to adulthood. There may be transitions that all young people experience (such as leaving school) or some that only happen to some individuals (such as experiencing parental divorce). There may be internal changes (such as biological changes of puberty) or external ones (such as expectations of society). The changes may be normative (that is, expected to occur at a particular age physiologically or as prescribed culturally) or idiosyncratic (person specific, such as illness). The transitions may be on-time or off-time and expected or unexpected. Generally, on-time and expected changes are less disruptive than off-time and unexpected transitions. There is consistent evidence that most young people manage the transition of adolescence without undue stress. Some of the behaviours of adolescence may be focused on because of the discomfort they generate in adults. Media representation of adolescents can also distort the realities.

In Western societies, the tasks of adolescence can be defined as follows:

- increasing educational demands, establishing adult vocational goals and thinking about how to achieve them (this may also mean preparing for financial independence and a career)

- adjustment to being a sexually mature adult (this includes developing sexual identity, sexual orientation and sexuality)

- developing peer relationships (sexual and non-sexual)

- developing a personal sense of identity

- acquiring a personal set of values and ethical system, a personal ideology

- increasing responsibility for one's own behaviour, which usually means desiring and achieving socially responsible behaviour

- achieving independence from parents and other adults (emotional, psychological, financial and otherwise)

- preparing for one's own marriage and family (can be widely interpreted and still applies to most young people).

Tasks are to an extent specific to a child's culture and family, and may present conflict for some individuals; for example, developing a sense of one's own sexuality as other than heterosexual when there is a societal or family expectation that one should be heterosexual.

Biological change is necessary for some of the above tasks to be completed. Some degree of psychological maturity is needed for all tasks. External conditions may strongly impact on achieving some tasks (economic conditions may dictate employment, and although an individual may be ready to separate from their parents, their personal finances may make that impossible). Socio-cultural forces impact all tasks, as each involves social expectations and definitions.

There is a period of rapid physical and intellectual growth in early adolescence. In middle adolescence, there is increasing self-reliance, which seems to promote the success of more intimate friendships and dating. By late adolescence a clear consistent sense of self has usually developed with ideas on roles and value systems as well as personal life goals. There are phases of adolescent maturity and these anticipate that between 10 and 13 years most young people are compliant with expectations of them. Rebellion usually occurs between 14 and 17 years. Between 17 and 21 years most young people mature and outgrow their need to rebel. Whether adolescents successfully complete the tasks expected of them will also to some extent depend on the way their parents and the wider community respond to them. Parents may struggle with balancing providing autonomy for the young person while still retaining a degree of control. Young people may also challenge the long-held value systems of their parents, thus leading to conflict. Interestingly, early puberty presents greater problems for girls than boys, and late puberty appears to present more difficulties for boys than girls.

CASE STUDY: Alison

Alison is 15 years old and has been complaining of a loss of interest in her schoolwork. She is questioning the point of being at school and feels it has no relevance to her now or in the future. You have known Alison for some time and this is quite a change from how you have seen her.

—   What would you do?

—   What might Alison's lack of interest be related to?

After talking further with Alison, you think she is struggling with aspects of her sexuality. What would you do next?

Developmental delay

Developmental disorders can be classified into three groups:

- general developmental delay

- specific developmental disorders

- unusual trajectory of development e.g. autism spectrum disorders, also known as pervasive developmental disorders.

General and specific disorders are outlined in this section and autism spectrum disorders in Chapter 11.

General developmental delay

Characteristics and presentation

Terminology for global developmental delay changes frequently in an attempt to avoid stigmatisation. It is now commonly known in the UK as intellectual disability, but is also referred to as developmental disability, learning disability (LD), mental handicap, or mental retardation. It is characterised by: global delay/slowing/hindered development (i.e. affecting all areas of physical, intellectual and psychological development) with preservation of the sequence of development. General developmental delay can present at different ages:

- routine antenatal screening for Down syndrome and other congenital abnormalities

- specific (at risk) antenatal screening of metabolic and genetic disorders

- at birth – physical characteristics of disorders commonly associated with developmental delay (such as Down syndrome)

- preschool – delay in expected milestones

- school-age – delayed speech/social development, poor scholastic achievement.

Assessment and diagnosis

The assessment is more than simply a measure of intelligence and should take into account the child's ability to function physically, socially, and in activities of daily living and self-care, such as washing and dressing, as well as academically. Further medical investigation of the known causes of developmental delay (see below) should be made. Diagnosis requires the following criteria to be met:

- Onset must be before the age of 18 years.

- There should be evidence of a significantly reduced level of intellectual functioning. A commonly accepted measure of intelligence is IQ (intelligence quotient) although there are concerns about its application and validity in different populations (Victor 2000). Table 4.3 shows the categories of intellectual functioning. However, assessment of severity should also take account of general adaptive functioning, without over-reliance on a single measure of function such as IQ.

- There should be evidence of a diminished ability to adapt to daily demands in areas such as self-care, communication, social competence, etc.

- A comprehensive assessment of functioning as a minimum requires physical and mental state examinations, information from parents and teachers, and observation in various environments. There may be additional need for more detailed testing of specific areas of function. This assessment must take account of cultural expectations and expected functioning for age. Assessment can be assisted by standardised informant-report inventories, such as the Vineland Adaptive Behaviour Scale (Sparrow, Balla and Cicchetti 1984), which gather information from parents or others who know the child well.

Table 4.3 IQ and severity of learning disability

IQ	Severity of learning disability
50–69	Mild
35–49	Moderate
20–34	Severe
<20	Profound

Causes of learning disability

There are two broad groups: inherited and acquired. These can be broken down further:

INHERITED

- Chromosomal disorders and chromosomal abnormalities (chromosomes are large packages of genetic material). Any syndrome characterised by malformation or malfunction in any of the body's systems may be caused by an abnormality in the number or structure of the chromosomes; for example Down syndrome (there is an extra chromosome) and fragile X syndrome (the structure of the X chromosome is altered).

- Genetic, causing chemical imbalances, such as phenylketonuria.

- Physical abnormalities, such as hydrocephalus and neuro-fibromatosis.

ACQUIRED

- Infection, such as rubella and encephalitis.

- Trauma, such as radiation, birth asphyxia, accidental or non-accidental injury.

- Poisoning, such as lead intoxication.

- Malnutrition.

- Environmental factors, such as poverty, poor housing, unstable family or under-stimulation.

More than one factor may mediate developmental delay. Psychological and environmental factors may account for variation in IQ of as much as 20 points. Studies of institutionalised young people suggest that providing more stimulating home and school environments can significantly increase IQ (Capron and Duyme 1989; Dumaret 1985; Garber 1988; Provence and Naylor 1983; Ramey, Campbell and Finkelstein 1984).

CASE STUDY: Julie

Julie is a seven-year-old girl who was brought to the attention of the school attendance officer as her school attendance had gradually fallen to less than 25 per cent. The school attendance officer learnt that Julie frequently attended her GP with non-specific 'ailments', often complaining that she could not do her schoolwork because of these. Her mother was anxious, often kept Julie off school because of this, and believed her difficulties were due to 'dyslexia', 'vitamin deficiency', and a list of some unsubstantiated very rare and unusual medical disorders. Julie's school reported that she was markedly behind in her schoolwork and had not made friends. She could not yet write her name or simple words, had poor pencil skills and could barely read books for preschool children. On further enquiry, Julie's mother reluctantly admitted that she still needed to dress Julie and assist her using cutlery.

– Who should assess Julie next? What is the likely diagnosis?

– Why do you think Julie's mother sought so many explanations for her difficulties?

– Why do you think Julie had so many non-specific physical ailments? What interventions would you recommend?

Specific developmental disorders

These include specific disorders of:

- speech and language – concerns about articulation, expression or understanding of speech and language indicate the need for a Speech and Language Therapy assessment

- reading, writing, spelling or arithmetic skills – difficulties arise in establishing these as there are many confounding factors, such as an under-stimulating environment

- motor function (physical movement) – developmental disorders of motor function usually present with clumsiness, and there may be impairment of hand-eye coordination

- a combination of the above – these all have an onset in the early stages of development, commonly present early, and are more common in boys: the specific delay should not be accounted for by a global developmental delay or an autistic disorder, also known as pervasive developmental disorder (PDD), and it is important to exclude medical causes, such as neurological and hearing abnormalities.

Strategies for use with developmental delay

Specific interventions in all types of developmental delay are largely aimed at maximising the young person's potential and supporting the family. Treatable causes of the delay should be identified. However, the majority of developmental delays are of unknown aetiology, and many known causes are untreatable.

Intervention to meet the young person's educational and social needs may include the provision of special education. In late adolescence and early adulthood, interventions may continue to focus on daily living skills with the provision of day care and sheltered housing. Issues of sex, sexuality and sexual orientation also need to be addressed in a developmentally appropriate way.

Physical and mental health issues, including emotional and behavioural problems have a markedly higher prevalence in young people with a developmental delay. These often need specialist intervention, particularly for multiple and complex problems.

Behaviour therapy is commonly used to encourage the development of skills needed for self-reliance and to discourage behaviours such as self-injury and stereotypies (intentional but pointless movements carried out in a repetitive manner). It is particularly important when working with young people with learning disabilities to follow the ethical guidelines outlined in the section on behaviour management in Chapter 14. Consent should be sought from parents who should be fully involved in planning and implementation.

Young people with learning disabilities frequently use their behaviour to communicate. A 'functional analysis' is a systematic method for developing an informed understanding of the function of the behaviour in terms of what the young person gains or avoids and is essential to the planning of an intervention.

Family issues in delayed development

The interaction between the young person and their family (which may include unrelated peers and others) is important, with particular reference to family development, culture and individual temperament. Families with a child with a learning disability may have difficulty accomplishing the tasks in one or more stages of family development (outlined in Chapter 5). This may be as a result of an interruption to the usual pattern of parent–child interactions due to one or more of the following factors:

Factors in the young person:

- reduced readiness to participate in social interaction

- impaired perceptual abilities

- impaired motor function

- impairment of general arousal

- abnormal expression of features of attachment in the first year of life.

Factors in the parents:

- parenting function impaired by guilt, depression, anxiety, or grief (of the loss of the 'normal' child expected) resulting in over-/under-involvement

- interruption of usual patterns of engagement from infancy, due either to parental failure to respond to the infant's socio-emotional needs because of lack of cues, or parents observing that their attempts to engage with their infant fail to elicit the expected response.

These are important features to assess and may require specific intervention.

The role of temperament in delayed development

The categories and features of the temperaments of infants are outlined in more detail in Chapter 6. 'Difficult temperament' predisposes infants to behavioural and conduct problems. 'Slow-to-warm-up' temperament predisposes infants to emotional problems. An important mediating factor in this is the family's response to these features.

A cycle of increased negative emotional response or of increased emotional distance between the child and other family members may perpetuate or exacerbate problem behaviours. The professional needs to understand the interactive nature of this cycle, elicit a clear history of family relationships and make interventions that reduce the problem behaviour and increase positive and appropriate behaviours. Parental stress and poor coping strategies may also need to be explored and support systems strengthened in order to allow the family to make the positive changes. The young person and their family may be aided by the provision of day services and activities or residential respite care.

References

Bronfenbrenner, U (1979) 'Contexts of child rearing: Problems and prospects.' *American Psychologist 34*, 644–850.

Capron, C. and Duyme, M. (1989) 'Assessment of effects of socio-economic status on IQ in a full cross-fostering study.' *Nature 340*, 552–554.

Dumaret, A. (1985) 'IQ, scholastic performance and behaviour of siblings raised in contrasting environments.' *Journal of Child Psychology and Psychiatry 26*, 553–580.

Eriksen, E. (1965) *Childhood and Society.* Harmondsworth: Penguin.

Garber, H.L. (1988) *The Milwaukee Project: Preventing Mental Retardation in Children at Risk.* Washington, DC: American Association of Mental Retardation.

Harris, P.L., Olthof, T., Meerum-Terwogt, M., and Hardman, C.E. (1987) 'Children's knowledge of the situations that provoke emotion.' *International Journal of Behavioural Development 10*, 319–343.

Kohlberg, L. (1973) *Collected Papers on Moral Development and Moral Education.* Cambridge, MA: Harvard University Press.

Miller, G.A., Galanter, E. and Pribram, K.H. (1960) *Plans and the Structure of Behavior.* New York: Holt, Rinehart and Winston.

Piaget, J. (1950) *The Psychology of Intelligence.* London: Routledge and Kegan Paul.

Provence, S. and Naylor, A. (1983) *Working with Disadvantaged Parents and Children: Scientific Issues and Practice.* New Haven, CT: Yale University Press.

Ramey, C., Campbell, F. and Finkelstein, N. (1984) 'Course and Structure of Intellectual Development in Children at High Risk for Developmental Retardation.' In P. Brooks, R. Sperber and C. McCauley (eds) *Learning and Cognition in the Mentally Retarded.* Hillsdale, NJ: Erlbaum.

Sparrow, S., Balla, D. and Cicchetti, D. (1984) *Vineland Adaptive Behaviour Scale.* Circle Pines, MN: American Guidance Service.

Victor, N. (2000) *Cross-cultural Neuropsychological Assessment: Theory and Practice.* Mahwah, NJ: Erlbaum.

Vygotsky, L.S. (1978) *Mind in Society: The Development of Higher Psychological Processes.* Cambridge, MA: Harvard University Press.

Further reading

Demetriou, A., Doise, W. and van Lieshout, C. (1998) *Life-span Developmental Psychology.* Chichester and New York: Wiley.

Gordon, J. and Grant, G. (eds) (1997) *How We Feel: An Insight Into the Emotional World of Teenagers.* London: Jessica Kingsley Publishers.

Heaven, P.C.L. (1996) *Adolescent Health: The Role of Individual Differences.* London: Routledge.

Henderson, A. and Champlin, S. with Evashwick, W. (eds) (1998) *Promoting Teen Health: Linking Schools, Health Organizations and Community.* Thousand Oaks, CA: Sage.

Hinde, R.A. and Stevenson-Hinde, J. (1988) *Relationships within Families: Mutual Influences.* Oxford: Oxford Science Publications.

Kimmel, D.C. and Weiner, I.B. (1994) *Adolescence: A Developmental Transition (2nd Edition).* New York: Wiley.

Mills, R. and Duck, S. (2000) *The Developmental Psychology of Personal Relationships.* Chichester and New York: Wiley.

CHAPTER 5

Family Development

Defining the family

Traditionally families have had at their heart a biological connection, but being part of a family extends far beyond this. Indeed, it is impossible to define the extent of the family, as this is personally, legally and culturally determined. For example, some cultures may regard members of the extended family, such as grandparents, as an important influence in their day-to-day life, while other cultures would regard this as unhelpful and intrusive. There are many routes into a family, such as birth, adoption, fostering, sexual relationships, and marriage. Generally speaking, it is much easier to become a part of a family than it is to stop being part of one. Whatever value an individual places on their membership of a family, they can never completely leave it except through death.

In Western societies, views on what is meant by family have been radically reshaped over the past few decades. In the UK, there has been a dramatic increase in families headed by one parent. In the US, stepfamilies now outnumber families made up of children living with both biological parents. In England and Wales in 2014, the divorce rate was 9.3 couples per 1000 married couples, with 111,000 divorces. This reflects a gradual decline in the number of divorces, which may be due to the increasing number of couples choosing to cohabit rather than marry. The median duration of marriage is 11.7 years. 48 per cent of divorcing couples had at least one child under 16 (Office for National Statistics 2014, 2015). This figure is an underestimate of this experience, as it does not take into account children of unmarried parents.

In many countries, legal definitions of what constitutes a family still reflect a view that it should have as its basis a heterosexual married couple, as the rights and responsibilities of unmarried fathers and same-gender parenting couples are severely curtailed.

The increasing diversity of the ways people choose to live together, as seen in single parent families, same-gender couples, stepfamilies, and couples choosing not to marry, is gaining acceptance to varying degrees. The way that people live their lives is challenging the view of what is 'normal'. Nevertheless, many families bear some resemblance to the 'traditional nuclear family' or are influenced by the idea in some way, as this powerful image shapes expectations of family life.

Personal definitions of the family are not static, as we all need to make sense of our changing circumstances. As well as the common experience of joining a new family via a relationship, there is also evidence from longitudinal studies of kinship networks that our views on family fluctuate depending on our differing needs throughout our lifetime.

For the purpose of working with children in a mental health context, a pragmatic definition of family would encompass all those involved in meeting the child's immediate emotional and developmental needs, which is a definition based on function rather than structure. This would usually include the household but can often extend to parents living elsewhere and, being mindful of issues of confidentiality, grandparents, close family friends, and child minders. Levin and Trost (1992) proposed a definition of family as two or more people who define themselves as family. In practice, families usually have little difficulty in defining themselves, but difficulties arise when the professional working with them does not share the family's views on membership because of their own cultural and personal expectations. It is also important to be mindful of the legal implications regarding who has the authority to make decisions for the family.

Family lifecycle

Much has been written on the development of the individual and, whilst there are fewer theories on family development, the notion of a cyclical progression through an individual's life has wide acceptance across cultures; a similar model adapted to describe family life has proven to be a useful perspective on how families live their lives. Carter and McGoldrick (1989) proposed an eight-stage lifecycle to describe an individual's journey through family life:

Stage One

Live in family of origin with focus on relationships with parents and siblings, and have shared experiences.

Stage Two

Leaving home, in which the individual establishes their own identity and creates a life beyond their family of origin.

Stage Three

Pre-marriage stage, which involves developing long-term relationships and deciding to live together/marry.

Stage Four

Childless couple stage, where couples develop ways of living together, becoming more influenced by their partner's extended family whilst loosening ties to their own family.

Stage Five

Family with young children where the couple have to adjust their own relationship to accommodate the children's needs. Adults find their relationship with their own parents is reshaped. Children are initially completely family-oriented but start to develop relationships outside the immediate family.

Stage Six

Family with adolescents. Children develop their autonomy and parent–child intimacy declines. Adults face mid-life issues regarding long-term relationships, and this is often the most demanding time in their working life.

Stage Seven

'Launching' children. Issues of loss for parents with children leaving and grandparents declining or dying, and reappraisal of their relationship as a childless couple. For children, the developing view of their parents as equals and ambivalence regarding their full independence.

Stage Eight

Later life, which involves adjustment to the effects of ageing for parents and the possible loss of their partner. For children, the growth of responsibilities towards parents and death of their parents.

There are many obvious criticisms of this model, such as its assumption of couples staying together and the ability or desire to have children, as well as assumptions about culture and sexuality – which could be seen as a white Western stereotype – but the concept of an evolutionary process of family development is fairly universal, with most cultures and societies recognising the importance of the passage of significant milestones such as birth, puberty, marriage and death, usually marking some or all of them with ceremonies.

All cultures have expectations that inform the way families think about resolving disputes, the extent of involvement of the extended family, and how marriages and parent–child relationships should be conducted. It is also important to recognise that families exist in a broader context. For example, a second-generation family of Indian origin living in Britain may have different family expectations from the family of origin, as their family expectations could be a mixture of the differing influences. As with all developmental models, there is a danger that families come to be pathologised if they are not progressing to the next stage. Despite these criticisms, the family lifecycle model remains a useful framework for thinking about the family context in which young people develop, as it poses the question, 'Why is this family/young person presenting now?'

Young people often present with mental health problems at points of transition in the family lifecycle (Carter and McGoldrick 1989). A family that is appropriately equipped with strategies may still find transition difficult, but will be able to achieve the tasks necessary to make the transition successfully. A family that does not have the necessary skills or finds itself thrown off course by unexpected events may struggle to meet the tasks to enable a successful transition. Alongside the more predictable transitional stressors there is likely to be a range of factors that impinge on a family's ability to negotiate transitions between stages of the lifecycle. These can be unpredictable life events such as a premature death, illness, disability and redundancy. The parents' own experiences in their families of origin has a significant influence on how they approach the task of helping their children through difficult times. For example, a mother's ability to help her daughter negotiate the transition into adolescence may be seriously compromised by the unexpected loss of a parent when she was an adolescent. Carter and McGoldrick (1989) described these as horizontal and vertical stressors.

CASE STUDY: Nigel

Nigel is 17 years old and you have been asked to see him because he has complained of feeling increasingly anxious in social situations. He has also been losing interest in seeing his friends and struggling to keep up with his college work. He is an able student and hopes to go to university later this year. He gets on well with his parents, but his father recently had to retire due to a chronic heart condition. Nigel's older brother is in his second year at university. His maternal grandparents lived nearby and had always been fit and well, but his grandmother died last year and his grandfather needs a lot of support from Nigel's mother.

–   What lifecycle issues, both predictable and unpredictable, can you identify and how might they be affecting Nigel and the family?

References

Carter, B. and McGoldrick, M. (1989) *The Changing Family Lifecycle: A Framework for Family Therapy (2nd edition)*. New York: Gardner.

Levin, I. and Trost, J. (1992) 'Understanding the concept of family.' *Family Relations 41*, 348–351.

Office for National Statistics (2014) and (2015) *Statistical bulletin: Divorces in England and Wales: Dissolutions and annulments of marriage by previous marital status, sex, age, children, facts proven and to whom granted.* ONS: London.

Further reading

Carr, A. (2000) *Family Therapy: Concepts, Process and Practice.* Chichester: Wiley.

Krause, I. and Miller, A.C. (1995) 'Culture and Family Therapy.' In S. Fernando (ed.) *Mental Health in a Multi-Ethnic Society: A Multidisciplinary Handbook.* London: Routledge.

McGoldrick, M., Pearce, J.K. and Giordana, J. (1996) *Ethnicity and Family Therapy (2nd edition).* New York: Guilford Press.

CHAPTER 6

What Causes Mental Health Problems in Young People?

There is no easy answer to this question; it requires an understanding of all the factors that can play a part in causing mental health problems. Until recently, those factors for which there were tangible interventions (such as cognitive behaviour therapy, family therapy, medication) were almost exclusively incorporated into theories to explain the cause (aetiology) of problems. For example, understanding a problem as being caused by how the family functions enables the professional to develop interventions based on improving family functioning. However, as this is a circular process, it can be difficult to evaluate the different components. Child mental health is becoming a more evidence-based discipline, which means that theories of understanding causation and treatment are not necessarily based on the same assumption as they have been historically.

So, what causes children and young people's mental health problems and disorders? Very few child mental health problems are caused by a single factor; most are multifactorial in origin, that is, several factors play a part in their development and often it may be the combination of factors that leads to problems. The impact of each factor varies from problem to problem and young person to young person. Traditionally there are three main areas that need consideration – biological, psychological and environmental – but whilst they are considered separately for clarity, it must be remembered that there is interaction between them all.

Biological factors

Biological factors refer to physical or physiological influences and may be inherited or acquired. They include:

- genetic (through one single gene or multiple gene inheritance)

- chromosomal abnormalities (chromosomes are large packages of genetic material; any syndrome characterised by malformation or malfunction in any of the body's system may be caused by an abnormality in the number or structure of the chromosomes)

- developmental (e.g. malformations of the brain)

- medical disorders, especially neurological (affecting the brain and nervous system) or endocrine (hormonal)

- physical or chemical trauma (especially affecting the brain); metabolic disorders (causing e.g. biochemical imbalance)

- toxic disorders (substance use, heavy metals such as lead, and chemicals)

- dietary deficiencies (e.g. vitamins).

A similar range of categories may also cause developmental delay, though the specific factors involved may differ (see Chapter 4). Genetic and chromosomal factors may directly influence the development of a specific mental health disorder, or their effect can be mediated by environmental factors. Physical abnormality or trauma to the brain is strongly associated with the development of mental health disorders, as are other disorders of the brain such as epilepsy. Other medical problems that may lead to mental health problems include:

- endocrine/hormonal (e.g. diabetes, thyroid dysfunction)

- infection

- chronic medical problems (e.g. cystic fibrosis, asthma)

- medication side-effects (e.g. steroids).

Specific medical problems are associated with particular presentations, for example hyperthyroidism (gives rise to raised levels of thyroxin) may cause anxiety; raised steroid levels (either owing to treatment or resulting from a primary endocrine disorder) may cause depression and aggression.

Developmental immaturity

There are also some presentations that are only defined as disorders should they continue beyond a certain age; for instance, temper tantrums are common at age two or three, but are less common and acceptable at age six. By adolescence young people are expected to have attained greater control of their emotions.

Psychological factors

Attachment theory

Babies are born with a biological drive to seek proximity to a protective adult for survival. They are dependent on the physical and emotional availability of the key adults who take care of them. Their relationships with adults are crucial to their trust of other people, their understanding of relationships generally and their feelings about themselves (Simmonds 2004). The drive for closeness promotes attachment behaviours, which help children feel safe.

Attachment theory was initially developed by Bowlby (1969, 1973) to try to understand how young people developed emotional links with their parents. Attachment is an adaptive biological process serving the needs of the child for protection and nurture. It is an interactive process, and though the attachment may be genetically determined, it is influenced by other factors (e.g. maternal mental health). It is of particular relevance in infancy, but features of attachment can be measured through childhood and into adulthood. The theory has been criticised as it centred on mothers, but it has relevance if the primary attachment figure (the person that the child has the closest attachment with, which is usually the primary caregiver) and other attachment figures are considered. The security of attachment is an important indicator of the quality of the parent–child relationship. Secure attachment predicts a better quality of the parent–child relationship in later years, as well as better skills at problem-solving, increased cooperation, compliance and sharing of positive emotions by the child with the parent. Children need a relationship with a caregiver who is sensitive and responsive, who comforts the child when distressed and who enables them to feel safe enough to relax, play and learn. This is the basis of a secure attachment.

Deficiencies in the quantity and quality of contact with the main attachment figure can give rise to specific problems in the short term and long term. Bowlby (1980) later identified three stages in the short-term response by infants to separation from the attachment figure, known as the separation response. These were:

- *Protest:* the child is distressed, often crying and agitated, and may seek or call out for the attachment figure

- *Despair:* the child expresses grief and misery at failure of the attachment figure to return, becoming listless with little interest and response to the immediate environment

- *Detachment:* if the child enters this stage, the child may appear to have adapted and become content, and will show no interest when the attachment figure returns.

These findings and other studies of child deprivation influenced social policy on child welfare and many aspects of childcare over the following decade, for instance, with the institution of parents sleeping in on paediatric wards. Previously, young people seen as 'troublesome' on separation from their parent(s) would later be reported – incorrectly – to have 'settled' as they reached the stage of detachment. Instead, priority is now given to maintaining contact of sufficient quality and duration in these circumstances.

Patterns of attachment

Ainsworth *et al.* (1978) described three main patterns of attachment that can be characterised by observation of the toddler's behaviour with the primary caregiver. These are based on the 12- to 20-month-old infant's reaction, in an experimental setting (known as the 'strange situation' procedure), over an 18-minute period to (a) exposure to a stranger while with the caregiver; (b) separation from the primary caregiver; (c) the return of the caregiver followed by departure of both; and (d) the return of the primary caregiver.

- *Secure attachment*
  The primary caregiver provides a secure base for exploration, and the child is readily comforted if distressed. When reunited with the primary caregiver the child will seek and maintain

contact if he/she has been distressed. The attachment is secure in that the child correctly anticipates that the primary caregiver will be there for them.

- *Anxious/resistant (clingy) attachment*
  In this pattern of attachment, the child is too anxious to leave the primary caregiver to explore his/her environment, and is more wary of new situations and people. When reunited after a separation the child may be aggressive, cry and refuse to be comforted, or remain very passive and withdrawn.

- *Anxious/avoidant (detached) attachment*
  The child explores readily, often ignoring the primary caregiver. The child is unduly friendly with strangers. After separation, the child will ignore or avoid the primary caregiver.

A fourth style of attachment, *disorganized attachment*, has since been described (Main and Solomon 1986) in which the child demonstrates conflict behaviour, confusion, fear of the caregiver and unusual, repetitive, unproductive behaviour. Here they are not able to 'organise' their behaviour and have difficulty regulating their emotions. Although this type of attachment is more likely to occur in children who have been maltreated, there are instances where there is no evidence of maltreatment – for example it can occur in children on the autism spectrum (Brown and Ward 2013).

It is important to emphasise that attachment disorder is not a diagnosis and is not a classification of the infant or of the behaviour, but of the relationship. An infant will show different characteristics in their attachments to different people, and, for instance, with parents the nature of each attachment is predicted by that parent's characteristics. The nature of the attachment is not a reflection of the child's temperament. During the course of childhood, the characteristics of the child's attachments become more unified, such that by adolescence and adulthood an individual's pattern of social interaction is more integrated.

Long-term consequences
Theories based on the importance of relationships in the first five years of life predict that early separation from attachment figures leads to poor outcomes in later childhood and adulthood. However, earlier studies of the long-term effects of separation are contradictory. Some

studies confirmed this prediction; for example, young people raised in institutions had higher rates of behaviour problems, related to adults with 'attention-seeking' or 'clingy' behaviour and were less attached to their mothers on return. However, young people from disrupted homes and young people adopted later in childhood had largely good outcomes, which depended on several factors and not solely early life experiences. Case studies of young people with profound deprivation (such as complete lack of contact with others, being locked in cupboards for prolonged periods) established that, over a period of time, with appropriate parenting they were able to catch up in their development and function normally at home and school.

The importance of secure attachment

Early attachment is important because it acts as an 'internal working model' for subsequent relationships. This model refers to a set of expectations and beliefs about the self and others. For example, a baby whose crying results in a prompt response will learn that certain of his behaviours are linked with the positive behaviours of his caregiver, and he will feel that he is loved and nurtured. A response that is unavailable or cold will lead to an internal working model of the attachment figure as rejecting, the self as unworthy of care and others as not to be relied on for help and support (Schofield and Beek 2014).

Children who are securely attached can benefit in a number of ways:

- they have higher self-esteem and empathy
- they can deal with stress more effectively
- they have faster memory recall
- they have higher impulse control
- they are reliable and likely to be popular with others.

Personality, temperament and self-identity

The psychological make-up of an individual, including their personality, may play a part in the development of mental health problems, so that a young person who has an anxiety trait may be more at risk of developing generalised anxiety or depression. An individual with a propensity for perfection may be at greater risk of developing obsessive compulsive disorder. This is often also a reason why young people who have experienced similar events may cope very differently.

How others perceive us and the concept of 'who I am' are important to child mental health because of their links with behaviour, emotion states and cognitions. Humans are essentially social, so our definition of self is necessarily in the context of relations with others, though the degree to which people see themselves as independent (or as individuals) varies between cultures. In Eastern societies, there tends to be a greater emphasis on self in the context of the family and society, whereas in Western societies the emphasis is more on individualism.

The terms which will be used in this section and their generally accepted definitions are:

- *Personality:* the totality of predisposing behavioural tendencies that is an identifiable ingrained pattern of response. Personality is not normally considered to be fully developed until late adolescence

- *Traits:* circumscribed aspects of personality (i.e. one's predictable behavioural response to a given event/situation)

- *Temperament:* components of personality for which there is an implied genetic contribution, further influenced by parental attitudes and child-rearing practices.

Characteristics of personality

The words personality and character are often incorrectly used inter-changeably. Personality refers to the whole pattern of psychological function, whilst character refers to distinguishing qualities. The concept of 'the whole' as being greater than the identifiable parts applies to personality, which confounds attempts to measure it. As with physical characteristics, we all differ, and yet share many qualities.

Personality and personality traits are much more useful concepts in adult mental health. In young people personality is not fully formed, and it is more helpful to refer to specific 'building blocks' of personality, known as temperament.

Characteristics of temperament

Temperament is probably inherited through many genes (polygenic), and there are also environmental influences. However, twin studies suggest that environmental influences lessen with time. Temperament is enduring, showing continuity throughout childhood.

In contrast to the assessment of personality in adults, which is largely based on self-report, the assessment of temperament relies on observers. The people likely to have the most complete set of observations and experiences of the child are usually parents. However, there are difficulties in relying on parental report of temperament because of the influence of factors such as the quality of the parent–child relationship, beliefs held by the wider family ('family myths'), and possibly the parents' relationship.

Nine categories of temperamental attributes have been identified: activity level, rhythmicity, approach/withdrawal, adaptability, threshold of responsiveness, intensity of reaction, quality of mood, distractibility, and attention span/persistence. The sum of these characteristics leads to a simple three-way classification of young people's temperament as 'easy', 'difficult', or 'slow-to-warm-up'. Most young people are described as having an easy temperament and this provides a relative protection against psychological problems. Difficult temperament predisposes to behavioural/conduct problems. Slow-to-warm-up temperament predisposes to emotional problems. However, these observations are limited by reliance on parent report, difficulty defining onset of a specific disorder (and thus distinguishing pre-existing factors from characteristics of the disorder), difficulties measuring specific characteristics (such as impulsivity), and interaction with environmental factors.

There is an interaction between the child's temperament and their emotional environment. 'Goodness of fit' describes a concept of how favourable this interaction is (Thomas and Chess 1977). A particularly important aspect of this is the interaction between the child and the parent: a dynamic pattern of behaviour is established and is prone to repetition.

The parent's behaviour in response to the child's behaviour influences the child's next behaviour, which in turn influences the parent's next behaviour, and so on.

Self-identity

Self-identity, or how we conceive of ourselves, is commonly considered to have two components. Self-image is the factual account of ourselves in physical terms (such as height, weight, etc.) and psychological traits (such as likes and dislikes). Self-esteem is the personal judgement of the quality and value of these traits, and the worth of oneself as a person.

Self-image

The assessment of our own factual traits may lead us to conclude that we differ significantly from the social group to which we belong. This may be on the basis of behaviour, beliefs, physical appearance, ability, sexuality, sexual orientation, ethnicity or other characteristics. This may or may not affect self-esteem. It may lead to attempts to modify those traits, modify the social group or change group. Self-image may also be distorted; for example, distortions of the concept of one's own physical size and shape are core features of anorexia nervosa.

Self-esteem

Self-esteem has been studied since the late 1960s, when a simple classification based on quantification (high, medium, and low) was found to correlate with behaviour. When boys were studied, those boys with high self-esteem were physically fitter, and more active, expressive, ambitious and successful. Boys with low self-esteem were more likely to experience headaches, insomnia and stomach complaints. There are also gender differences in attribution in that girls attribute negative events to themselves and positive events to other influences (either the environment or factors such as luck), whilst boys do the reverse. Young people with high self-esteem are more likely to have involved parents, who are clear and firm at setting limits and have higher expectations of their child. Low self-esteem in turn can influence patterns of thinking, and with more likelihood of identifying failure there may be a relationship with the development of disorders such as depression.

We learn about ourselves through the relationships that we have with others, and this is true from early infancy. Our concept of 'self' changes with the constantly changing nature of these relationships and the experiences we have. We learn more about ourselves from each new experience. This is of great importance in childhood, with relatively fewer experiences on which to base the concept of self. Increased autonomy accompanies the child's growth of the concept. The development of relationships and the development of the concept of self may be two sides of the same coin.

Psychoanalytical factors

These derive from the work of Freud but have been developed further by Anna Freud, Klein and many others. Some of the theories developed by Eriksen and Bowlby have transformed psychoanalytical theory so that they now have only a tenuous link with Freud's original ideas.

One of the enduring features of Freud's work was the development of the concept of defence mechanisms – that is, strategies that individuals use to cope with difficult situations or feelings. There are several defence mechanisms. One example is projection, in which one's own unacceptable thoughts or feelings are transferred to another person. So instead of acknowledging one's own anger, an individual may state that someone else is angry. Displacement is another commonly used defence mechanism where aggression or anger is transferred from the real issue to another. Most people use defence mechanisms at some time or another and this can be healthy. Their use is only a problem if they continue to be used as a long-term measure, thus preventing the resolution of issues that may cause conflict.

Behavioural theories

Behavioural theories assert that behaviour and emotional expression are learned as a result of experience. Four theories predominate.

Classical conditioning

First described by Pavlov (1927), this involves the repeated introduction of a neutral stimulus alongside one that is known to induce a physiological or behavioural response – until the neutral stimulus alone induces the same response, and is then known as the conditioned stimulus.

Operant conditioning

First described by Skinner (1953), this is a process whereby the frequency of behaviour is influenced by its consequences. A behaviour becomes more frequent if it commonly leads to a reward (positive reinforcement), or avoidance of an undesirable or unpleasant consequence (negative reinforcement). A behaviour becomes less frequent if it commonly leads to no reward (extinction), or an undesirable or unpleasant consequence (punishment). Of these four, positive reinforcement and extinction are the most influential on the frequency of behaviour. Positive reinforcement is more potent when it is intermittent and irregular.

Social learning theory

First described by Bandura (1977), this emphasises the importance of human relationships in behaviour and the observations people make of each other. In this way, vicarious experience leads to learning – a process known as modelling. Participant modelling, in which the person also actively takes part, has the highest learning rate. Patterson (1982) described the dynamic interplay between parent and child as each influences the other's behaviour. These findings, which were the result of systematic observations of parent–child interactions, have influenced the development of family behavioural interventions over the last two to three decades and informed the further exploration of the parent–child relationship.

Cognitive learning

This underpins cognitive-behavioural approaches and recognises the importance of cognitions that accompany behaviour, which may be generally positive (e.g. self-congratulatory) or negative (e.g. self-denigratory). Cognitive learning theory regards learning as a process of thinking about and understanding behaviours and of consciously seeking solutions to problems, rather than seeing acquired behaviours as a series of unconscious responses to environmental stimuli.

Environmental factors

Social theory states that the young person's environment plays a part in the development of their problems. Environment may include the family, school, peer group, community, and life-events such as bereavement, traumatic events and serious accidents and so on. Young people on the margins of normative or cultural (in the very broadest sense) groups may also be at increased risk of developing mental health problems.

Family theories

For young people, the family (or the lack of it) plays a key role in their development. Family theories conceptualise that processes and communications that go on within families may result in the development of problems within the family. These problems may be presented through the identification of a problem in one family member, who is usually a child. Sibling order can also play a part in the development of some problems, although the reasons for this are not clear. In clinic samples, young people who live in families under stress are more likely to be referred than young people with the same level of problems who live in well-functioning families.

Styles of parenting

Research studies have shown that parenting styles and resilience can influence mental health. Young people's need for affection and control is well established. These qualities have been described in families in terms of parenting style (Carr, 2006; Darling and Steinberg, 1993; Joshi, Sharma and Mehra 2009). Using these two qualities, it is possible to describe four different styles of parenting and the likely outcomes for young people subjected to these styles.

AUTHORITATIVE PARENTING

When parents combine lots of warmth with a degree of control. This tends to provide the most beneficial environment for a child's emotional development.

PERMISSIVE PARENTING

When parents are warm and accepting of their children but exert little control on their behaviour. These children often fail to develop sufficient self-control and problem solving skills.

AUTHORITARIAN PARENTING

When parents are warm but over-controlling and over-involved. These young people develop a way of interacting with the world that avoids conflict and demonstrates little initiative.

NEGLECTING PARENTING

When a lack of parental warmth is combined with control, which is sometimes harsh but always inconsistent. This style is associated with the worst outcomes for young people and can be a significant factor leading to their presentation with mental health problems in childhood and adolescence.

These styles can develop from the parents' own experience of being parented and can result from differing parental beliefs about bringing up children, parental relationship difficulties, parental mental health problems (such as depression, which can cause the parent to feel emotionally detached and lacking in motivation) or as a reaction or response to a temperamentally difficult child. The positive impact of authoritative parenting is not dissimilar to the effects of secure attachment on the child's healthy emotional development.

Family lifecycle events

A family's difficulty in negotiating the transition between the stages of the family lifecycle (as described in Chapter 5) can often be a point at which a child presents with mental health problems. What seems to make a difference at these transitions is a family's level of flexibility. The family's ability to manage change and the perceptions of individuals about the family vary at different stages. For example, this ability begins to decline as young people enter adolescence and reaches its lowest point just as young people are preparing to leave home.

Family structure changes

Changes in family structure may result from death of a family member, separation, divorce, fostering and adoption. Structural changes in families are an increasingly common experience for young people, therefore it is important to consider the consequences for them of these events. Generally speaking, if the parental relationship is chronically acrimonious, irrespective of whether the parents stay together or separate, the impact on their children will be considerable. This impact is compounded if young people are caught up in continuing hostility and its consequences. The age at which the young person experiences the separation will also influence the different issues that young people may face as a result of parental separation or divorce.

It is difficult to disentangle the effect of separation from the effect of socio-economic disadvantage (Wadsby 1993) as the two are so closely linked in the UK. The experiences in countries where the socio-economic effect of separation is lessened by a more generous welfare and benefit system suggest that many of the negative effects associated with separation (such as poorer mental health outcomes) are linked more to social disadvantage than to the emotional turmoil. This view, however, is contradicted to some extent in other studies (Amato 1993).

Rodgers and Pryor's (1998) wide-ranging review of outcome studies points to a strong association between parental separation and conduct disorders in young people and an association with higher levels of distress and unhappiness. Most studies suggest that this effect is temporary and begins to fall after 18 months to two years. With adolescents and young adults there is good evidence of a relationship between parental separation and mental health problems and substance abuse. The link between parental separation and a higher risk of depressive symptoms in adolescence is well established in UK studies.

The experience of losing a parent through death increases the likelihood of behavioural problems in young people and adolescents. However, taken overall the impact is less than that of a child experiencing parental separation, especially when considering the longer-term mental health consequences.

Stepfamilies also have long- and short-term implications for young people and young people's mental health. While re-partnering can go some way to lessen the socio-economic effects of separation and single parenthood, many of the protective factors for families and young people are reduced, with attendant risks for the child and the adult relationship. Most difficulties in relationships and adjustment to transitions in stepfamilies occur when young people are in early adolescence. When compared with single parent families, on the other hand, children tend to fare better in stepfamilies.

Overall, it is the experience of multiple changes in family structure that significantly increases the likelihood of adverse outcomes. Young people of separated families are more likely to experience these multiple changes because of the greater chances of subsequent parental relationships breaking down.

Peer influences

Whilst the importance of a warm and positive relationship with a significant adult is widely acknowledged, the development of social relationships outside the family from middle childhood onwards is a significant protective factor in young people's mental health. The ability to make and keep friends can counter extremely adverse experiences. Studies on the mental health of children affected by war has shown that social support is an important protective factor – for example, children living in camps in Uganda who reported higher levels of social support tended to have lower levels of depression and post-traumatic stress disorder (Betancourt *et al.* 2012).

Young people who fail to develop friendships and acquire some skills in peer relationships are at greater risk of developing mental health problems in adolescence and early adulthood. Peer relationships are where most young people learn about managing conflict and early peer interaction is important for the development of self-esteem and a child's sense of place in the wider world. Unpopular young people often get caught up in a pattern of poor peer relationships because of their limited social skills and fixed models of interacting with their peers; as a consequence, unpopularity is often a long-term experience. Two types of unpopular child are identified by Carr (2006): the aggressive, disruptive child and the sensitive, anxious, often bullied child. This pattern has been noted across several cultures and both types have been shown to have low self-esteem. Carr estimates that 10–15 per cent of young people could be described as unpopular and are rejected by their peer group.

In adolescence, peer culture has been shown to have a strong influence, both positive and negative, on educational outcomes, which in turn is a clear factor in young people's mental health. However, there is evidence that peer influences are not merely accidental and that there is a large degree of choice about peer group selection. By the age of 12–14 years, in Western societies, there is a sharp decline in the young person's choice of a parent as the primary confidant and a marked preference for peers. The desire to conform to the peer group peaks around the ages of 13 and 14. Both of these factors are important considerations when working with young people and mental health.

Impact of school

School plays a big part in young people's lives. It is often the first exposure to the world outside the family, which for many children will begin with nursery school. The way children settle into this environment is a good predictor of longer-term outcomes. Those children that have peer difficulties or behavioural problems are likely to continue to have them in later years unless the problems are addressed. For most young people, school is a positive experience. For many, though, it can be a very difficult environment, either because they struggle with the work or because the environment is too challenging for them. To function well in school, young people need to be able to tolerate rules and boundaries as well as sustain relationships with peers and adults. They may also have to cope with stressors such as bullying. It is well recognised that young people who struggle with their schoolwork are at increased risk of behavioural problems. There can be a tendency to focus on the behaviour rather than consider why the child is struggling.

Young people with neurological disorders, including epilepsy, are particularly vulnerable to struggling in school, which impacts negatively on self-esteem and self-confidence. It also means that young people miss out on developing appropriate peer relationships. An educational or school psychologist, where these exist, should be the first point of contact for school staff who have concerns about a young person's educational progress or behaviour problems. The educational psychologist can then assess the young person to clarify whether he or she has a learning disability or specific learning problems. It is usually necessary for the young person's cognitive ability to be assessed. The psychologist, school staff and parents can then work together to develop the best strategies to help the young person make the most of their educational experience.

Schools can impact positively on young people by providing them with a supportive and challenging environment. A positive relationship with a teacher can mitigate the impact of less positive experiences. School exams and coursework can generate stress in young people, and it is important that they are helped to address this, as they are likely to come across it again in their lives. Schools should consider addressing it in a proactive way through the development of workshops that help young people recognise their stress and deal with it appropriately. Schools are also well placed to enhance social development through 'buddy' systems and 'circle of friends' in the classroom in younger children, and the use of social skills groups in older children and adolescents.

The impact of culture

Defining culture is difficult. Each individual has their own assigned meaning of culture. For some it is defined by skin colour, religion or ethnic background; for others country of origin, sexuality, and so on. It is likely to be a combination of all of these with some aspects playing a more dominant part than others. Whatever group an individual may belong to, they remain unique because of their experiences and interpretations of their experiences.

Studies in the UK have found that in Gujarati preschool children, there may be less psychological disturbance than in peers from a non-Gujarati background (Hackett and Hackett 1993). It is possible that there is no difference in the behaviours of the children, but what is culturally bound is the parental responses to the behaviours. For example, Gujarati parents may tolerate different levels of non-compliance than their English counterparts. However, whether this is changing, as second and third generation individuals become parents, remains to be seen.

Culture strongly influences the role of parents and of young people. Whilst traditional domestic routines may continue to be of great importance to young people of British minority ethnic groups growing up in the UK, this is not seen as the only way to do things and they are increasingly exposed to other cultures. Ethnically Indian adolescents had lower rates of all types of mental health problems, with the exception of eating disorders, compared with their white counterparts (5% vs. 13% and 21% vs. 30% for abnormal Strengths and Difficulties Questionnaire and Short Mood and Feelings Questionnaire scores, respectively) and substance misuse (18% vs. 57%, 5% vs. 15% and 6% vs. 9% for regular alcohol, smoking and drug use, respectively) (Dogra et al. 2013). South Asian young people may be brought up with a strong sense of family responsibility implicit in particular relationships. The roles of brother/sister, son/daughter, maternal uncle/paternal aunt involve particular duties and privileges (Jackson and Nesbitt 1993). However, in wider society they are exposed to different expectations. Where there is a tendency for the family to have a central role, the needs of the family and the needs of the individual may conflict. Asian girls, and especially those who find their choices restricted because of cultural expectations, can experience considerable distress. This can be compounded by the unwillingness of minority groups to discuss this openly. However, culture can also provide young people with a sense of belonging and some appreciation of their role.

Less research has been undertaken on African-Caribbean young people in the UK. It is, however, clear that African-Caribbean young people are more likely to be excluded from school than all other groups and more likely to get caught up in the criminal justice system. It is possible that being excluded from school, and the attendant risks associated with that, is a more significant factor than being African-Caribbean. In adult mental health, there is a question as to whether professionals are more likely to attribute mental health diagnoses to African-Caribbean individuals than to other ethnic groups. This is a question that in child mental health remains largely unaddressed.

American studies have investigated the help-seeking behaviour in African-American, Latino and Caucasian youth. Minority parents appeared more reluctant to access services. This may be for several reasons, including concerns that they will not be understood, previous experience, and differing cultural interpretations of behaviours and methods to manage them. However, services for young people may need to engage these populations more actively.

The impact of the community

There is a higher prevalence of mental health problems in economically disadvantaged areas and in communities where there is a lack of a stable population. Support networks in these communities tend to be poorly developed. Urbanisation of society has led to changes in community structures. National crime rates tend to be positively correlated with the proportion of the population in urban residence. Young people may find themselves at increased risk of being involved in crime, both as perpetrators and victims. Urbanisation is also associated with an increased differential between living standards of the affluent and the poor, and increased residential segregation by class and minority group.

CASE STUDY: Leanne

Leanne is an 11-year-old girl whose mother had been diagnosed with breast cancer several months ago. Leanne's family had told her that her mother was 'poorly' but had sought to protect her from the details of the extensive treatment her mother had to undergo. This was now complete and Leanne's mother's progress was very positive. Previously Leanne had been getting on well at school and had an active social life, but over the past two months she had been increasingly reluctant to go to school and leave the house. This had culminated in Leanne refusing to go to school when she needed to move up to secondary school. She also experienced several episodes of acute anxiety when her father tried to get her to go to school.

Reflect on Leanne's presentation of anxiety and what this might be related to. What might be the key factors that contribute to how she is feeling?

The economically disadvantaged areas have larger schools and bigger classes, with less parental involvement than wealthier areas. This may result in poor education, and especially affected will be those with special educational needs. There may also be increased exposure to violence (both domestic and non-domestic), discrimination and parental mental health problems (related to issues of stress). All of these factors are interrelated and can significantly impact on the development of mental health problems in young people. However, for some young people, urbanisation can offer diversification of educational and recreational opportunities.

References

Ainsworth, M.D.S., Blehar, M., Waters, E. and Wall, S. (1978) *Patterns of Attachment: A Psychological Study of the Strange Situation.* Hillsdale, NJ: Lawrence Erlbaum Associates.

Amato, P.R. (1993) 'Children's adjustments to divorce: Theories, hypotheses and empirical support.' *Journal of Marriage and the Family 55,* 23–28.

Bandura, A. (1977) *Social Learning Theory.* Englewood Cliffs, NJ: Prentice Hall.

Betancourt, T.S., Carmel, S., Buka, S., Leaning, J., Dunn, G. and Earls, F. (2012) 'Connectedness, social support and internalising emotional and behavioural problems in adolescent displaced by the Chechen conflict.' *Disasters 36,* 4, 535–655.

Bowlby, J. (1969) *Attachment and Loss. Vol.1: Attachment.* London: Hogarth Press.

Bowlby, J. (1973) *Attachment and Loss. Vol.2: Separation: Anxiety and Anger.* London: Hogarth Press.

Bowlby, J. (1980) *Attachment and Loss. Vol.3: Loss: Sadness and Depression.* London: Hogarth Press.

Brown, R. and Ward, H. (2013) 'Decision-making within a Child's Timeframe. An overview of current research for family justice professionals concerning child development and the impact of maltreatment.' London: Childhood Well-being Research Centre, Institute of Education.

Carr, A. (2006) *Family Therapy: Concepts, Process and Practice (2nd Edition)*. Chichester: Wiley.

Darling, N. and Steinberg, L. (1993) 'Parenting style as context: An integrative model.' *Psychological Bulletin 113*, 487–496.

Dogra N., Svirydzenka N., Dugard P., Singh S.P. and Vostanis P. (2013) 'The characteristics and rates of mental health problems among Indian and White adolescents in two English cities.' *British Journal of Psychiatry 203*, 44–50.

Hackett. L, and Hackett. R. (1993) 'Parental ideas of normal and deviant child behaviour. A comparison of two ethnic groups.' *The British Journal of Psychiatry 162*, 3, 353–357.

Jackson, R. and Nesbitt, E. (1993) *Hindu Children in Britain*. Stoke on Trent: Trentham Books.

Joshi, H.L, Sharma, M., and Mehra, R.K. (2009) 'Depression among adolescents: Role of self-efficacy and parenting style.' *Journal of SIS-Projective and Mental Health 16*, 13–17.

Main, M. and Solomon, J. (1986) 'Discovery of an Insecure Disorganized/Disorientated Attachment Pattern: Procedures, Findings and Implications for the Development of Behaviour.' In M. Yogman and T.B. Brazelton (eds) *Affective Development in Infancy*. Norwood, NJ: Ablex.

Patterson, G.R. (1982) *Coercive Family Process*. Eugene, OR: Castalia.

Pavlov, I.P. (1927) *Conditioned Reflexes* (translated by G.V. Anrep). Oxford: Clarendon Press.

Rodgers, B. and Pryor, J. (1998) *Divorce and Separation: The Outcomes for Children*. York: Joseph Rowntree Foundation.

Schofield, G. and Beek. M. (2014) *The Secure Base Model: Promoting Attachment and Resilience in Foster Care and Adoption*. Norwich: BAAF.

Simmonds, J. (2004) *Fostering: Attachment SCIE Guide 7*. Available at www.scie.org.uk/publications/guides/guide07, accessed on 15 June 2017.

Skinner, B.F. (1953) *Science and Human Behaviour*. New York: Macmillan.

Thomas, A. and Chess, S. (1977) *Temperament and Development*. New York: Brunner/Mazel.

Wadsby, M. (1993) 'Children of Divorce and their Parents.' Linkoping University medical dissertations, Number 405. Linkoping: Linkoping University.

Further reading

Helman, C.G. (2000) *Culture, Health and Illness: An Introduction for Health Professionals (4th edition)*. Abingdon: Bookpoint.

Main, M. (1996) 'Overview of the field of attachment.' *Journal of Consulting and Clinical Psychology 64*, 237–243.

Parkes, C.M. and Stevenson-Hinde, J. (1982) *The Place of Attachment in Human Behaviour*. London: Tavistock Publications.

Research in Practice (2014) *Attachment Theory and Research*. Available at www.fosteringandadoption.rip.org.uk/topics/attachment-theory-research, accessed on 15 June 2017.

Parkes, C.M., Stevenson-Hinde, J. and Marris, P. (1991) *Attachment across the Life Cycle*. London: Routledge.

Rutter, M. (ed.) (1995) *Psychosocial Disturbances in Young People: Challenges for Prevention*. Cambridge: Press Syndicate of the University of Cambridge.

Steinhausen, H-C. and Verhulst, F. (1999) *Risks and Outcomes in Developmental Psychopathology*. Oxford: Oxford University Press.

CHAPTER 7

Protective and Adverse Factors Relating to Child Mental Health

Introduction

There is evidence that some factors or characteristics are likely to lead to an increase in mental health problems, whilst some protect against the development of problems and enable children to build resilience. Resilience is something that is acquired through experience, although there may be some inherited aspects. However, continuous and extreme adversity is very likely to be a drain on the most resilient of children. Rutter argued that resilience is created when risk is reduced through protective factors. Unfortunately, it is still not known how protective factors work. It is likely to be a complex relationship between an individual and their environment. It is useful to be aware of protective factors because staff in universal services can try to ensure they are in place or maximised to enable young people to break the cycles of adversity they might face and thereby reduce the incidence of mental health problems.

The Resilience Framework, developed by Hart, Blinrow and Thomas (2012), clearly sets out the many protective factors that can contribute to developing a child's resilience. There are groups of young people who are more likely to experience mental health problems. However, this does not mean that all young people from these groups experience problems.

Protective factors

Generally, protective factors include factors within the child, their family and those around them – their support networks and communities that they live in:

Within the child

- Being female (in prepubertal children).

- High intellectual ability and academic success, and being able to celebrate successes: this gives the young person opportunities to focus on long-term goals and build up a positive self-image. Academic success is often also seen as a way out of poverty and may present greater opportunities.

- Easy temperament as described in Chapter 6.

- Having special skills or a particular talent (sporting or musical talents may be especially useful in giving young people opportunities to leave difficult circumstances behind).

- Good communication skills and sociability.

- Being a planner and having a belief that they have some control over their own lives.

- Having and using humour.

- Problem solving skills.

- Capacity to reflect.

- Faith or spirituality.

Within families

- Developing a warm and confiding relationship with a trustworthy and reliable adult (not necessarily within the family): this enables the young person to develop a support mechanism as well as developing trust with an adult.

- Affection.

- Clear and consistent parenting and discipline.

- Support for education.

- An absence of discord.

- A supportive family that is able to manage change.

Within networks and communities

- Peer relationships and friendships: adults can often underestimate the support that young people provide for each other, especially during adolescence; positive peer relationships give young people an opportunity to share their concerns and consider alternative ways of managing stress or difficulties, added to which, peer relationships also enable young people to have fun.

- Wider support networks.

- Good housing and high standard of living.

- High school moral and positive approaches to managing behaviours, attitudes and bullying.

- Accessing a range of sport and recreational activities.

Family resilience

Just as factors can lead to resilience in young people, there are factors that can indicate a family's level of resilience – their healthy functioning in situations of adversity, and ability to cope with crisis and high levels of stress. Highlighting and developing a family's strengths can promote a more collaborative way of working with the family compared with earlier ideas of dysfunctional families.

So how can we explain the different outcomes for families who have broadly similar experiences? First, this will depend on a family's ability both to maintain its core structures, strengths and values and at the same time to balance this with a capacity to develop new patterns and structures flexibly. Second, the way in which the family interprets or ascribes meaning to events is an indicator of their resilience. Connected with this is a family's ability to contemplate alternative perspectives to a given event. Studies of families who have experienced divorce suggest that there are better outcomes for those that have a coherent family 'story' about the breakdown of the marriage and responsibilities, both before and after the divorce. Third, Olson (1988) identified what he termed 'critical family resources', which enable families to weather periods of stress. These resources varied to some extent across the family lifecycle but broadly speaking can be identified as:

- parental relationship strengths, such as good communication, financial management and a mutually satisfactory sexual relationship
- family accord
- the subjective experience of satisfaction with the couple relationship and quality of family life.

Walsh (2003) also suggested that family resilience can be strengthened when its members:

- make meaning out of adversity
- have a positive outlook
- are flexible
- have connectedness and mutual support
- have social and economic resources
- are clear, and consistent
- have open emotional expression
- have collaborative problem solving.

Adverse factors
Adverse factors that can affect children's mental health include:

External to the individual
- Lack of stable placement.
- Lack of appropriate parenting.
- Parental illness (especially mental illness).

- Domestic violence.

- Experiencing abuse (physical, sexual or emotional).

- Low socio-economic status.

Individual factors

- Poor strategies to cope with stress or difficulty.

- Poor educational attainment.

- Poor peer relationships.

- Developmental delay.

- Physical health problems.

Vulnerable young people who have experienced or face adversity

Young people who have experienced or face adversity are at increased risk of developing mental health problems and are often considered to be vulnerable. They are considered to be vulnerable because they have certain attributes, or have had past or present negative or traumatic experiences, or they are growing up in the face of adversity. Sometimes they may have a combination of attributes or experiences (Vostanis 2007). Young people from these vulnerable groups are some of the most disturbed and distressed young people in society. Their problems often stay with them into their adult lives and may re-emerge when they themselves become parents.

In addition, vulnerable young people can also experience a number of challenges that can exacerbate the complexity of their needs. These challenges can include the experience of increased stigma, movement of their location and displacement, difficulties in communicating their needs and having them understood, poor and unstable living conditions and school circumstances, and being subject to violence, abuse and sexual exploitation or even disaster.

Young people may often be given incomplete explanations of what is happening around them, thus compounding their difficulties. Adverse factors do not lead to a specific mental health problem but increase general vulnerability to experiencing problems. Young people can also face difficulties in accessing services that are appropriate to their needs. The best way for professionals to provide services that are responsive to these young people's needs is to provide them through close working partnerships, thus ensuring collaborative approaches that do not allow them to slip through gaps in provision (Vostanis 2007).

It is important to emphasise that not all young people in these at-risk groups will experience mental health problems. Some show 'resilience' and have sufficient protective factors. It may be that even during such complex and difficult life circumstances, young people will be able to have enduring friendships, achieve educationally or have some life experiences that still offer some stability, for instance regular communication with a relative or stability within the school environment.

Groups of young people at high risk of developing mental health problems are highlighted here so professionals are better able to consider the needs of these young people. Some young people may belong to more than one group. However, it cannot be over-emphasised that each young person needs to be viewed as an individual and stereotyping young people and their needs should be avoided.

Young people who have experienced abuse

The numbers of young people who have experienced physical, sexual or emotional abuse, or a combination of these, vary depending on the definition of abuse. It is difficult to obtain figures for sexual abuse as much of it may not be disclosed until adulthood; and figures for emotional abuse are even less reliable as much of it is not even identified. It is suggested that in the UK approximately 10 per cent of young people have been sexually abused.

The response of adults to disclosure of abuse may affect how young people themselves cope with the issues. Young people may find that disclosure of abuse may lead to retribution against them in the form of further abuse, rejection or bullying. They may find themselves in care and may perceive this as a punishment. The internet has increased the possibility of more young people experiencing abuse through sharing of indecent images.

Young people in care

There are over 70,000 young people in the care of local authorities in England and Wales at any one time; in the UK this group is currently called 'children looked after', or Children in Care. Around 11 per cent of these young people live in residential units and community placements (Coram BAAF 2016), and a large majority (74%) live with foster carers. There is evidence to show that looked-after young people have complex health and social needs, including higher rates of mental health problems. Their needs may be significantly higher, with between 60 and 80 per cent having significant mental health problems and requiring specialist treatment, which is often lacking.

Young people who are homeless

It is difficult to be sure of the numbers of young people who are homeless as the definition of homelessness varies. However, a significant number of these young people are also likely to have been in care. They have often witnessed domestic violence, experienced abuse, have substance use problems, or have unmet mental health needs. In addition to homeless families with young people, there will be adolescents who are living in temporary hostels or living on the streets.

Young offenders

The needs of this group are not dissimilar to those of the looked-after group in that these young people often also have multiple and complex needs. Young offenders have significantly higher rates than their non-offending peers of serious mental illness, problem substance use, educational failure, past abuse, which has often been more persistent and deviant than that experienced by other abused young people, and social isolation or deviant peer contact (Kroll 2004). Many of these needs are not recognised by professionals working with them, and even when recognised they can be difficult to address. There are worryingly high rates of suicide and self-harm by young people in custody. There can be reluctance by professionals to accept that these young people should be entitled to the same level of services as other young people, which, coupled with young people's own ambivalence, can be difficult to overcome.

Young people excluded from school

These young people already have significant problems, which led to their exclusion from school. Exclusion compounds the problems of poor peer relationships and poor educational achievement. These young people are at increased risk of becoming involved in crime as well as developing mental health problems.

Young people with physical disorders

Young people with physical disorders, including neurological conditions, experience mental health problems more often than physically healthy young people. The rates of mental health problems in an Isle of Wight study were 7 per cent for physically well young people, 12 per cent for young people with physical disorders and 34 per cent for young people with brain disorders, including epilepsy (Rutter 1977). Disorders of emotion and conduct were more common in the epilepsy sample and severity of central nervous system damage was a better predictor of developing mental health problems than site of damage. Many of the physically ill young people without a neurological condition had levels of functional disability similar to those with epilepsy, but they had lower rates of mental health problems. This may indicate that brain damage plays an important aetiological role, although the nature of the damage may be difficult to identify (Rutter, Tizard and Wightmore 1970). The support available to young people with epilepsy may also influence their emotional adjustment and management of the disorder. Recent studies have found that young people with physical health problems continue to have higher rates of mental health problems (Cadman *et al.* 1987; Gortmaker *et al.* 1990; Office for National Statistics 2005).

Young people who are refugees or asylum seekers

Young refugees or asylum seekers are at high risk of developing mental health problems. These may be related to the reasons for leaving their home (such as witnessing or experiencing violence and other atrocities, guilt about surviving when others did not, bereavement, and loss of contact with family) or related to settling into a new community (such as isolation, lack of access to positive aspects of their culture, racism and discrimination, poor housing, poverty and parents under stress).

There has been an increase in numbers of unaccompanied asylum-seeking children in England. In 2016, 4,210 unaccompanied children were looked after. The majority were male (93%) and 75 per cent were over 16 (Coram BAAF 2016).

References

Cadman, D., Boyle, M., Szatmaris, P. and Offord, D. (1987) 'Chronic illness, disability and mental and social well-being: Findings of the Ontario Child Health Study.' *Paediatrics 79*, 5, 805–812.

Coram BAAF (2016) *Children in Public Care: Statistics.* Available at www.corambaaf.org.uk/res/statengland#pc, accessed on 15 June 2017.

Gortmaker, S.L., Walker, D.K., Weitzman, M. and Sobol, A.M. (1990) 'Chronic conditions, socioeconomic risks, and behavioural problems in children and adolescents.' *Paediatrics 85*, 3, 267–276.

Hart, A., Blincow, D., and Thomas, H. (2012) *The Resilience Framework.* Available at www.boingboing.org.uk/index.php/component/phocadownload/category/9-resilience-frameworks?, accessed on 15 June 2017.

Kroll, L. (2004) 'Needs Assessment in Adolescent Offenders.' In S. Bailey and M. Dolan (eds) *Adolescent Forensic Psychiatry.* London: Arnold.

Olson, D. (1988) 'Family Types, Family Stress and Family Satisfaction: A Family Development Perspective.' In C. Falicor (ed.) *Family Transitions.* New York: Guilford Press.

Office of National Statistics (2005) *The Mental Health of Children and Young people in Great Britain, 2004.* Basingstoke: Palgrave McMillan.

Rutter, M., Tizard, J. and Wightmore, K. (1970) *Education, Health and Behaviour.* London: Longman.

Rutter, M. (1977) 'Psychosocial resilience and protective mechanisms.' *American Journal of Orthopsychiatry 57*, 3, 316–611.

Vostanis, P. (ed.) (2007) *Mental Health Services and Interventions for Vulnerable Children and Young People.* London: Jessica Kingsley Publishers.

Walsh, F. (2003) 'Family resilience: A framework for clinical practice.' *Family Process 41*, 1–18.

Further reading

Hester, M., Pearson, C. and Harwin, N. (2000) *Making an Impact: Children and Domestic Violence – A Reader.* London: Jessica Kingsley Publishers.

Hinde, R. and Stevenson-Hinde, J. (1988) *Relationships within Families: Mutual Influences.* Oxford: Clarendon Press.

Jackson, S. and Thomas, N. (2000) *What Works in Creating Stability for Looked After Children (2nd edition).* Ilford: Barnardo's.

Kurtz, Z. (1996) *Treating Young People Well.* London: Mental Health Foundation.

McGee, C. (2000) *Childhood Experiences of Domestic Violence.* London: Jessica Kingsley Publishers.

National Children's Bureau (1998) *Review of the Gatsby Investment in 'Young People Living in Public Care'.* London: National Young People's Bureau, Young People's Residential Care Unit 1996–1998.

Richardson, J. and Joughin, C. (2000) *The Mental Health Needs of Looked After Children.* Focus College Research Unit, London: Gaskell.

Rutter, M. (ed.) (1995) *Psychosocial Disturbances in Young People: Challenges for Prevention.* Cambridge: Press Syndicate of the University of Cambridge.

Vostanis, P. and Cumella, S. (eds) (1999) *Homeless Children: Problems and Needs.* London: Jessica Kingsley Publishers.

Young Minds (n.d.) Handout: Resilience. Available at www.youngminds.org.uk/resources/tools-and-toolkits/academic-resilience-resources, accessed on 17 July 2017.

CHAPTER 8

Legal and Ethical Aspects Relevant to Young People and Mental Health

Introduction

This chapter begins by outlining relevant international legislation before covering the principles of legislation related to England and Wales, with some reference to Scotland that is relevant to child mental health. The ethical principles of consent and confidentiality are described before we conclude by considering child protection as it relates to child mental health.

International legislation

The Human Rights Act 1998

The Human Rights Act (HRA) came into force on 2 October 2000 and incorporates directly into English law most of the provisions of the European Convention on Human Rights (known as Convention rights). There are 13 specific human rights 'articles'. Some are absolute rights and others are qualified, which means that there may be situations where an infringement of rights is justified. It protects every member of society against a breach of the rights by public authorities but not by private individuals. The Act applies to all authorities undertaking functions of a public nature, including all care providers in the public sector.

The Human Rights Act and children

The HRA supports the protection of the health and welfare of young people throughout the United Kingdom (Home Office 1999). Young people are amongst the most vulnerable members of our society; the HRA puts measures in place to protect them and to improve their lives. Although the HRA is not particularly child-focused, it will affect the way in which decisions are made involving young people. Only those articles relating to young people are outlined here.

Article 3 – freedom from torture and inhuman or degrading treatment

Article 3 states that 'no one shall be subjected to inhuman or degrading treatment or punishment'. Legislation in the UK already protects children from abuse and harm. Article 3 raises questions regarding physical chastisement by those acting on behalf of public bodies. Although common law defends lawful chastisement or correction, degrading and harmful punishment can never be justified.

This article will also be related to complaints arising from children and young people who have been subject to restraint, seclusion or detention. To fall within this article the 'treatment' must attain a minimum level of severity, which will depend upon the circumstances of the treatment, its physical or mental effects, and the age, sex and health of the victim. This is something that those providing such methods of intervention will need to consider carefully when developing protocols and policies.

Article 5 – the right to liberty, and Article 6 – the right to a fair hearing

Both articles are relevant to young people detained under a section of the Mental Health Act, the Children Act or within the youth justice system. In terms of those young people detained under the Mental Health Act, the European Court of Human Rights has held that such detention must:

- be based on a medical opinion

- be for a mental disorder, of the kind or degree that warrants confinement

- continue only as long as the mental disorder persists

- be in accordance with the law – in the UK, the Mental Health Act.

Article 8 – the right to private and family life

Article 8 guarantees the right to respect for private and family life and will have implications for children and their mental health in several areas, especially in situations of family separation or breakdown. For example, a court making a residence order in favour of one parent will need to take account of the right to family life for the child and for both parents, and consider the child's wishes. It will often strike a balance between conflicting rights, although there will not always be an obvious or easy answer.

Article 10 – freedom of expression

Article 10 states that 'everyone has the right to freedom of expression'. This serves to encourage young people to make their views known and to impart their ideas about the services they get and what they feel would be beneficial to them. Young people's views are increasingly sought, but professionals have a duty to ensure that these views are heard and appropriately acted on.

Article 14 – freedom from discrimination

Article 14 states that 'the enjoyment of the rights and freedoms set forth in this Convention shall be secured without discrimination on any ground. It is every professional's duty to ensure that they employ anti-discriminatory practices in the work that they undertake with children and their families, and apply the legislation with respect to service provision for mental health problems'.

The United Nations Convention on the Rights of the Child

The HRA needs to be considered alongside the United Nations Convention on the Rights of the Child (UNCRC) which is the most complete statement of children's rights and is the most widely-ratified international human rights treaty.[1] However, just because a policy has been ratified does not mean it is implemented in the spirit it was

---

1   www.unicef.org

intended, as implementation is dependent on the value placed on a child in any given context.

The Convention has 54 articles that cover all aspects of a child's life and set out the civil, political, economic, social and cultural rights that all children everywhere are entitled to. Every child has rights, whatever their ethnicity, gender, religion, language, abilities or any other status.

The Convention must be seen as a whole: all the rights are linked and no right is more important that another. There are four articles in the convention that form the 'General Principles' through which all the other articles are interpreted and they are:

- Non-discrimination (article 2)

- Best interest of the child (article 3)

- Right to life survival and development (article 6)

- Right to be heard (article 12).

It is worth reflecting on how the HRA and UNCRC are applied in whichever context you work. It is likely that some rights will be implemented more enthusiastically than others. Implementation of children's rights has financial implications and again, whatever the intentions may be, the reality is that many children do not have a voice and live in circumstances that are not conducive to positive mental health.

England- and Wales-specific legislation

Although this section covers legislation specific to England and Wales, many countries will have similar legislation that enshrines the principles outlined below. Acts specific to context or particular groups are not covered here, except, of course, those relating to mental health.

The Children Act 1989

The main principles of the Children Act are that:

- the welfare of the child is paramount

- children should be brought up and cared for within their own families wherever possible

- children should be safe and protected by effective interventions if at risk

- courts should avoid delay

- courts should only make an order if this would be better than making no order

- children should be kept informed about what happens to them and involved in decisions made about them.

Parents continue to have parental responsibility for their children even when their children are no longer living with them. Parents should be kept informed about their children and participate in decisions regarding their future. Parental responsibility is a fundamental principle and concept of the Children Act. Consequently, parents with children in need should be helped to bring up their children themselves, and help should be provided as a service to the child and family.

Such help should:

- be provided in partnership with the parents

- meet identified needs

- be appropriate to the child's race, culture, religion and language

- be open to effective independent representation and complaints procedures

- draw upon effective partnerships between agencies.

Orders within the Act
The Act provides for various court orders:

- Care Order – places the child into the care of a local authority

- Supervision Order – places the child under the supervision of Social Services or a probation officer

- Assessment Order – enables the child to have an assessment but the child is not obliged to consent to the assessment.

Factors to consider when assessing the best interest of the child under the Children Act

» The child's own ascertainable wishes, feelings and views

» The child's ability to understand the treatment

» The child's potential to participate

» Risk to or from the child

» Views of parents and family

» Implication of non-treatment (including risks to the child).

Good practice

Principles of good practice set out the context in which children's needs should be considered. These acknowledge that children and young people need to be kept fully informed about their care and treatment in an age-appropriate way. Therefore, they should be encouraged to share their concerns and preferences, which should be taken into account as appropriate. Accordingly, professionals should be prepared to give people time to make decisions and consider their options (if appropriate).

Children have the right to:

- child-centred care

- be looked after appropriately without discrimination (on the basis of race, culture, gender, religion, disability or sexuality)

- develop their full potential

- be involved as appropriate in decision-making (and have the right to decline involvement)

- express their opinions without fear

- receive support and information in reaching decisions

- confidentiality.

Refusal by a child whose competence may be in doubt, for example because of mental illness, leads to consideration of whether parental consent is enough, or whether the Mental Health Act (MHA) should be used. There are views that in such cases the Children Act should be used as it focuses on the wishes of the child and does not carry the stigma and sequelae of the MHA. The Children Act also expects a guardian *ad litem* to consider all of the relevant factors in a child's case. However, it is debatable whether the Children Act protects against possible stigmatisation and it does not have the appeal procedures inherent in the MHA.

The benefits of using the Children Act when mental illness is present include:

- focus on the child

- applicability to children who do not have a formal psychiatric diagnosis but who may benefit from intervention

- provision for a guardian *ad litem* to be appointed to ascertain the child's wishes and make recommendations about the child's best interests

- particular aptness for younger children (especially those under 12 years of age)

- a perception that it is potentially less stigmatising than the MHA.

However, the disadvantages of using the Children Act are that it does not:

- address mental disorders

- provide specific powers to enforce treatment

- provide safeguards for the rights of detained patients

- provide for treatment without consent as it can only be used to hold a child in a place of safety.

The Children Act (2004)

The Children Act (2004) essentially strengthens the 1989 Act, encouraging more partnerships between agencies and establishing greater accountability. This act created the role of the Children's Commissioner.

The Children and Families Act (2014)

Children and Families Act (2014) was created to make provision about children, families, and people with special educational needs or disabilities. The Act introduced a single assessment process and an Education, Health and Care (EHC) Plan to support children, young people and their families from birth to 25 years. The EHC plan will replace statements of special educational needs.

Principles of consent and confidentiality

Consent

There are governing principles of good clinical practice, which include providing information in an age-appropriate and accessible way to young people. Their views need to be ascertained and clear explanations provided of what is happening. It is worth asking children to explain their understanding of consent and confidentiality so any misconceptions can be corrected. Children may respond better to communicating their concerns through non-verbal methods.

Under the Mental Capacity Act (2005) all individuals over age 16 are assumed to have capacity to make their own decisions to consent to or refuse treatment unless there is evidence to the contrary. The key elements of capacity to be able to consent are that:

- the patient understands the information presented to them

- the patient can retain the information

- the patient can weigh the information in the balance and come to a decision based on this

- the patient can communicate their wishes (note that this can be through any means and not just verbally).

Although they do not acquire full adult rights to make their own decisions until they are 18, young people in England and Wales aged 16 and 17 are also presumed to be competent to give consent and should be treated as such unless there is evidence to suggest otherwise, such as severe intellectual disability or temporary inability to consent due to severe mental illness. There is no lower age limit in Scotland. A 16- or 17-year-old only needs to be 'capable of expressing his own wishes'. If a young person cannot fulfil the above criteria, their capacity to give consent is questionable. If the young person is under 16, the decision will need to be made by whomever is responsible for the child.

An expert government committee has suggested that the presumption of competence to consent should arise at around age 10 or 12. This may be more appropriate in some conditions and situations than others. Whilst younger children may not be in the position of giving informed consent, it is still important to seek their views as they may have fears or worries, which, if addressed, could improve compliance. Consent to healthcare assessments and interventions for people under 16 years of age is normally obtained from parents and the young person's wishes are, where possible, taken into account. The assumption is that parents usually make appropriate decisions for their children and give consent for treatment on their behalf.

In child mental health, any therapeutic input is limited unless the young person is engaged in the work. It is therefore often useful to engage with the family to explore some of the issues around what they find difficult. However, there may be instances where the young person wishes to consent but does not wish the parents to be involved (and professional opinion respects this wish), or the parents are unavailable or decline or are unable to consent. It is good practice to involve parents or caregivers unless there is a compelling reason not to do so. In such instances, and where assessment or intervention is desirable, the young person should first be assessed as to whether they have the capacity to consent. This is known as 'Gillick competence' – a shorthand way of referring to the landmark judgement in a legal case in England in the 1980s, which ultimately stated that 'the parent's right yields to the child's right to make his own decision as he reaches sufficient understanding and intelligence' (*Gillick v West Norfolk* 1985). This is a developmental concept and does not fluctuate from day to day but can be developed over time. A judgement about a young person's competence to consent would have to be reconsidered for each different treatment. Whilst there is no lower age limit to Gillick competence, it would be unusual for a child under 12 years to be Gillick competent. The 'Fraser Guidelines' (named after the Law Lord making the judgement) refer specifically to the area of sexual health advice, which was the medical issue in the Gillick case, and have been taken as a guide for all health professionals, not just doctors, and in other specialties. Thus, 'Gillick competence' has taken on a more general meaning. In many cases the terms have become inter-changeable.

Useful checklists for consent taking account of factors that can influence capacity to give consent, including stage of development, have been developed (Department of Health 2009; Pearce 1994). A modified version of Pearce's (1994) checklist is shown in Figure 8.1.

Does the young person have a satisfactory understanding of:	**Other factors**
• nature of illness? • own needs and needs of others? • risks and benefits to treatment? • own self-concept? • significance of time (past, present, future)?	• Is the parent–child relationship supportive and affectionate? • Is there trust and confidence in the doctor–patient relationship? • Whose opinion influences the child, and how? • How disabling, chronic or life-threatening is the illness? • Is more time/information needed? • Is a second opinion required?

Figure 8.1 Factors affecting ability to consent

Confidentiality

You must have a clear understanding of your organisation's policies on confidentiality. Young people are entitled to limited confidentiality. What this means is that young people are entitled to confidentiality as long as maintaining it does not put them at risk of harm from themselves or others. Confidentiality is very important to young people and they often want to know how much of what they say to you is going to be repeated to other adults. You should start by explaining what information will be passed on to others, what will be recorded in notes and how the notes will be stored. At the outset, establish that any information you receive that raises child protection issues must be reported to adults and colleagues to ensure the safety of the young person and others. Indeed, guidelines from professional bodies are clear that in these situations young people have a right to be protected. Even when a child is judged to be generally able to make their own decisions, in situations where child protection is an issue, child protection overrides confidentiality. Promising confidentiality is unhelpful as this is not a promise that professionals can keep. If confidentiality is promised but later broken, the child may find it difficult to trust professionals again. If there is a need to break confidentiality, it is important that this is explained to the child and the reasons for breaking it given. It is also important to ensure that the child is not put in the position of having to take responsibility for sharing the information. Even in a situation where older children state they do not want action taken as they are no longer at risk, the safety of other children potentially still at risk needs to be considered. If abuse is an issue it may be useful to have an initial conversation with the local social services department before referring on to them. It will then be up to social services to decide whether further investigation or action needs to be taken.

The Mental Health Act 1983 and other legal provisions

This section outlines the use of the Mental Health Act 1983 (MHA) and other legal provisions as applied in England and Wales (but not necessarily in other parts of the UK).

Mental Health Act 1983

Parts IV and V of the MHA provide for compulsory (know as 'formal') admission and continued detention where a patient is deemed to have, or is suspected of having, a mental disorder and where other criteria are met, depending on the section used. The mental disorder must be specified as mental illness (this is not further defined by the MHA), psychopathic disorder, mental impairment (learning disability), or severe mental impairment. Full assessment (Section 2) and treatment (Section 3) orders require an application to be made by the nearest relative or a social worker approved under the MHA, and medical recommendation by two doctors, one of whom must be approved under the MHA. Table 8.1 summarises those sections of the MHA most likely to be used in young people. With reference to young people, the MHA:

- applies to all ages – except guardianship and aftercare in the community (only applies if over 16 years)
- defines children (minors) as aged under 18 years
- has special application for those aged 16 and 17 years.

Sections 135 and 136 may be used by non-specialist mental health staff, such as the police, to take someone from a private place or a public place respectively to a place of safety for a mental health assessment because of concerns about their mental health and/or risk to self and/or others.

Table 8.1 Sections of the Mental Health Act 1983 that commonly apply to young people in practice

(Details of admission and discharge procedures are not described here.)

Purpose	Section	Requirements in addition to presence of mental disorder	Powers
To ensure safety	135	Mental health assessment and can be used by police	To take someone to a place of safety from a private place for an assessment for up to 72 hours
To ensure safety	136	Concerns about mental health and risk to self or others	To take someone from a public place to a place of safety for assessment for up to 72 hours
Assessment	2	Admission is necessary for patient's own health and safety or for the protection of others	Up to 28 days admission for assessment, or assessment followed by medical treatment – not renewable
Emergency order for assessment	4	As for Section 2 (used when only one doctor is available)	Up to 72 hours admission for assessment – not renewable
Emergency detention of an informal patient	5(2)	As for Section 2 (used when only one doctor and no social worker is available)	Up to 72 hours admission for assessment – not renewable
Emergency detention of an informal patient	5(4)	As for Section 2 (used when no doctor and no social worker available (nurses holding power))	6 hours
Treatment	3	Inpatient treatment is appropriate; and the disorder is treatable;[1] and as for Section 2 and treatment cannot otherwise be provided	Up to 6 months admission for medical treatment – renewable

[1] Includes alleviation and prevention of deterioration.

Mental Health Act 2007

The Mental Health Act 2007 includes some important amendments to the Mental Health Act 1983 that relate to children and young people under the age of 18 years.

16- and 17-year-olds who do not consent to their informal admission to hospital for the treatment of mental disorder cannot be admitted to hospital for such treatment on the basis of consent from someone with parental responsibility for them.

This means that where a young person aged 16 or 17, who has the capacity to make a decision on their healthcare, decides that they do not want to consent to treatment for mental disorder, the young person cannot be admitted to hospital for that treatment unless they meet the conditions to be detained under the Mental Health Act 1983 as amended, even if a person with parental responsibility is prepared to consent.

It also means that where a young person aged 16 or 17, who has the capacity to make a decision on their healthcare, consents to being admitted to hospital for treatment for mental disorder, they should be treated as an informal patient in accordance with Section 131 of the Mental Health Act 1983 as amended, even if a person with parental responsibility is refusing consent. This should offer young people better safeguards.

Staff responsible for detaining a young person under the Act must ensure that they consult a person with knowledge or experience of cases involving patients under the age of 18 years. Courts who may be detaining a young person can also ask for information about the availability of hospital facilities 'designed so as to be specifically suitable for patients who have not yet attained the age of 18 years' (Mental Health Act 2007).

Common law

Common law is not legislation, but a term used to describe a body of law in a country or state that is based on custom and on law court decisions. In healthcare, this has particular application where there is an expectation on professionals (and the general public) to act in another's best interests in circumstances where legislation either does not exist or cannot be implemented swiftly enough to prevent serious harm. Common law is rarely applicable in child mental health.

Guiding principles are:

- there must be a degree of urgency together with safety/protection issues

- intervention must end immediately when the situation is safe

- the rights of the person being treated must be protected at all times.

For instance, a person with a suspected serious mental disorder who is aggressively disturbed and with whom it is not possible to reason may be restrained under common law if that person presents an immediate danger to themselves or others. Restraint should preserve the dignity of the person and be relaxed the moment the situation is safe. The issue for the professional is both legal and clinical: would he or she be able to defend their action or inaction in a court of law?

Admission to hospital for mental health problems

If admission to hospital is required for mental health problems the following situations may arise:

- Young people below 16 years may be admitted with consent of their parent or legal guardian. Consent of the young person is usually sought but not legally required.

- Young people may consent to admission in the absence of parental consent, providing they have the capacity to do so: parental objections are considered but normally 'will not prevail' (MHA 2007). Whilst this applies to giving consent, young people under 16 years of age cannot refuse consent to treatment where their parents have given consent.

- If both the child and parent refuse to consent to admission, an order under the MHA should be considered.

- If the young person is on a care order, then the parents and local authority should negotiate. (Note: the local authority may restrict parents' exercise of parental responsibility if there is evidence that the parents do not act in the child's interests).

- A competent child cannot arrange to be discharged against parents' wishes: 'contrary wishes of any person who has parental responsibility will ordinarily prevail' (MHA 2007).

INFORMAL ADMISSION OF 16- AND 17-YEAR-OLDS

This age group has the same rights as adults with respect to consent. If the young person does not consent but needs admission, consider using the MHA (parental wishes do not need to be sought, as the young person's wishes cannot be overridden by the parent's wishes (MHA 2007); however, in practice it is unlikely their views would not be sought). If the young person is incapable of giving consent, the MHA should be used above the Mental Capacity Act (2005).

FORMAL ADMISSION UNDER THE MENTAL HEALTH ACT 2007

General principles for the formal admission of all young people (below 18 years) are the same as for adults:

- The decision process is the same.

- Consider if admission or treatment is needed but refused by the young person or parent.

- If the parents consent, but the young person, through illness, is unable to give consent, it may be in the young person's best interest to use the MHA, as it provides certain safeguards.

- Keep the young person and parents informed at all times.

- Use the least restrictive intervention.

Consent to treatment: below 16 years

The issues of consent and refusal are the same as for admission (discussed above). An additional consideration is that consent has to be separately sought for each aspect of treatment. Permission from the court may be needed if the child is neither 16 nor Gillick competent and the parents cannot be identified, are incapacitated, or are not acting in the child's best interests.

Child protection (safeguarding)

We do not cover child protection/safeguarding in detail as this is not the specific remit of child mental health. However, all those working with children need to have an understanding of child abuse and be aware when a child may present with mental health problems as a result of abuse. The report on the Consultation on Child Abuse Prevention Geneva, March 29–31, 1999 (WHO 1999) defined child abuse in ways shown below. Abuse can be physical, emotional and/or sexual. In thinking about abuse one has to be aware of wider societal and cultural factors. A very obvious example is the practice of what is called female circumcision in parts of North Africa but is called female genital mutilation in the UK. The National Society for the Prevention of Cruelty to Children in the UK has excellent resources regarding child abuse[2] and for readers outside the UK, it can be helpful to identify equivalent organisations in your context to access such resources.

GENERAL DEFINITION

Child abuse or maltreatment constitutes all forms of physical and/or emotional ill-treatment, sexual abuse, neglect or negligent treatment or commercial or other exploitation, resulting in actual or potential harm to the child's health, survival, development or dignity in the context of a relationship of responsibility, trust or power.

PHYSICAL ABUSE

Physical abuse of a child is that which results in actual or potential physical harm from an interaction or lack of an interaction, which is reasonably within the control of a parent or person in a position of responsibility, power or trust. There may be a single incident or repeated incidents.

EMOTIONAL ABUSE

Emotional abuse includes the failure to provide a developmentally appropriate, supportive environment, including the availability of a primary attachment figure, so that the child can develop a stable and full range of emotional and social competencies commensurate with her or his personal potentials and in the context of the society in which the child dwells. There may also be acts towards the child that cause, or have a high probability of causing, harm to the child's health or physical, mental, spiritual, moral or social development. These acts must be reasonably within the control of the parent or person in a relationship of responsibility, trust or power. Acts include restriction of movement, patterns of belittling, denigrating, scapegoating, threatening, scaring, discriminating, ridiculing or other non-physical forms of hostile or rejecting treatment.

---

2   www.nspcc.org.uk

NEGLECT AND NEGLIGENT TREATMENT

Neglect is the failure to provide for the development of the child in all spheres: health, education, emotional development, nutrition, shelter, and safe living conditions, in the context of resources reasonably available to the family or caretakers, and causes, or has a high probability of causing, harm to the child's health or physical, mental, spiritual, moral or social development. This includes the failure to properly supervise and protect children from harm as much as is feasible.

SEXUAL ABUSE

Child sexual abuse is the involvement of a child in sexual activity that he or she does not fully comprehend, is unable to give informed consent to, or for which the child is not developmentally prepared and cannot give consent, or that violate the laws or social taboos of society. Child sexual abuse is evidenced by this activity between a child and an adult or another child who by age or development is in a relationship of responsibility, trust or power, the activity being intended to gratify or satisfy the needs of the other person. This may include but is not limited to:

- the inducement or coercion of a child to engage in any unlawful sexual activity

- the exploitative use of a child in prostitution or other unlawful sexual practices

- the exploitative use of children in pornographic performances and materials.

EXPLOITATION

The World Health Organisation states:

> Commercial or other exploitation of a child refers to use of the child in work or other activities for the benefit of others. This includes, but is not limited to, child labour and child prostitution. These activities are to the detriment of the child's physical or mental health, education, or spiritual, moral or social-emotional development. (World Health Organization. Violence and Injury Prevention Team Global Forum for Health Research 1999, p.16)

Anyone working with children needs to be familiar with the safeguarding policies local to their context and be aware of how to manage any concerns related to actual abuse or the risk of abuse.

THE CHALLENGES OF TECHNOLOGY AND CHILD PROTECTION

Safeguarding children from online abuse is presenting significant challenges. They are at risk of online grooming, but also exploitation of images sent in one context being used inappropriately in another. Bullying in the form of cyberbullying continues beyond school or social contexts and can impact on the child in all contexts. Increasingly, young people's relationship with new technology is being researched so we can better understand both the benefits and risks this may present to their mental health.

References

Department of Health (2009) www.gov.uk/government/publications/reference-guide-to-consent-for-examination-or-treatment-second-edition, accessed 3 July 2017.

Gillick v West Norfolk [1985] Accessed on 21 September 2017 at www.bailii.org/uk/cases/UKHL/1985/7.html

Home Office (1999) *Human Rights Act: How it will Help Children.* Home Office News Release, 26 January 1999.

The Mental Health Act (2007) London: Office of Public Sector Information.

Pearce, J. (1994) 'Consent to treatment during childhood. The assessment of competence and avoidance of conflict.' *British Journal of Psychiatry 165*, 713–716.

World Health Organization. Violence and Injury Prevention Team Global Forum for Health Research (1999) Report of the Consultation on Child Abuse Prevention. 29–31 March 1999, WHO Geneva, Geneva, World Health Organization.

Further reading

Bainham, A., and Cretney, S. (1993) *Children: The Modern Law.* Bristol: Jordan Publishing.

Black, D., Wolkind, S. and Hendricks, J.H. (1998) *Child Psychiatry and the Law (3rd edition).* London: Gaskell.

British Medical Association (2001) *Consent, Rights and Choices in Health Care for Children and Young People.* London: BMJ Books.

Department of Health and Welsh Office (1999) *Code of Practice to the Mental Health Act 1983 (Pursuant to Section 118 of the Act).* London: HMSO.

Department of Health (1989) *An Introduction to the Children Act 1989.* London: HMSO.

Hoggett, B. (1984) *Mental Health Law (2nd edition).* London: Sweet and Maxwell.

Hoggett, B. (1993) *Parents and Children: The Law of Parental Responsibility (4th edition).* London: Sweet and Maxwell.

The Mental Capacity Act (2005) London: Office of Public Sector Information.

The Mental Health Network (2007) *Maintaining the Momentum: Towards Excellent Services for Children and Young People's Mental Health.* London: The NHS Confederation.

CHAPTER 9

Emotional Problems

Defining emotional problems

'Emotional disorder of childhood' has commonly been used as an all-embracing term for the variety of emotional problems with which young people can present. The reasons for such a broad category have been that:

- presentations vary with age and development

- young people often present with a mixture of symptoms that include significant changes in the young person's mood, changes in behaviour, and physical symptoms

- the mixture of symptoms (i.e. their presence and relative significance) varies considerably between young people, to a point that makes further categorisation potentially complex.

Despite these issues, different types of emotional problem have recently been more clearly distinguished, and these are usually defined on the predominant change in mood. These may include anxiety, worry, fear, sadness, misery, depression and anger. Anger does not usually feature as a mental health problem but is included here as intervention is often made with young people to help emotional or social development.

The next question in defining emotional problems is, 'When is a problem a problem?' There are two aspects to the young person's presentation that are helpful in defining this: first, whether the symptoms cause the young person (or others) a significant degree of distress; and second, whether the symptoms have an adverse effect on social or educational function. A third factor may be assessed in longer-term issues: that of the effect on the young person's psychological or physical development. The case of Richard (below) describes features that are helpful in determining the distress caused to him and the impact of his symptoms on function and potentially on development.

CASE STUDY: Richard

Richard is an 11-year-old boy who was seen by his school nurse after he was reported by his teacher to be tearful on a number of occasions in playtime and after school. Over two appointments Richard began to describe how he feels worried at night, often cries himself to sleep, has nightmares about his family being in a car accident and on two occasions has had panic attacks. He is tired a lot, finds it difficult to concentrate on his schoolwork, and is particularly upset with himself because he 'just can't be bothered to do things any more' – despite being very conscientious normally. He thinks this is all 'silly' and can no longer face playing with his friends because he is afraid of what they might think of him. He has managed to hide it from his parents, thinking that they would tell him off.

Richard was first upset watching a TV programme two months ago about how stress might cause cancer, which is what his grandfather died of a few weeks before that. He was very close to his grandfather, who had given Richard some good advice on lots of things. Richard had even wondered whether he was a stress to his grandfather and therefore caused his death. This thought was very painful and kept coming back to him – 'even in class'.

- What should the school nurse also enquire about?

- How should Richard's concern about telling his parents be approached?

- What specific interventions should be made?

Types of emotional disorder

There are two broad groups of emotional disorders – anxiety disorders and depressive disorders. In addition, there are some disorders that are partly defined by an identified precipitant, such as adjustment reaction, abnormal bereavement reaction and post-traumatic stress disorder. Depression is covered in Chapter 13.

Anxiety and anxiety disorders

Anxiety serves as a biological function in ensuring survival, which is mediated by a number of observed mechanisms such as attachment, learning, physiological response, and avoidance of danger. The degree to which we experience and use anxiety is influenced by our genetic inheritance, temperament and life experiences. Anxiety can become habitually maladaptive, causing distress and dysfunction, at which point it may be defined as a disorder. There is a high prevalence of reported anxiety in population studies, but a relatively low presentation in clinics, which implies that most anxiety-related problems are tolerated and do not cause significant dysfunction. This may partly explain the many and varied definitions to distinguish an anxiety disorder from the normal experience of anxiety.

Anxiety disorders may present in young people in a variety of ways. Some are situation-specific and some are general. The four most common anxiety disorders in young people are separation anxiety, phobic disorders, social anxiety and generalised anxiety (previously called overanxious disorder). Panic disorder can also present in childhood.

Features of anxiety disorders include affective, cognitive and physical (or somatic) components. Affective features necessarily include a subjective experience of anxiety, which may be reported – especially in younger children – as fear, scared feelings, being afraid or worry. Young people also commonly report misery, sadness and sometimes anger, when it is important to exclude depressive disorders. Cognitive features may include the belief that self or a family member is at risk of death or illness, that an event has occurred or will occur as a result of the young person's own action (or inaction), and fear of imminent (though not necessarily definable) disaster. Somatic features include headaches, stomachaches, shortness of breath, a choking sensation, pins and needles in hands or feet, dry mouth, blurred vision, a repeated sense of the need to urinate or defecate, tremor, sweating, muscular tension, and hot and cold flushes. The relative prominence of affective, cognitive and somatic features varies with type of disorder, between young people, and within the same young person over time.

Anxiety disorders may co-occur with each other and with other disorders such as depression, behaviour disorders and attention deficit disorder. There may be at least one common path in the aetiology of anxiety and behaviour problems in young people presenting with both. If no clear limits are set to expected behaviour then, as well as showing undesirable behaviour, the young person experiences a sense of potentially unlimited control, which is in itself anxiety-provoking. Instituting clear limits to behaviour, with predictable consequences if these are breached, not only results in a diminution of the undesirable behaviour, but can also lead to reduced anxiety without the need for a specific intervention. Each anxiety disorder has a different predominant age of onset, which implies a developmental influence on presentation.

Separation anxiety

PRESENTATION

This is the most common anxiety disorder, affecting 2–4 per cent of children. It most commonly presents in preschool or early school years and is characterised by repeated, unrealistic and preoccupying anxiety associated with actual or anticipated separation from a particular adult, usually a parent. The anxiety may result in difficulty settling at night, and reluctance to go to school or to be alone – this can be to the extreme of refusing to be alone in a room when others are in the house. Parents may report that the child follows them to the bathroom; younger children may physically cling to the parent. It may reach the point where the child is habitually allowed to sleep with the parents when this is not the cultural norm. The child may experience repeated intrusive nightmares, which in young children are usually non-specific, such as monsters. There may be associated cognitive and physical symptoms. The child may believe that harm will befall their parent or themselves if separated. The parent may also experience anxiety at the prospect of separation.

ASSESSMENT

Assessment should explore the presenting features and likely precipitants. The child and the parents should ideally be interviewed, together and, if possible, separately. It may, however, have to be one of the aims of intervention to accomplish an individual interview with the child. The school may have additional information, even if the young person has not attended school for some time. The dynamics of the parent–child relationship need exploration, particularly regarding the transmission of anxiety between them and to identify parental behaviours and anxieties that perpetuate the problem.

TREATMENT

Treatment should consist of two strands, which may run simultaneously. One is specific treatment of the separation anxiety and the other is to address any presumed precipitants. These may include the birth of a sibling, a recent loss or threat of loss, illness in the family, and change of house or school. These issues should be addressed in further appointments and at home.

Specific interventions are mostly behavioural and usually involve graded exposure to separation starting in the situations defined by the family as least distressing.

Unintentional rewards for clingy behaviour should be identified and avoided. Separation should be rewarded with positive comment and praise, and the use of a star chart may be indicated. Cognitive treatment may be warranted, and can include identifying phrases that the young person may use for self-reassurance. Should parental expectations, anxiety or behaviour be a significant factor, then these should be addressed. There is insufficient evidence to support the use of medication. Outcome is usually good, with no evidence of continuity with adult disorders.

Phobic anxiety

PRESENTATION

Young people may develop specific phobias, often of particular objects, animals or situations. These commonly include spiders, dogs, blood, needles, enclosed spaces, and heights. General phobias include being in a crowded place, going outside (as distinct from separation anxiety), and public performance. Phobias are present in 2–4 per cent of young people. Whilst girls and younger children report more fears, there are no clear gender or age patterns.

ASSESSMENT

Assessment should include checking the range of situations to which the anxiety relates, the degree of anxiety experienced in the situation or in anticipation of it, and to what extent this impedes the young person's function. The important feature of phobic disorders is that the anxiety leads to habitual avoidance of the situation. This is because anxiety increases as the situation is anticipated and further as the situation/object is approached – the young person finds that their anxiety lessens on leaving the situation, which effectively rewards the young person for leaving it. Eventually, anxiety levels will increase sufficiently on anticipation of the object/situation that the young person will avoid it altogether.

TREATMENT

Simple phobias are common and do not require treatment, providing they do not cause significant distress or dysfunction. In situations where treatment is required, the most successful treatment is graded exposure to the feared object. The principle here is that the young person becomes accustomed to situations that initially promoted moderate degrees of anxiety to the point that their discomfort is less and anxiety levels fall more quickly, thus making it easier to pass on to the next most anxiety-provoking situation from a hierarchy of situations drawn up by the child and parent.

The young person may be unable to complete this regime without assistance, and the most appropriate person to support the intervention should be identified. This may be the professional, a parent or someone else in whom the young person has confidence and who has the requisite support skills. Cognitive interventions may include identification of automatic negative thoughts pertaining to the object identified by the young person at times of exposure, and active selection of alternative (positive) thoughts. Younger children may also find selected phrases to assist self-reassurance helpful. Again, there is usually no indication to support the use of medication, and outcome is normally good.

Social anxiety disorder

PRESENTATION

Although social anxiety disorder and social phobia are not technically the same, they greatly overlap with each other – and indeed with generalised anxiety disorder and with marked shyness. It is, however, important to exclude disorders in which young people may avoid or fail to seek social contact, such as pervasive developmental disorders. In social anxiety disorder, there is a persistent fear of being with unfamiliar adults and peers in social situations, which may be expressed in the young person's behaviour: crying, tantrums or freezing. The young person may experience anxiety, fear or panic attacks in the situation, which are commonly accompanied by somatic symptoms. The disorder is present in about 1 per cent of the population, and more commonly presents in late childhood and early adolescence.

As well as a comprehensive assessment of the child, in social anxiety there is also a strong reliance on corroborative accounts as the young person may not be aware of the extent of their limitations.

TREATMENT

Treatment should include an explanation of anxiety and its function, anxiety management and social skills training. Self-esteem work is also often undertaken. These treatments are most effectively delivered as group therapy, which has been shown to have positive effects that generalise beyond the group.

School refusal

School refusal may present at any age, though most often during early adolescence, when it represents a combination of adolescent stress and the revival of an earlier overdependent parent–child relationship. The increased need for independence and autonomy posed by the demands of secondary school precipitates an avoidance of school. Although it is most common in early adolescence, it can occur at times of school transition, with no gender differences.

PRESENTATION

The problem can manifest after a time of change at school or a period of illness. The unwillingness to go to school is often expressed openly and the young person may say there is a particular student or lesson that they dislike or find anxiety-provoking. Although not strictly defined as a mental health problem, it can be associated with anxiety symptoms or with associated physical complaints such as headaches or abdominal pain. The prompt exclusion of medical problems is essential in order to prevent the secondary elaboration of physical symptomatology. Delay in the recognition of the underlying psychological basis for the problem greatly exacerbates the difficulties.

MANAGEMENT

School refusal is most appropriately managed by the education welfare service. There should be a clear and consistent approach to returning young people to school. The school should involve the parents, and if appropriate the child, in devising programmes or plans. Parents need to support the programme to introduce the young person back to school. They need to be firm about what is expected of the young person and resist the temptation to accede to the young person's distress. If there are concerns about parental commitment, this may be appropriately discussed with social services or addressed legally.

Sometimes it is helpful to devise a phased return into the school environment. There should be clear expectations for the child, and parents and teachers need to be consistent and firm in this. It is important to try to encourage the young person to return to school as soon as possible. The longer it is left, the more the young person will feel that getting back is insurmountable. The prognosis is not good for a significant minority of adolescents, up to one third failing to maintain regular school attendance. Follow-up studies of young people into adult life have shown that they may have a predisposition to mental health problems including anxiety or agoraphobic symptoms (Fremont 2003). Where there have been long absences, the school should involve the education welfare service and the education psychology service to advise on the process of reintegration. Tuition at home is usually an unhelpful strategy, as it can perpetuate the problem and impedes appropriate social and educational development. Cognitive-behavioural techniques can assist the young person to gain understanding of their difficulties and control over the situation. If there are concurrent problems with anxiety, they will need to be addressed using cognitive behaviour therapy and anxiety management. The role of CAMHS is usually to manage severe anxiety or phobia associated with school refusal.

Generalised anxiety disorder

PRESENTATION

Young people experience generalised anxiety and tension that is not limited to one event or situation. This is often accompanied by somatic symptoms and non-specific complaints of ill health. Young people often seek reassurance and worry about their performance – past, present and future. Most studies estimate prevalence at 3 per cent, but some as high as 6 per cent.

ASSESSMENT

A comprehensive assessment as described above. A family history may be very significant and a family may describe itself as being 'worriers'.

TREATMENT

Treatment includes anxiety management and cognitive therapy to address specific anxieties where present. If a family is made up of several people who worry, family therapy can be useful in helping them manage their anxieties rather than generate even more anxiety. However, for many young people, symptoms continue on into adult life.

CASE STUDY: Tom

Tom is a 15-year-old boy with recurrent and intense fears of failure. This causes him to panic in situations requiring public performance, such as answering questions in class. He experiences gripping headaches in anticipation of situations where there is just the slightest chance of him being judged by others, and this has led to avoidance of these situations and resulted in poor school attendance.

–   Identify the likely distorted cognitions that Tom may have. How would you help him to identify these?

Attachment disorders

Based on the work of Bowlby and Ainsworth already discussed in Chapter 6, it follows that if attachment with caregivers does not develop there might be sequelae. O'Connor and Zeanah (2003) argue that whilst there is a greater understanding of the needs of children who experience early deprivation, there is not an equal understanding about the nature of attachment-related disturbances or strategies for intervention.

PRESENTATION

Broadly, there are two types of attachment disorder identified. The first is where children are indiscriminate about who they form 'attachment' to – they are inappropriately friendly with everyone and show little wariness. The second is where attachment is more defined in relation to the child's behaviour toward the caregiver. Children with insecure attachment, especially disorganised attachment, are at significant risk of later emotional and behavioural problems. Many children who do not form secure attachments may be children who are institutionalised or have a lack of consistent care (Allen 2007). However, attachment disorder may also be present when primary caregivers have a history of postnatal depression, unwanted pregnancy and/or other adverse perinatal events.

ASSESSMENT

Assessment is often not comprehensively undertaken. O'Connor and Zeanah (2003) support the use of multiple methods of assessment, including a comprehensive history of early childhood (which may often be lacking for children who have experienced early neglect and deprivation), a history of concerning behaviours and observations. Questionnaires may also be useful but need to be used in conjunction with clinical history and observations. It is important that attachment disorder is not diagnosed without clarity of context, as attachment is a two-way process. Children will show developmentally inappropriate social relationships and may also present as having an anxious relationship with caregivers and/or disinhibited behaviour (behavioural problems, inattention, poor concentration, aggression) or asocial behaviour (lack of empathy or ability to see another perspective) in which attention deficit hyperactivity disorder or autism spectrum disorder may be mistakenly diagnosed. Learning disability may also need to be excluded as children who demonstrate friendliness to strangers may be doing so as they do not understand the contexts for different social relationships.

TREATMENT

To date there is no known effective treatment for attachment disorders although several psychotherapeutic techniques are used based on very little evidence (Croft and Celano 2005). O'Connor and Zeanah (2003) are particularly critical of the dominance of holding therapy despite the lack of evidence. They argue that those that use it purport that it can facilitate attachment relationships, but that they have not examined the extent to which there is an improvement in the quality of attachment relationship (using reliable measures of attachment quality). Family therapy may be appropriate in some contexts but would be inappropriate if there is ongoing abuse (emotional or otherwise). Social cognitive treatment approaches may be more beneficial given that there is greater evidence of efficacy for changing specific behaviours (such as peer rejection).

From a front-line perspective, it is important that terms such as attachment disorder are not loosely used and there is awareness that other disorders need to be excluded before such a diagnosis should be made.

Panic disorder

Panic disorder is not commonly present in young people without other features of anxiety, and may accompany agoraphobia (fear of being in a place without immediate escape, e.g. outside the home, in a crowd). Panic disorder can be with and without agoraphobia. A panic attack is a discrete, intense experience of fear or anxiety, with sudden onset, typically peaking at five to ten minutes and accompanied by several physical symptoms and cognitive features, particularly the fear held by the young person that he or she is going 'mad' or 'crazy'. Panic disorder is the recurrent, unexpected experience of panic attacks. Other possible causes of panic attacks, such as medical disorders and substance use, should be excluded. Panic attacks may occur in simple phobias or social anxiety.

Panic disorder most commonly presents in the mid- to late-teens and there is frequently a family history. Treatment, in addition to anxiety management and behavioural and cognitive therapy, may include tricyclic antidepressants or selective serotonin reuptake inhibitors, which 'block' panic attacks.

Obsessive compulsive disorder

Counting rituals, magical thinking and repetitive touching occur normally in childhood, and what are often referred to as obsessions (such as with idolised figures such as pop stars and with subjects or beliefs) are not technically obsession (see definition below), but rather preoccupations or fixations; they are a part of normal socialisation in adolescence.

None of these show any relationship or continuity with obsessive compulsive disorder (OCD).

Obsessions are recurrent, intrusive thoughts that are distressing and recognised by the young person as being their own thoughts (as distinguished from psychosis – described in Chapter 13) and not simply worries about everyday life. The young person may recognise them as thoughts that come into their head over and over again and will not go away. They often take up a significant amount of time and impair social and educational function. Unlike adults with the disorder, young people do not necessarily recognise that the content of the thoughts is excessive or irrational. Obsessions may also be in the form of images (e.g. a visual representation of an imagined road accident) and impulses that the young person has no conscious desire to act on (e.g. a strong urge to shout out obscenities in school assembly, or to break a valued object).

Compulsions are actions that the young person feels compelled to repeat, usually in a very specific way in accordance with rules that the young person has generated to reduce the distress that is usually associated with obsessions. These compulsive actions are either physical (typically hand-washing, arranging or checking objects) or mental (typically counting, repetition of words or phrases to oneself in a specific way). The young person (or parent) may recognise the problem as something that they have to do over and over again or that they have to do in a particular way, starting again if they do not get it right. By performing the compulsion, the young person aims to prevent an imagined undesirable or traumatic event, which either has no bearing on the compulsive behaviour or is an extreme response to it. Again, unlike adult patients, the young person does not necessarily recognise the excessive or irrational nature of the behaviour.

A diagnosis of OCD can be made with the presence of either obsessions or compulsions. Young people with OCD usually present with a long history, not uncommonly dating to preschool years. The problem is usually identified because of their eventual inability to complete tasks at school or home, spending excessive time washing or dressing, and possibly engaging other family members in their rituals. Other causes of similar ritualistic behaviours and obsessions, such as occur in autism, schizophrenia and Tourette's syndrome, need to be excluded. Depression and anxiety can also cause symptoms of OCD.

Treatment is more effective for compulsions than obsessions. The core component of intervention is 'response prevention': the young person draws up a hierarchy of compulsions and – starting with the least distressing – aims to stop the behavioural response. A greater degree of anxiety is experienced immediately on doing so, for which anxiety management and cognitive therapy may be helpful. The programme should be such that the anxiety is tolerable, and repeated blocking of the behavioural response will result in reduced experience of anxiety, allowing progress to the next most challenging behaviour in the hierarchy.

Complex or prolonged behaviours may be considered as a series of separate behaviours and broken down into their constituent parts, again addressing the least distressing component first. Medication has a role in many cases, and may even do so in children as young as six years. Long-term outcome is poorer than for other emotional disorders, particularly where there is a predominance of obsessions, and many young people continue to experience symptoms into adulthood.

Further details on psychotherapeutic and pharmacological interventions for OCD are outlined in Chapter 15.

Adjustment reaction

Adjustment reaction can be diagnosed when there is a significant emotional response to a stressful event. The symptoms abate within six months of onset. The event usually involves loss or harm, such as bereavement, family separation, a serious accident or abuse. There is disagreement as to the maximum interval from the event to the onset of symptoms, which ranges from one month (ICD-10: WHO 2016) to three months (DSM-V: APA 2013). The symptoms may include depression, anxiety and behavioural disturbance in any combination. If the diagnostic criteria are met for other disorders, such as those listed above, or major mental disorders, then they 'trump' adjustment reaction.

CASE STUDY: Jodie

Jodie is eight years old. Her mother, Ms Mortimer, requests to see you in your role as the school nurse. Ms Mortimer tells you that she is concerned that Jodie is unhappy at school and not learning as well as she could because of this. She feels the schoolteachers are not concerned with Jodie's lack of progress. She would like you and the school to sort things out.

As the school nurse, what further information might you like?

It becomes clear that Jodie had been progressing well until four months ago when her schoolwork deteriorated a little. At school, she is noted to be a little quieter but settles as the school day progresses. Ms Mortimer separated from Jodie's father about four months ago and Jodie has had no regular contact with her father since that time.

What would you do next?

Abnormal bereavement reaction

Abnormal bereavement reaction may be considered if there is a significant departure from the 'normal' sequence of grief, which is similar across age groups.

There are several stages of grief recognised in a 'normal' reaction to bereavement. Different authors describe these differently, with between three and six stages depending on what they include in each. There is an initial stage of shock, during which the young person may be in denial, numb and detached from events, and may direct much of their mental and physical activity towards the deceased person. Young people may talk about the deceased as if they were still alive, and act accordingly. This stage may last from several minutes to days, and can be returned to from later stages of grieving. Rituals associated with the death, such as formalised mourning and funerals, are invariably found across cultures. These assist young people in moving on from this stage in particular.

Many Western societies have 'sanitised' death to the extent that young people may be deprived of this important aspect of socialised mourning. Common issues for families are whether to allow a child to see the dead body, and whether the child would understand what it is all about. There is evidence that young people have an understanding of the permanence of death from toddlerhood, and increasingly adopt cultural beliefs throughout childhood. One benefit of a child seeing the body, if they so choose, is that it enables them to say goodbye. It also prevents distressing elaborations of what the body might look like. Apart from most Western societies over the last 150 years, custom has been to involve young people in all aspects of bereavement.

In the next stage, the young person may express despair, anger, guilt, sadness, hopelessness, self-blame and worthlessness. There may be changes in behaviour, appetite and sleep. Children may have an egocentric view of the death, whereby they believe that something they did, or did not do (often unrelated or very remotely related), directly caused the death. This belief may persist, despite reassurance, for several years. Young people commonly have visual and auditory hallucinations of the deceased, which may be either comforting or distressing. Sometimes professional reassurance is needed that they are not going 'crazy'.

The final stage of adjustment, in which the young person takes on and enjoys usual activities, with a reduction of the distressing emotions, may take several months or even years to achieve. At each stage, there may be a return to aspects of previous stages, particularly at the anniversary of the death and other times such as birthdays and religious festivals. The content and duration of each stage varies considerably.

What differentiates a 'normal' from an 'abnormal' bereavement reaction is difficult to define, and it is not usually helpful to talk in these terms. Three features, however, can distinguish a significant departure from a normal reaction. First, the reaction may follow a normal course, but the young person experiences marked distress or greater than expected dysfunction, particularly slowing of physical and mental activity (psychomotor retardation). Second, one or more stages may be prolonged. For instance, there may be a marked or prolonged belief held by the young person that he or she is worthless or should have died too. Third, there may be additional features not normally found, such as distressing emotions, negative cognitions or hallucinations unrelated to the death.

The young person and their family may seek support in the form of simple counselling about the nature of grief and how best to manage. Assessment should include a full history of events about the death itself (the nature of the death, beliefs held by each family member about it, how the young person heard of the death), the family's response to the death (how the funeral was managed and who attended, how the family have grieved and how they tolerate each other's grieving) and any other changes in the family. Intervention should be directed to specific aspects of the grief that have not been achieved in addition to general education or counselling about the nature of grief.

Post-traumatic stress disorder

Post-traumatic stress disorder (PTSD) occurs in young people in response to experiencing or witnessing events that caused a threat of death or serious harm, such as a disaster, gross violence, traumatic accident, abuse, war, serious illness and medical procedures. To diagnose PTSD there must have been such an event and the response must persist for at least one month and involve at least one aspect of each of the following features:

- intense fear, helplessness, horror, disorganised or agitated behaviour

- repeated re-experience of the event through intrusive images, thoughts, repetitive play; or frightening dreams (which in young people may or may not be related to the event); or a reliving of the experience with hallucinations and flashbacks

- re-enactment of the event, particularly by young children; or intense distress at reminders of the event; or marked physiological arousal at reminders of the event

- persistent avoidance of things that may be associated with the event or which may be a reminder of it, such as places, objects, activities, people and conversations; or inability to recall important aspects of the event, feelings of detachment, restricted range of feelings, or sense of foreshortened future

- persistent symptoms of arousal, including poor sleep and concentration, irritability, exaggerated startle response and markedly increased vigilance.

Onset is defined as delayed if it presents more than six months after the stressor, and the disorder is defined as chronic (or persisting) if symptoms last more than three months. Screening instruments have been developed but are not sensitive at detecting PTSD compared with screens for other disorders, particularly when completed by parents and teachers. Young people should be assessed individually, where possible, as well as in parent and family interviews. They are more likely than in other disorders to hide symptoms to protect friends or family members from their own suffering or out of feelings of loyalty to anyone implicated in a trauma.

Before specific interventions can be made, it is important to ensure the young person's general welfare, safety and protection. There may be issues to address within the family, particularly if the event was abuse, serious harm, or murder. The young person may be reassured at how common such symptoms are – generally found in about 30–40 per cent experiencing a natural disaster, higher than this in war, displacement and violence, and between 40 per cent and 50 per cent in repeated sexual abuse (Davis and Siegal 2000; Rodriguez, Vande Kemp and Foy 1998). Talking over the event may be helpful but premature counselling or formal debriefing may 'block' the natural resolution of symptoms. Sharing experiences with others who experienced the same or similar events in therapeutic groups may help the young person. Young people can be helped to understand the event further through play and verbal therapies. Behavioural and cognitive therapies can be helpful in managing anxiety and avoidance of specific places, and managing dreams, distressing emotions and intrusive thoughts.

References

Allen, J. (2007) 'Interventions for Foster Carers and Adoptive Parents of Children Who Have Experienced Abuse and Trauma.' In P. Vostanis (ed.) *Mental Health Interventions and Services for Vulnerable Children and Young People.* London: Jessica Kingsley Publishers.

American Psychiatric Association (2013) *Diagnostic and Statistical Manual of Mental Disorders (5th edition).* Washington DC: American Psychiatric Association.

Croft, S. and Celano, M. (2005) 'Evaluating and Managing Attachment Difficulties in Children.' In S.S. Sexson (ed.) *Child and Adolescent Psychiatry (2nd edition).* Malden, MA: Blackwell Publishing.

Davis, L. and Siegel, L.J. (2000) 'Post-traumatic stress disorder in children and adolescents: A review and analysis.' *Clinical Child and Family Psychology Review 3,* 3, 135–154.

Fremont, W. (2003) 'School refusal in children and adolescents.' *American Family Physician 68,* 8, 1555–1561.

O'Connor, T. and Zeanah, C.H. (2003) 'Attachment disorders: Assessment strategies and treatment approaches.' *Attachment and Human Development 5,* 3, 223–244.

Rodriguez, N., Vande Kemp, H. and Foy, D.W. (1998) 'Post-traumatic stress disorder in survivors of childhood sexual and physical abuse: A critical review of the empirical research.' *Journal of Child Sexual Abuse 7,* 2, 17–45.

World Health Organization (2016) *The International Classification of Diseases, ICD-10 Classification of Mental and Behavioural Disorders.* Published 1992 and revised 2016. Geneva: World Health Organization.

Further reading

Dwivedi, K.N. (2000) *Post-Traumatic Stress Disorder in Children and Adolescents.* London: Whurr.

Flament, M.F. (1999) 'Obsessive-Compulsive Disorders.' In H-C. Steinhausen and F. Verhulst (eds) *Risks and Outcomes in Developmental Psychopathology.* Oxford: Oxford University Press.

Hill, P.D. (2002) 'Adjustment Disorders.' In M. Rutter, and E. Taylor (eds) *Child and Adolescent Psychiatry (4th edition).* Oxford: Blackwell Science.

Klein, R.G. and Pine D.S. (2002) 'Anxiety Disorders.' In M. Rutter, and E. Taylor (eds) *Child and Adolescent Psychiatry (4th edition).* Oxford: Blackwell Science.

Rapoport, J.L. and Swedo, S. (2002) 'Obsessive-Compulsive Disorder.' In M. Rutter, and E. Taylor (eds) *Child and Adolescent Psychiatry (4th edition).* Oxford: Blackwell Science.

Seligman, L.D. and Ollendick, T.H. (1999) 'Anxiety Disorders.' In H-C. Steinhausen and F. Verhulst (eds) *Risks and Outcomes in Developmental Psychopathology.* Oxford: Oxford University Press.

Yule, W. (2002) 'Post-Traumatic Stress Disorders.' In M. Rutter, and E. Taylor (eds) *Child and Adolescent Psychiatry (4th edition).* Oxford: Blackwell Science.

CHAPTER 10

Behavioural Problems

This chapter has two parts. In the first we consider behavioural problems related to developmental aspects and in the second we focus on disorders that have a behavioural component to their presentation.

Behavioural problems

Defiance, temper tantrums, impulsivity, breath holding, sleep problems and perceived lying are frequently noted around the ages of two to four years, when children need autonomy but do not have the skills for successful independence. Around 5 per cent of three-year-olds display severe tantrums (Richman, Stevenson and Graham 1982). Most of these behaviours are considered appropriate at certain developmental levels. They are often as a result of anger and frustration. Studies of US preschoolers show that around 8.3 per cent of children have behaviour difficulties at some point, with an excess of oppositional defiant disorders seen in this age group (Lavigne *et al.* 1993, 1996).

Temper tantrums, defiance, oppositionality, impulsivity
Presentation
These behaviours are frequently shown by children of 18 months to three years. They often feel frustrated by conflicting desires to be, on the one hand, in control of their environment and, on the other hand, taken care of and pampered in a developmentally regressed way. Children of two to five years may show aggression in the form of temper tantrums, screaming, hurting others, or destroying toys or furniture. Aggressive behaviour is frequently a product of particular frustrations and a toddler's inability to manage them. It is usually directed toward parents during preschool years, and later towards

siblings or peers. Verbal aggression increases between two and four years, and after three years revenge and retaliation can be prominent acts of aggression.

Risk factors

When temper tantrums become overwhelming and persistent, there are often other contributing factors to continuing outbursts. These can be related to risk factors such as:

- family disruption

- inconsistent parental management

- witnessing of 'out-of-control' or aggressive behaviour in the family

- separation anxiety

- abuse

- developmental delay

- poor interpersonal relationships.

Assessment and management

When undertaking an assessment, as well as exploring parental expectation of behaviours for a given age, behaviours that parents are concerned about should be specifically clarified in detail. It is important to observe parental management of behaviours as part of the assessment, as that will prove useful in planning the management with the parents. Parental responses to the above behaviours determine the likelihood of the behaviours recurring and persisting. A parent who responds with punitive anger runs the risk of reinforcing the idea that emotionally 'out of control' responses are acceptable. Children can often be frightened by the strength and intensity of their own angry feelings, as well as those that they raise in their parents. Parents need to model and control their own anger and aggressive feelings, if they wish children to follow. Most parents of children with such problems can become frustrated and horrified by their children's loss of control and displays of anger. Most problematic behaviour can be modified by consistent application of behavioural techniques discussed in Chapter 14.

Breath holding

Breath holding is very common during the first years of life. Infants and toddlers may frequently use it in an attempt to control their environment and their parents.

Presentation

This behaviour can become problematic and concerning, as children may hold their breath until they lose consciousness. This can sometimes lead to seizures, which can in turn lead to parental panic. However, there is no increased risk of later development of a seizure disorder in children.

Management

Parents are best advised to ignore the behaviour and leave the room in response. This eradicates most breath holding. This response should not be used if the child is physically unwell or has a respiratory problem. If breath holding continues and is coupled with other disruptive behaviours and psychosocial factors then more intensive behavioural strategies may be necessary.

<u>CASE STUDY</u>: Jacob

Ms. Collins is a 21-year-old single mother. She has approached her health visitor for help. Her son Jacob, age three, has started to refuse to do anything she asks him. He often hits out when he has to do things that he does not like. She sends him to his room but he screams for hours and strips the wallpaper off the walls of his room. He has also started to use abusive language, but Ms Collins does not know why. He is fine at nursery and gets on well with other children. Ms Collins' partner left recently and Ms Collins is concerned that Jacob has heard arguments between her and his father. She feels that she is a useless mother. She no longer goes out with friends, as she is afraid that Jacob may treat a babysitter as he has treated her. She gives in to him a lot and feels he has now got the better of her; she is at the end of her tether and doesn't know what to do next. She feels there may be something wrong with him.

- What should the health visitor do?

- What would you do differently if Jacob's father were still part of the family?

Lying and stealing

Lying can often be used by two- to four-year-olds as a way of playing with language, therefore it is important to keep it in perspective. Preschoolers learn cognitively and affectively by observing the reactions of parents. Lying is also a form of fantasy for young people, when describing the way they would wish things to be rather than how they are.

Before the age of five years, the concept of personal property is likely to be poorly developed. Therefore, the concept of stealing in this age group cannot be meaningfully employed. From the age of six years onwards, stealing in its real sense can be possible. In the earlier age groups, it can become confused with borrowing without permission. Children around the age of seven to nine years can become involved in stealing from shops or taking money from the home.

Presentation and management

Regardless of age and development, intervention is warranted when lying becomes a frequent way of managing conflict and anxiety. Children should be given a clear message of what is acceptable. Sensitivity and support are important because children are developmentally vulnerable and therefore open to embarrassment and shame. When parents become unable to resolve or understand the situation, then professional intervention is indicated.

Stealing can be impulsive, but the gratification derived does not satisfy underlying need. It can also be an expression of anger or revenge for real or imagined injustices or misrepresentations. In many instances, children wish to be caught, as it is one way for the child to manipulate and attempt to control interactions with parents. It is important to deal with an escalating problem as early as possible before the child raises the stakes and resorts to greater secrecy. Stealing can also be an indication of emotional or physical neglect.

Sleep problems and disorders

There are three distinct areas of sleep problems – difficulty in getting a child to go to bed, nightmares, and night terrors and sleepwalking, which together have rates of approximately 10 per cent in preschool children and 4 per cent in five- to nine-year-olds (Richman 1981; Richman *et al.* 1982). There can be different cultural and family expectations that determine whether problems with the onset of sleep are presented to professionals or not.

Night time sleeping

When there are problems with getting a child to bed, this is usually part of a wider picture, which includes defiance in several areas. The management is usually behavioural and the parents are encouraged to parent with consistency and clarity.

Nightmares

These can occur at any age and are common in young childhood without identified triggers, though may also be associated with specific life events. Following trauma, they may occur in association with flashbacks and anxiety. A child who has experienced a nightmare is usually able to describe their nightmare to you. Their management involves identifying potential causes for the nightmares and addressing those issues. Recall of a nightmare may lead to some anxiety and the parents need to provide explanation or education, perhaps with reassurance, in a way that does not reinforce the anxiety.

Night terrors and sleepwalking

These are most common between the ages of six and nine years. Night terrors present with a history of the child often issuing a 'blood curdling' scream, sitting bolt upright while asleep, and appearing terrified. They may awake with no recall of what has just taken place. The child is not 'engageable', and appears disoriented and to be 'in a different world'. A child who has night terrors may also sleepwalk; these occur in the same stage of sleep. Most children outgrow night terrors and sleepwalking. Management largely comprises reassuring the parents and helping them to ensure that the child is safe if they sleepwalk. Parents can be informed that they do not need to wake the child during a night terror, though there are no dangers in doing so.

Eating problems in younger children

Problems encountered by preschool and younger children may range from being picky or faddy about food to severe problems such as non-organic failure to thrive (when there is no identified medical cause to explain the reason that a child is failing to grow). It is unlikely that a child with a feeding problem other than the latter will become nutritionally deficient. Around 10 per cent of preschool children can show difficulties or problems with their feeding at some stage. However, the majority of these children will improve their eating habits as they get older, with no lasting consequences on their health (Butler and Golding 1986; Kedesdy and Budd 1998).

Feeding problems in early infancy (0–3 months)

Transient problems and minor setbacks in early feeding are common. Persistent and more severe problems are rare and require careful assessment. Some problems can be as a result of an underlying physical problem. However, if they are not, these difficulties may be a prelude to other behavioural problems.

Early eating or feeding problems include:

- rejection of the bottle or breast

- failure to suck

- crying – leading to difficulty in getting the child to feed

- diarrhoea

- colic

- constipation

- vomiting

- abdominal pain.

Rumination

Rumination can be defined as a repeated voluntary regurgitation of food, without associated nausea or gastrointestinal disorder, with a failure to gain weight. It usually occurs between the ages of 3 and 12 months and is possibly a reflection of the mother–child relationship. The relationship can be bound up with the symptoms in a complex interaction of cause and effect. For the parent of a child who ruminates, their failure to feed the child successfully may render the act of feeding aversive. There is also a noxious odour of vomit, and clothes can become saturated. In severe cases treatment is urgent, as there are potential medical complications and the condition can become fatal.

Pica

Pica is the persistent ingestion of substances that have no nutritional value. Although onset is usually at 12–14 months, a diagnosis should not be made before the age of two years because infants often put objects in their mouths. Diagnosis is made if the behaviour occurs at least twice weekly and persists for more than one month.

Pica can be associated with psychiatric conditions such as autism, schizophrenia and Kleine–Levin syndrome. It is, however, more commonly associated with learning disability. Pica is important when recognising associated mental health issues such as autism. In children who do not have a learning disability it may also be a behavioural indicator of neglect or abuse. It can also be associated with poverty and parental mental illness.

Food avoidance emotional disorder

This disorder is restricted to early childhood. There is often a previous history of food restriction in the home and a presence of emotional disturbance such as phobias, obsessional behaviour, and refusal to attend school or depression. The avoidance is often of the same intensity as in older anorexic young people. However, distorted body image and fear of gaining weight are absent.

Pervasive refusal syndrome

The status of this as a syndrome is not yet determined and is controversial. This occurrence is rare and can be life-threatening. It consists of a profound and pervasive refusal to eat, drink, walk and talk. The child shows similar characteristics to anorexia, but rapidly manifests the other avoidant behaviours. The child may become totally regressive, and efforts to intervene may be met with terror or anger.

Childhood obesity

Childhood obesity is of concern primarily because of its persistence into later life. There are psychological and physiological consequences to obesity that can be adverse. Psychological consequences can be missed and are usually related to negative peer group interactions, though not exclusively. Children in nursery have already learned to associate obesity with a variety of less desirable traits, and obese children are the least popular in the peer group. Therefore, obesity can result in low mood and poor self-esteem.

Risk factors

The common risk factors for children developing more serious problems include:

- problems with social relationships

- adverse living conditions, such as overcrowding

- maternal mental health problems

- anxiety focused on the baby

- lack of social support.

Management of eating problems in preschool or younger children

Children may be born prematurely or have physical problems at birth, which can make parents anxious, especially in relation to weight gain. Minor problems can usually be addressed by providing parents with support and advice about feeding routines. Difficulties may arise from repeated battles at mealtimes, and children may miss stages in developing their own taste or in gaining a normal feeding routine. Behavioural techniques can be effective in establishing a normal eating pattern. Usually the less fuss made the better.

Disorders with a behavioural component on presentation in school age children and adolescents

The problems presented here may be part of a broader problem, which is presented through some of the behaviours discussed here.

Lying and stealing

Lying and stealing in isolation may be a problem in this age group. The presentation and management are not dissimilar to that in younger age groups, so a description is not repeated here. Generally, however, lying and stealing tend to be part of a wider picture with other associated problems, such as conduct disorder or family relationship difficulties.

Aggression

Aggression is probably one of the most concerning and distressing behaviours in this group of problems. Young people who are aggressive are often overly sensitive and may have a low threshold for perceiving and understanding aggression in others. They sometimes have poor social and problem solving skills and tend to have automatic and impulsive responses. Often, they will have difficulty in estimating the consequences of their behaviour and will use such behaviour to relate to their peer group. Intentional aggression may be primarily either a means to an end or to inflict physical or psychological pain. Hyperactive and clumsy children may be deemed aggressive due to the unintended results of their behaviour. Aggression is often evidence of parental display of anger, aggression or punishment, which they may initiate when physically or psychologically hurt. Aggressive behaviour is also commonly associated with:

- conduct disorder
- attention deficit disorder
- specific learning disabilities (or difficulties)
- developmental delay.

Risk factors

Aggression in childhood is also positively correlated to family unemployment, discord, criminality and mental health disorders (Farrington 2000; Stormont 1998). Factors that contribute to aggression include:

- gender – boys are reported more aggressive than girls, but aggression in girls is often less tolerated and more likely to be seen as abnormal or pathological

- size – large children are often more aggressive than smaller ones

- more active and impulsive children are perceived as more aggressive, which in turn leads to them being more aggressive

- difficult temperament in infancy has been shown to be related to later aggressiveness

- family size – children from larger families are often more aggressive than those from smaller families

- marital discord between parents and aggression in the home

- exposure to aggression in play and, somewhat controversially, on TV and electronic media and games.

Management

The causes and motives of aggression should be identified. The management of aggression involves enabling young people to understand their problem. It includes the use of cognitive-behavioural techniques, which enable the young person to self-monitor their behaviour and to understand difficult situations. A method called self-instruction or self-talk (an internal dialogue that is used as a coping strategy to decrease the experience of anger arousal and to enhance the ability to manage an angry situation) is utilised to help them get through the difficulty. Usually the young person will benefit from learning problem solving techniques and methods of relaxation.

The management plan within the home or school environment should focus on using a consistent approach, with defined boundaries and rules that reward appropriate behaviour and encourage the young person's responsibility and autonomy.

Fire-related behaviour

Fire-related behaviour is on a continuum of severity from normal fire interest at one end of the spectrum to fire setting at the other. There are three sequential phases of fire behaviour: fire interest, fire play and fire setting. Some children may never progress beyond the first level, whilst others may develop a career of risky and dangerous fire setting behaviour. The value of defining the level of fire-related behaviour is that it can help professionals to identify potential risk factors and the most appropriate care pathway.

Presentation

FIRE INTEREST

Many children show what is considered to be a normal interest in fire at an early stage in their development. Studies of children aged five to nine years show that fire interest is almost universal. This includes: the desire to play with matches, interest in fire-related themes, making attempts to watch fires, and lighting matches or other combustibles. Children may express their curiosity in several ways; for example, they may ask questions in relation to fire or they may incorporate fire scenarios into their play. Most children experiment with fire and, due to their inability to comprehend the inherent hazards of such an activity, experimentation can result in fire that is more serious than the child's level of risk would suggest. Interest should start to diminish around the age of nine or ten years; a high level of interest beyond this age requires investigation.

FIRE PLAY

When fire interest extends to experimentation it becomes fire play and is potentially serious, occurring mostly in boys between the ages of five and nine years. Fire play may also include the collection of, and experimentation with, incendiary materials to see which are the most flammable or produce the most flamboyant effects. First-time fire play seldom produces significant fire; however, the probability of this increases with subsequent fire play.

FIRE SETTING

Children older than ten years should have learned the rules of fire safety and prevention. Should they continue with inappropriate behaviour beyond this point, with or without intervention, then this is a more risky and dangerous behaviour, known as fire setting. The most concerning fire setting is when a child sets fires on their own, in an aggressive or angry manner or in an attempt to harm others.

Risk factors

Young people may show a general pattern of behaviours – impulsive, overactive, mischievous, more prone to temper outbursts and destructive behaviour. Certain risk factors may also be present and these include:

- single-parent family

- absent father (e.g. working away from the family home)

- high level of marital discord

- overprotective parent who administers inappropriate harsh punishment

- parental mental illness

- domestic violence

- social isolation

- low self-esteem

- abuse

- early inappropriate fire modelling within the family.

Management

Some local fire services run programmes for children and young people who start to show an interest in setting fires. It can be helpful for the child to be referred at an early stage. Whilst early fire play can be addressed by the fire service, sustained fire setting requires specialist CAMHS intervention. In complex cases of fire setting it is important to have a multi-agency approach to managing the child's problems due to the potential danger to self and others.

Truancy

Truancy is defined as when young people stay off school without parental knowledge or permission or valid reason. It can start to become a problem for some young people during their secondary school years, usually during the final years of compulsory schooling, occurring more commonly in inner-city schools. Persistent truancy is unlikely in primary school children.

Young people who truant often get ready for school, sometimes going in to register and then leaving the school premises. They commonly also exhibit other problem behaviours. Young people tend to truant in groups and will often say that they are bored with school. Those who spend their time alone are in a minority but are at greater risk of becoming involved in criminality. There is only a role for CAMHS when there is a clearly defined mental health disorder.

Conduct disorder

Nearly all young people at some time exhibit difficult or antisocial behaviour. Most have brief episodes of stealing or lying. Some may be involved in bullying or aggressive behaviour. The difference in a young person with conduct disorder is in the extent and severity to which difficult and antisocial behaviours are displayed and persist. However, there is considerable debate about whether this is a mental health disorder, although it appears in international classifications of diseases (Loeber et al. 2000). Up to 11 per cent of young people over ten years old could be described as having a conduct disorder, depending on the defining criteria.

Presentation

Conduct disorders are classified as either unsocialised or socialised. In unsocialised conduct disorder the young person usually presents with a pervasive difficulty in relating to their peer group, and in socialised conduct disorder they are usually well integrated with their peers. The diagnostic criteria include persistence of the behaviour difficulties for over six months and the presence of behaviours representing major violations of age-appropriate expectations, not just mischief or adolescent rebelliousness. Conduct disorder also often coexists with depression and/or substance misuse. Behaviours include:

- excessive levels of bullying or fighting

- often initiating physical fights

- use of a weapon to harm others

- severe deliberate destructiveness to property

- stealing from a victim during a physical confrontation (e.g. mugging)

- forcing someone into sexual activity

- repeated stealing and lying

- deliberate fire setting with the intention to cause harm

- repeated truancy

- repeatedly staying away from home overnight against parental instruction

- cruelty to other people or animals

- unusually frequent and severe temper tantrums

- defiant or provocative behaviour

- severe and persistent violation of rules.

Risk factors

In conduct disorders, there is usually the coexistence of several of the following risk factors:

- socio-economically disadvantaged communities

- familial discord and large families

- poor parental child-rearing practices and modelling

- poor educational attainment or opportunities (especially specific reading disorders)

- genetic factors

- difficult temperament and personality

- poor physical health.

Management

Any form of treatment offered will depend on the motivation of the young person and the family; unfortunately, this is often lacking. Cognitive-behavioural techniques can be helpful in a minority of cases, as can other forms of psychotherapy, such as behaviour and family therapy. Medication sometimes has a limited role to play in the treatment of conduct disorders, especially in those who have severe aggressive outbursts not associated with epilepsy, but this should only be given in consultation with specialist services. There has been recent discussion that parenting programmes based on social learning models are more effective than other types of parenting programmes (Scott 2008). However, much of this applies to those children under 12 years of age.

CASE STUDY: Jack

Jack is a seven-year-old boy who lives with his mother, younger sister and maternal grandmother, who dotes on him. He reminds his mother of his father, from whom she separated after he was convicted of violent assault; consequently, she prefers the company of his younger sister. His mother brought Jack to see the GP because he frequently bites his sister at home and other children in the playground. Other parents have complained, and Jack is at risk of being expelled from school. During the interview, she was angry with Jack and kept demanding to know why he continued to behave as he did, despite her attempts to stop his bad behaviour. She has shouted at him, slapped and bitten him 'to show him what it's like' but his behaviour continues. However, on recounting an episode that she witnessed of him biting at school she smiled, and admitted that sometimes she finds it amusing and laughs at his behaviour. At this point, Jack looked up at her and grinned.

- What behavioural techniques has Jack's mother unwittingly used that have encouraged the biting?

- How effective are the techniques that she has used to discourage the biting?

- How should this be further assessed?

- What is this assessment likely to demonstrate?

Outline an intervention to reduce the frequency of biting. Does Jack's grandmother have a role to play, and if so what? What advice should be given to the school?

Multisystemic therapy (MST) offers promise for older children with conduct disorder but has yet to be used in non-specialist contexts (Scott 2008). The proactive nature of MST supports the engagement of unmotivated families.

References

Butler, M.R. and Golding, J. (eds) (1986) *From Birth to Five: A Study of Health and Behaviour in Britain's Five-Year-Olds.* London: Pergamon Press.

Farrington, D.P. (2000) 'Adolescent Violence: Findings and Implications from the Cambridge Study.' In G. Boswell (ed.) *Violent Children and Adolescents: Asking the Question Why.* London: Whurr Publishers.

Kedesdy, J.H. and Budd, K.S. (1998) *Childhood Feeding Disorders: Biobehavioural Assessment and Intervention.* Baltimore, MD: Brooks Publishing Company.

Lavigne, J.V., Binns, H.J., Christofel, K.K., Rosenbaum, D. *et al.* (1993) 'Behavioural and emotional problems among pre-school children in paediatric primary care: Prevalence and pediatricians' recognition.' *Pediatrics 913*, 649–655.

Lavigne, J.V., Gibbons, R.D., Christofel, K.K., Arend, R. *et al.* (1996) 'Prevalence rates and correlates of psychiatric disorder among pre-school children.' *Journal of the American Academy of Child and Adolescent Psychiatry 35*, 2, 204–214.

Loeber, R., Burke, J.D., Lahey, B.B., Winters, A. and Zera, M. (2000) 'Oppositional defiant and conduct disorders: A review of the past 10 years, Part I.' *Journal of the American Academy of Children and Adolescent Psychiatry 39*, 12, 1468–1484.

Richman, N. (1981) 'A community survey of one to two-year-olds with sleep disturbances.' *Journal of the Academy of Child Psychiatry 20*, 281–291

Richman, N., Stevenson J. and Graham, P. (1982) *Pre-school to School: A Behavioural Study.* London: Academic Press.

Scott, S. (2008) 'An update on interventions for conduct disorder.' *Advances in Psychiatric Treatment 14*, 61–70.

Stormont, M. (1998) 'Family factors associated with externalising disorders in preschool children.' *Journal of Early Intervention 21*, 3, 232–251.

Further reading

Burke, J.D., Loeber, R. and Birmaher, B. (2002) 'Oppositional defiant disorder and conduct disorder: A review of the past 10 years, Part II.' *Journal of the American Academy of Child and Adolescent Psychiatry 41*, 11, 1275–1293.

Kazdin, A.E. (1997) 'Practitioner Review: Psychosocial treatments for conduct disorder.' *Journal of Child Psychology and Psychiatry 38*, 2, 161–178.

Neville, D., King, L. and Beak, D. (1995) *Promoting Positive Parenting.* Aldershot: Arena.

Neville, D., King, L. and Beak, D. (1995) *Promoting Positive Parenting of Teenagers.* Aldershot: Arena.

Sutton, C. (1999) *Helping Families with Troubled Children.* Chichester: Wiley.

Turk, J., Graham, P. and Verhulst, F. (2007) *Child and Adolescent Psychiatry: A Developmental Approach (4th edition).* Oxford: Oxford University Press.

CHAPTER 11

Neurodevelopmental Disorders

The term *neurodevelopmental disorders* encompasses a heterogeneous group of disorders of genetic, environmental, mixed or unsubstantiated aetiology that usually present in infancy or early childhood and have a chronic course, often into adulthood. Neurodevelopmental disorders may affect up to 3 per cent of the population and typically affect boys more frequently than girls. Interestingly, for many neurodevelopmental disorders, the male-to-female sex ratio approximates to 3:1. These disorders can cause considerable health, social and economic problems, many of which are preventable or treatable. Their impact is experienced by the individual, the family, the community and society.

There are many disorders included in this group, and this chapter will focus on two that are more likely to present with mental health problems: Attention Deficit Hyperactivity Disorder (ADHD) and Autism and related disorders.

Attention Deficit Hyperactivity Disorder

The definition and classification of Attention Deficit Hyperactivity Disorder (ADHD) have changed significantly over the last two to three decades. The Diagnostic and Statistical Manual of Mental Disorders (DSM) and International Classification of Diseases (ICD) classifications have come somewhat closer to each other in how they define the disorder. ICD uses the terminology Hyperkinetic Disorder and DSM uses Attention Deficit Hyperactivity Disorder. The core features of ADHD comprise a triad of:

- inattention (decreased concentration and cognitive focus)

- hyperactivity (restlessness, overactivity relative to that required)
- impulsivity (lack of or significantly reduced forethought or consideration of consequences), which may be expressed verbally or behaviourally.

These cardinal features of ADHD are common characteristics of the behaviour of toddlers and preschool children. As the brain matures, the child is able to regulate motoric behaviour, increase attention, and delay behavioural responses while consequences are considered. Hence, ADHD can be described as a neurodevelopmental disorder and presenting features should always be assessed relative to what would be expected for the individual's age. As in many other areas of development, this maturation is slower in boys than girls, and boys are at greater risk of developing the disorder.

Controversy endures about the definition of this disorder, diagnostic processes, and terms used to describe children with hyperactivity. There is also a wide variation of opinion on the aetiology and management of this disorder. There is debate about whether ADHD is a discrete diagnosis and whose interests are served in making the diagnosis and treating it using medication (Timimi *et al.* 2004). Professionals apply the diagnostic criteria with varying precision, and there is criticism that some apply the criteria too flexibly. There may also be differences in the way professionals are trained to identify the disorder (Prendergast *et al.* 1988). The controversy is compounded by the amount of media attention this particular disorder receives. Sometimes parents and non-mental health professionals make an inaccurate diagnosis for themselves. This may lead to a lack of clear understanding among professionals and between professionals and families. The publication of practice guidelines (e.g. BMJ 2016; NICE 2009, with updates 2013 and 2016; Pliszka 2007) goes some way to achieving a more consistent approach.

Differences in the definition of ADHD between countries and over time have resulted in wide variation (Green *et al.* 1999) in estimates of prevalence from as low as 1.3 per cent to 1.7 per cent in Europe (Gillberg, Carlstrom and Rasmussen 1983; Taylor *et al.* 1991) to 11 per cent or more in the US (Zametkin and Ernest 1999). A survey of 10,438 children in the UK between the ages of 5 and 15 years found that 3.62 per cent of boys and 0.85 per cent of girls had ADHD (Ford, Goodman and Meltzer 2003). Generally, community prevalence rates are estimated at around 4 or 5 per cent using DSM criteria, and around 2 per cent using the more stringent ICD criteria. ADHD has consistently been found to be approximately three times more common in boys than girls, with a peak in childhood, reducing in adolescence. A systematic review of international studies of prevalence (Polanczyk *et al.* 2007) found relatively minor variability and an overall rate of around 5.3 per cent.

Presentation

Inattention, overactivity, and impulsivity in excess of that seen in similarly-aged peers generally become apparent from mid-toddlerhood and later preschool years. These features may present in the following ways:

Inattention

- Poor concentration (manifested by significantly reduced ability to stay on task unprompted compared with peers).

- Easily distracted (by extraneous stimuli and own thoughts).

- Often shifts from one incomplete activity to another.

- Recurrent difficulty in following instructions, particularly multistep tasks (as distinct from oppositionality, though this may be difficult to distinguish from the history even with detailed questioning).

Hyperactivity

- Often physically overactive (relative to peers).

- Often talks excessively.

- Often finds it difficult to play quietly.

- Often fidgets or squirms.

Impulsivity

- Often interrupts or intrudes on others (adults or peers).

- Frequent difficulty turn-taking (e.g. in games with other children, or blurting out answers to questions in class).

- May engage in potentially hazardous activities without considering consequences (e.g., running across a road, climbing out of windows).

Not all of the above features are required to make a diagnosis. Children may present to services with consequences of ADHD rather than its core features. A careful enquiry for features of ADHD should be made in any of the following presentations, which may represent consequences of ADHD:

Schools

- Delayed educational attainment in the absence of a specific learning disability or developmental delay.

- Disinterest in sustained academic activity.

- Apparent forgetfulness or difficulty following instruction.

- Poor relationships with peers (who are intolerant of the child's behaviour, particularly impulsivity).

Social services or social welfare non-governmental organisations

- Difficult-to-manage behaviour (that is impulsive or hyperactive).

- Increasingly harsh discipline used in ineffective attempts to manage these behaviours.

- Poor family relationships.

- Frequent apparent non-accidental injuries.

Youth justice system (police, youth courts, or justice social workers)

- Recidivistic offending.

- Substance use.

Risk factors

Several factors are implicated in the aetiology of ADHD or associated with it. These include:

Family history

- Biological parents of children with ADHD are more likely to exhibit ADHD or have a related disorder than are adoptive parents (van den Oord, Boomsma and Verhulst 1994).

- Siblings of children with ADHD are two or three times more likely to have ADHD than are normal controls (Faraone and Biederman 1994).

- Twin studies (Faraone *et al.* 2005) suggest that around 75 per cent of the variation in ADHD symptoms are due to genetic factors (with heritability estimated at 0.7 to 0.8 per cent).

Physical problems, particularly affecting the brain

- These include Cerebral Palsy, epilepsy, developmental disabilities, specific genetic syndromes, prenatal exposure to alcohol, drugs and cigarettes, lead poisoning, and zinc deficiency.

- 25 per cent of children with traumatic brain injury have ADHD.

Family factors

- Disruptions to early care giving (Jacobvitz and Sroufe 1987).

- Parenting that is hostile, aversive and power assertive (Buhrmester *et al.* 1992), and disrupted family relationships have been associated with higher rates of ADHD.

Although diet is often cited by parents as having an influence, studies of this have been inconclusive. Most evidence arises from older studies with poor methodology. One recent study found generally increased levels of hyperactivity in preschool children as a result of eating food colouring and benzoate preservatives (Bateman *et al.* 2004). Children with pre-existing hyperactive behaviour were no more vulnerable to this effect.

ADHD is associated with structural and functional brain changes in neuroimaging studies, mostly involving frontal and prefrontal cortical structures and connections (Cortese and Castellanos 2012; Mana, Paillere-Martinot and Martinota 2010; Weyandt, Swentosky and Gudmundsdottir 2013).

Assessment

Assessment is multifaceted and should comprise multidisciplinary and ideally multi-agency input (Taylor *et al.* 2004). Assessment should be led by a trained specialist and should include a clinical interview, medical assessment, and standardised parent-, teacher-, and, if appropriate, self-rating scales. The clinical interview should comprise careful history taking that specifically identifies symptoms of inattention, impulsivity and hyperactivity. This history should be obtained from multiple informants who know the young person well, including caregivers/parents and teachers, and where feasible the child or young person themselves. This history may be supported by direct professional observations of the child at home and at school and by standardised rating scales completed by caregivers and teachers. Repeated use of the same scales at intervals is also useful in monitoring response to treatment. Neuropsychological testing and academic assessment may be indicated in some cases. Sometimes psychometric assessments that directly test concentration and ability to control impulses can also be informative, though the diagnosis rests on careful elucidation of the history.

Other disorders may cause behaviours that can look like ADHD and should be excluded as possible causes of the presentation. Medical problems, such as hearing loss and congenital conditions, should be considered. Some psychiatric disorders include behaviours that might present with one or more features that need to be distinguished from ADHD, including oppositional and conduct disorders, anxiety, depression, substance use, attachment, autism, bipolar disorder, and intellectual disability. These disorders are also found at higher rates in people with ADHD.

Management

Management of ADHD should also be multifaceted and is ideally delivered by the multidisciplinary team that has completed assessment

(Taylor *et al.* 2004). Caregivers, teachers and any other adults directly involved with the young person should be provided with sufficient information (including written) about ADHD and its management in support of their interactions with the child. The family may be further supported by contact with support groups.

Psychosocial interventions include provision of education about ADHD for the family and school, behaviour management programmes, family-based interventions, school-based interventions, interpersonal psychotherapy, cognitive behaviour therapy, and general support. Some children may additionally need support in specific areas of development and in managing consequences of ADHD, such as social skills training and occupational or speech and language therapy, and some families may need additional social support.

Although controversy still surrounds the use of psychostimulant medication in ADHD (Timimi *et al.* 2004), they are now more widely accepted. Stimulant medication is one of the most highly researched and evidence-based interventions in medicine. More recent studies have been larger with more robust designs and have reconfirmed that medication is more effective on the core symptoms of ADHD than psychosocial treatment alone (Jensen *et al.* 1999). Whilst generally not recommended for preschool children, medication is a recommended first-line intervention for school-age children with severe symptoms and functional impairment, followed by psychosocial intervention, which may be required in the treatment of co-existing disorders.

The most commonly prescribed psychostimulants are methylphenidate and dexamphetamine, which are sold under a variety of trade names and in a variety of formulations. However, up to 30 per cent of children with ADHD show no, or minimal, response to either psychostimulant medication. Effectiveness may be limited by unwanted side effects, which can include decreased appetite with weight loss, sleep disturbance, agitation, nausea, abdominal pain, tics, palpitations, headache, dizziness and increased blood pressure. Second-line treatments include atomoxetine and clonidine. There is no evidence to support the use of so-called 'drug holidays' for avoiding long-term effects. However, monitored periods off medication are valuable at intervals across adolescence in determining continued effectiveness and, therefore, the ongoing need for medication, and some families prefer to stop medication over school holiday periods. Although there are concerns that psychostimulants are a drug of abuse, their use in ADHD can reduce the risk of onset of substance use disorders in adolescence (Faraone and Wilens 2003), though some studies have not replicated this finding.

There may be subgroups of children with ADHD that particularly benefit from psychosocial intervention (Swanson *et al.* 2002), which may influence long-term outcome (Swanson *et al.* 2001). Effective psychosocial interventions include group-based parent training (Sonuga-Barke *et al.* 2001) and strategies for reducing adult demands and intrusion (Morrell and Murray 2003). Although parent involvement has a low impact on ADHD symptoms, it can have a significant impact on internalising symptoms and academic problems (Corcoran and Dattalo 2006).

The evidence that elimination or supplementation diets when compared with placebo may reduce ADHD symptoms is inconclusive. Studies of diet and dietary supplement, including omega-3 fish oils, have shown uncertain benefit (Clayton, Hanstock and Garg 2007). There is some limited evidence that electroencephalograph (EEG) biofeedback can be beneficial.

Strategies to support the child in the classroom should be based on specialist assessment, taking account of teacher and teacher aide reports and direct observation. They should be tailored to the individual child and may include:

- the use of clear, simple statements

- breaking down multi-step tasks and instructions

- ensuring that the child understands what they are required to do

- arranging the classroom so that the child sits away from extraneous distractions

- breaking activities down to shorter time periods with frequent timed breaks (e.g. 'ten minutes on, ten minutes off' in younger children)

- providing stimulating activities and avoiding repetitive tasks

- following a defined, regular timetable

- giving frequent positive feedback

- token behaviour reward system

- avoid group work; instead consider collaborative work in pairs.

These strategies can enhance the likelihood of success in reducing disruptive behaviour and improving on-task behaviour (Miranda, Jarque and Tárraga 2006), which should be rewarded as frequently as possible. A detailed Educational Psychology assessment is invaluable where there have been significant problems in school. There is some evidence to support the effectiveness of self-regulation interventions (self-monitoring with reinforcement, self-management and self-reinforcement) in children with ADHD (Reid, Trout and Schartz 2005).

CASE STUDY: Oliver

Oliver is a six-year-old boy who is frequently teased by his peers and acts like the 'clown of the class'. He often blurts out in class, runs around, fails to complete tasks set in class, is unable to sit still during 'quiet time', and in the playground has been observed to disrupt other children's games, which they don't tolerate. His teacher has discussed this with his parents, who have described Oliver's behaviour at home as stressful; they don't feel able to have family days out because he often runs off. And yet, he becomes more disruptive when they try to keep him indoors for his own safety.

- If you were Oliver's teacher, how might you approach this with the parents? Who else might you discuss this with?

- What would be the most appropriate service to refer Oliver to? And who might be best placed to make this referral?

- How might you be involved in Oliver's ongoing management?

Autism and related disorders

This is a group of disorders around which there is considerable controversy and misunderstanding (Wing 1996). These disorders are not common, although their impact can be considerable. Two (not necessarily contrary) ways of considering autism and related disorders are to view them as discrete disorders or to view them on a broad spectrum from 'no disorder' through to core autism, which is becoming the more accepted approach and is reflected in recent changes to DSM-5. Terminology for the group includes Autism Spectrum Disorders (ASD) and Pervasive Developmental Disorders (PDD).

Characteristics and presentation of autism

Autism is characterised by a triad of features that affect functioning in a range of domains (see Table 11.1):

- impairment of social interactions (with impaired ability to understand social behaviour and contexts)

- impairment of reciprocal communication (with impaired ability to understand and use verbal and non-verbal communication)

- restricted, repetitive repertoire of interests, behaviours, or activities (with impaired ability to think and behave flexibly); and/or abnormal sensory responses, including hypersensitivity, such as intolerance of noise, preoccupation with texture, and hyposensitivity, such as a high pain threshold; and preoccupied self-stimulation, such as spinning self (balance) or spinning objects (visual).

There is usually:

- an abnormal development from infancy, though this often these features may not be recognised at the time

- a history manifesting in preschool years, though this may not present to services until later years.

In addition to the core features, young people with autism may also present with associated (i.e. not diagnostic) features, which include fears, phobias, sleeping and eating disturbances, tantrums, aggression and self-injury. There may additionally be cognitive impairment; although this may be associated, it is not a diagnostic feature and many people on the autism spectrum have average or above average intelligence.

There is evidence that the prevalence of autism (and related disorders) has increased since the late 1980s (Fombonne 1999), though it is unclear whether this reflects an increased incidence in the population rather than a broadening of the definition or improved detection. Recent studies estimate the prevalence of autism at 6–9 per 10,000 individuals. The condition is three to four times more common in boys.

Table 11.1 Core triad of symptoms of autism

Impairment of reciprocal social interactions	Impairment of reciprocal communication	Abnormal repertoire of interests or activities
• Inadequate appreciation of socio-emotional cues • Poor use of social signals • Lack of social or emotional reciprocity • Lack of emotional response to others • Failure to form developmentally-appropriate peer relationships • Lack of spontaneous sharing of interests, achievements, or enjoyment	• Delayed development or lack of language • If language is present, lack of social use of language (verbal and non-verbal) • Poor flexibility in expression (repetitive use of idiosyncratic language) • Poor variation in cadence and gesture • Impairment of imaginative play	• Adherence to rigid routine in daily activities • Preoccupation with unusual objects or parts of objects • Non-functional rituals or routines • Preoccupation with unusual interests and non-functional aspects of objects • Resistance to change • Repetitive stereotyped mannerisms (e.g. hand flapping)

Assessment and diagnosis of autism

Assessment should comprise a full history from informants (parent, caregivers, teachers). Standardised rating scales and semi-structured interviews can assist in accurately identifying symptoms and assessing functional ability. Diagnosis requires qualitative impairment of functioning in all symptom areas with onset (though not necessarily presentation) before the age of three years.

Early detection is important: there is evidence that earlier interventions lead to better functionality in later life (National Research

Council 2001). Thus, primary care workers and preschool teachers can promote better outcomes through early detection by having a 'high index of suspicion' if parents report that 'something is odd or different' about their infant. Early features that distinguish infants who later receive a diagnosis of autism are (Baranek 1999; Werner *et al.* 2000):

- repeated failure to respond to their name being called

- sustained failure to distinguish a parent's voice (and parents frequently calling the infant's name)

- reduction in use of language (including preverbal language) after one year

- having an unusual response to at least one of the senses.

Causes of autism

Autism (and related disorders) has a greater genetic basis compared with other mental health disorders in childhood (Rutter 2000). There are many studies that support this. Siblings of a child with autism have substantially higher rates of the disorder than the general population (2–6%). It is likely that there are multiple interacting genes involved on more than one chromosome.

Autism is also associated with the presence of medical disorders. One study was erroneously reported to have found an association between the MMR (measles, mumps and rubella) vaccine and autism. Further study has not supported this link. However, the MMR vaccine is given around the time of onset of symptoms and it is a question parents may raise. Neither is there evidence to support the earlier theories held mid last century of 'refrigerator parents', whose supposed emotional frigidity induced autism in their children.

Other disorders on the autism spectrum

- *Atypical autism* is similar to autism but not all diagnostic criteria are fulfilled, or onset may be after three years of age.

- *Asperger syndrome* is characterised by impairment of social interaction and an abnormal repertoire of interests and activities, as in autism. There is no delay in cognitive development or the development of speech and language (though use of language may appear odd, being over-formal or stilted).

- *Childhood disintegrative disorder* presents with normal development in the first two years of life and marked sustained regression with an onset after toddlerhood and before the age of ten years. There is progressive loss of language, behavioural changes, incoordination, and loss of bowel or bladder control.

- *Rett's syndrome* is the most discrete of the autism diagnoses. It has an onset following normal development at 7–24 months and presents in girls only with impairment of speech and hand skills, with hand wringing and other midline hand movements, and loss of purposeful movement. Social development stops in toddlerhood. The cause of Rett's syndrome is unknown.

DSM-5 refers to Autism Spectrum Disorder as a single classification, with specifiers for accompanying features, and a severity defined from Level 1to Level 3 depending on the degree of support required.

Management

Whilst there are no specific treatments for autism spectrum disorders, there is an array of effective interventions available to assist in their management. The specific interventions selected should be tailored to the individual child and based on a detailed assessment of need. Needs may change over time and with circumstance, and they will depend on the child's developmental attainment. There are also many unproven 'cures' that are periodically touted: caution must be exercised when claims are made, particularly about amelioration of core features of autism, often based on one poorly-designed study. Effective interventions include:

Education – teaching the child specific skills and behaviour is the most beneficial and potent intervention (National Research Council 2001). This is usually highly intensive, repetitive work, delivered individually or in a small group setting. Examples include:

- *Contemporary Applied Behaviour Analysis* (ABA; which incorporates language, developmental and milieu approaches into a behavioural framework)

- *Developmental-Social Pragmatic* (which utilises cognitive and socio-cultural approaches).

Whilst each school for children with autism may have its own 'package' of programmes, these should be delivered flexibly to meet the individual child's needs.

Family and parent/caregiver support and advocacy – the provision of information about the disorder, its management and resources available locally improves outcome (Whitaker 2002). Parents may need support in acceptance of their child having the disorder, support in the management of behaviour, and financial support or advice. Parent-run support groups are increasingly available and able to meet these needs. There are many charities and nongovernmental agencies that work in support of families with a family member with autism. For instance, in the UK, the National Autistic Society[1] and the Autism Alliance[2] provide access to resources and networking.

Specific individual therapies – the child or adolescent with autism may benefit from a therapy directed at a particular need: physiotherapy, occupational therapy, speech and language therapy, behaviour therapy, and, in some older adolescents, industrial or vocational therapy aimed at achieving optimal gainful employment.

Medication

Whilst there is no psychopharmacological 'treatment' of autism, some autistic features that pose significant risk or dysfunction in the individual warrant a trial of medication as an adjunct to behaviour therapy. Antipsychotic medication can be used in the management of aggressive, self-injurious and repetitive behaviours; SSRIs in anxiety, obsessions, and repetitive behaviours; and clonidine (and to a lesser extent stimulant medication) might be of benefit in overactivity. Benefit from medication is often limited by side effects, which is an

---

1   www.autism.org.uk
2   www.autism-alliance.org.uk

indication for starting at a low dose and increasing slowly. Medication is considered after a failed or partial response to behavioural intervention, environmental modification, and provision of respite, though it may be used sooner in serious repetitive self-injurious behaviour. Co-existing disorders should receive appropriate treatment.

CASE STUDY: Peter

Peter is nearly three years old and his parents have been concerned for some time that he is not as engaged with them as they would have hoped. They are unable to identify a particular time from when this first became apparent. He used to call out 'Dada' and 'Mama' during parent–child interactions, but this has stopped. He seems to be more interested in the flickers made by shadows moving behind his bedroom blinds than he is in his toys. And if he were to pick up a toy car, for instance, he doesn't play with it as they might have expected him to; instead he'll spend inordinate periods of time fascinated by spinning the wheels on it. They were particularly upset when the parents of another child at a recent third birthday party made a disparaging remark about Peter after he had shown no interest in playing with the others there.

Peter's parents decide to chat about him with the nurse at their local Health Centre. What should the nurse advise them?

– What form of assessment should be planned and what investigations undertaken?

– What is the most likely diagnosis?

A comprehensive assessment might take several months and indeed some aspects of the developmental assessment would necessarily be postponed. What could be achieved in the interim?

References

Baranek, G.T. (1999) 'Autism during infancy: A retrospective video analysis of sensorimotorand social behaviours at 9–12 months of age.' *Journal of Autism and Developmental Disorders 29*, 213–224.

Bateman, B., Warner, J.O., Hutchinson, E., Dean, T. *et al.* (2004) 'The effects of a double-blind, placebo-controlled artificial food colouring and benzoate preservative challenge on hyperactivity in a general population sample of school children.' *Archives of Diseases in Childhood 89*, 506–511.

BMJ (British Medical Journal) (2016) *BMJ Best Practice: Attention Deficit Hyperactivity Disorder* (web publication). Available at www.bestpractice.bmj.com/best-practice/monograph/142/treatment/step-by-step.html, accessed on 3 July 2017.

Buhrmester, D., Whalen, C.K., Henker, B., MacDonald, V. and Hinshaw, S.P. (1992) 'Prosocial behaviour in hyperactive boys: Effects of stimulant medication and comparison with normal boys.' *Journal of Abnormal Child Psychology 20*, 103–121.

Clayton, E.H., Hanstock, T.L. and Garg, M.L. (2007) 'Long chain omega-3 polyunsaturated fatty acids in the treatment of psychiatric illnesses in children and adolescents.' *Neuropsychiatrica 19*, 2, 92–103.

Corcoran, J. and Dattalo, P. (2006) 'Parent involvement in treatment for ADHD: A meta-analysis of the published studies.' *Research on Social Work Practice 16*, 6, 561–570.

Cortese, S. and Castellanos, F.X. (2012) 'Neuroimaging of Attention-Deficit/Hyperactivity Disorder: Current neuroscience-informed perspectives for clinicians.' *Current Psychiatry Reports 14*, 5, 568–578.

Faraone, S.V. and Biederman, J. (1994) 'Is attention deficit hyperactivity disorder familial?' *Harvard Review of Psychiatry 1*, 271–287.

Faraone, S.V., Perlis, R.H., Doyle, A. E., Smoller, J.W. *et al.* (2005) 'Molecular genetics of attention-deficit/hyperactivity disorder.' *Biological Psychiatry 57*, 1313–1323.

Faraone, S.V. and Wilens, T. (2003) 'Does stimulant treatment lead to substance use disorders?' *Journal of Clinical Psychiatry 64*, Supp 11, 9–13.

Fombonne, E. (1999) 'The epidemiology of autism: A review.' *Psychological Medicine 29*, 769–782.

Ford, T., Goodman, R. and Meltzer, H. (2003) 'The British Child and Adolescent Mental Health Survey 1999: The prevalence of DSM-IV disorders'. *Journal of the American Academy of Child and Adolescent Psychiatry 42*, 1203–1211.

Gillberg, C., Carlstrom, G. and Rasmussen, P. (1983) 'Hyperkinetic disorders in children with perceptual, motor and attentional deficits.' *Journal of Child Psychology and Psychiatry 24*, 233–246.

Green, M., Wong, M., Atkins, D., Taylor, J. and Feinleib, M. (1999) *Diagnosis of Attention-Deficit/Hyperactivity Disorder. Technical Review No. 3* (Prepared by Technical Resources International, Inc.) AHCPR Publication no. 99–0050. Rockville, MD: Agency for Health Care Policy and Research.

Jacobvitz, D. and Sroufe, L.A. (1987) 'The early caregiver–child relationship and attention-deficit disorder with hyperactivity in kindergarten: A prospective study.' *Child Development 58*, 1496–1504.

Jensen, P.S., Arnold, L.E., Richter, J.E., Severe, J.B. *et al.* (1999) 'Moderators and mediators of treatment response for children with attention-deficit/hyperactivity disorder: The multi-modal treatment study of children with attention-deficit/hyperactivity disorder.' *Archives of General Psychiatry 56*, 1088–1096.

Mana, S., Paillere-Martinot, M.L. and Martinota, J.L. (2010) 'Brain imaging findings in children and adolescents with mental disorders: A cross-sectional review.' *European Psychiatry 25*, 345–354.

Miranda, A., Jarque, S. and Tárraga, R. (2006) 'Interventions in school settings for students with ADHD.' *Exceptionality 14*, 1, 35–52.

Morrell, J. and Murray, L. (2003) 'Parenting and the development of conduct disorder and hyperactive symptoms in childhood: A prospective longitudinal study from 2 months to 8 years.' *Journal of Child Psychology and Psychiatry 44*, 4, 489–508.

National Research Council (2001) *Educating Children with Autism.* Washington, DC: National Academy Press.

NICE (National Institute for Health and Clinical Excellence) (2009, updated 2013 and 2016) *Attention Deficit Hyperactivity Disorder: The NICE guideline on diagnosis and management of ADHD in children, young people and adults.* Clinical guideline [CG72]. London: The British Psychological Society and The Royal College of Psychiatrists.

Pliszka, S. (2007) 'Practice parameter for the assessment and treatment of children and adolescents with attention-deficit/hyperactivity disorder.' *Journal of the American Academy of Child and Adolescent Psychiatry 46*, 894–921.

Polanczyk, G., de Lima, M.S., Horta, B.L., Biederman, J. and Rohde, L.A. (2007) 'The worldwide prevalence of ADHD: A systematic review and metaregression analysis.' *American Journal of Psychiatry 164*, 6, 942–948.

Prendergast, M., Taylor, E., Rapoport, J.L., Bartko, J. *et al.* (1988) 'The diagnosis of childhood hyperactivity: A US–UK cross-national study of DSM-III and ICD-9.' *Journal of Child Psychology and Psychiatry 29*, 3, 289–300.

Reid, R., Trout, A.L. and Schartz, M. (2005) 'Self-regulation interventions for children with attention deficit/hyperactivity disorder.' *Exceptional Children 71*, 4, 361–377.

Rutter, M. (2000) 'The genetic studies of autism: From the mid-1970s into the millennium.' *Journal of Abnormal Child Psychology 28*, 3–14.

Sonuga-Barke, E.J.S., Daley, D., Thompson, M., Laver-Bradbury, C. and Weeks, A. (2001) 'Parent-based therapies for preschool attention-deficit/hyperactivity disorder: A randomized, controlled trial with a community sample.' *Journal of the American Academy of Child and Adolescent Psychiatry 40*, 4, 402–408.

Swanson, J.M., Kraemer, H.C., Hinshaw, S.P., Conners, C.K. *et al.* (2001) 'Clinical relevance of the primary findings of the MTA: Success rates based on severity of ADHD and ODD symptoms at the end of treatment.' *Journal of the American Academy of Child and Adolescent Psychiatry 40*, 168–179.

Swanson, J.M., Arnold, L.E., Vitiello, B., Abikoff, H.B. *et al.* (2002) 'Response to commentary on the multimodal treatment study of ADHD (MTA): Mining the meaning of MTA.' *Journal of Abnormal Child Psychology 40*, 168–179.

Taylor, E., Döpfner, M., Sergeant, J., Asherson, P. *et al.* (2004) 'European clinical guidelines for hyperkinetic disorder – first upgrade.' *European Child and Adolescent Psychiatry 13*, Supplement 1, 7–30.

Taylor, E.A., Sandberg, S., Thorley, G. and Giles, S. (1991) *The Epidemiology of Childhood Hyperactivity.* London: Oxford University Press.

Timimi, S. and 33 coendorsers (2004) 'A critique of the International Consensus Statement on ADHD.' *Clinical Child and Family Psychology Review 7*, 59–63.

van den Oord, E.J., Boomsma, D.I. and Verhulst, F.C. (1994) 'A study of problem behaviours in 10–15 year old biologically related and unrelated international adoptees.' *Behaviour Genetics 24*, 193–205.

Werner, E., Dawson, G., Osterling, J. and Dinno, N. (2000) 'Brief report: Recognition of autism spectrum disorder before one year of age – A retrospective study based on home videotapes.' *Journal of Autism and Developmental Disorders 30*, 157–162.

Weyandt, L., Swentosky, A. and Gudmundsdottir, B.G. (2013) 'Neuroimaging and ADHD: fMRI, PET, DTI findings, and methodological limitations.' *Developmental Neuropsychology 3*, 4, 211–225.

Whitaker, P. (2002) 'Supporting families of preschool children with autism.' *Autism 6*, 4, 411–426.

Wing, L. (1996) *The Autistic Spectrum: A Guide for Parents and Professionals.* London: Constable and Robinson.

Zametkin, A.J. and Ernest, M. (1999) 'Current concept problems in the management of attention deficit hyperactivity disorder.' *New England Journal of Medicine 340*, 1, 40–46.

Further reading

Attwood, T. (2007) *The Complete Guide to Asperger's Syndrome.* London: Jessica Kingsley Publishers.

Frith, U. (2003) *Autism: Explaining the Enigma (2nd edition).* Oxford: Blackwell.

Gillberg, C. (2003) *Clinical Child Neuropsychiatry.* Cambridge: Cambridge University Press.

Munden, A. and Arcelus, J. (1999) *The ADHD Handbook: A Guide for Parents and Professionals.* London: Jessica Kingsley Publishers.

Volkmar, F.R. (ed.) (2007) *Autism and Pervasive Developmental Disorders (2nd edition).* Cambridge: Cambridge University Press.

Websites

www.autism.org.uk (National Autistic Society)
www.autism-alliance.org.uk (Autism Alliance)

CHAPTER 12

Self-harm

Self-harm is a term that covers a variety of behaviours, with a multitude of different functions and a wide range of intentions. Self-harm in adolescence is common, whereas completed suicide is relatively uncommon, especially in those under 16 years of age. The terms deliberate self-harm (DSH) and suicide/parasuicide are falling out of fashion. The first is often felt to be pejorative and implies blame, which can be unhelpful. The second term is misleading as most people who self-harm do not intend to kill themselves.

Self-harm is recognised internationally as a common problem in health services as well as a contributory factor to the high number of deaths by suicide worldwide. Self-harm is one of the most common causes of hospital admission. It is often repeated and is associated with a range of personal and social costs.

In England, there may be over 200,000 presentations for self-harm of all ages to emergency departments annually (Hawton *et al.* 2007). In the UK, young people account for around 5 per cent of non-accidental self-harm episodes referred to hospital (Hawton, Fagg and Simkin 1996). Some 7–14 per cent of adolescents will self-harm at some time in their life, and 20–45 per cent of older adolescents report having suicidal thoughts at some time (Hawton and James 2005). Many attempts at self-harm remain hidden and therefore accurate prevalence figures are difficult to establish. Hawton *et al.* (2002) found that 6.9 per cent of a school population of 15- and 16-year-olds had engaged in an act of deliberate self-harm in the previous year. Only 12.6 per cent of these episodes had led to a hospital visit. These figures are comparable with US data (Centers for Disease Control 1990). Young people might avoid the Emergency Department because of their fear or shame in doing so, amongst other reasons (Owens *et al.* 2016).

There is a question as to whether these rates are increasing: a survey of 6,000 11-, 13- and 15-year-old children in England in 2013– 14 (Inchley *et al.* 2016), as part of an international series of studies of health-related behaviour, found that 20 per cent of 15-year-olds reported having self-harmed. These figures may reflect a real change in the rate of self harm, or they might reflect the way in which the study was designed compared with previous surveys, i.e. such as how questions were asked and how the data were collected. Rates prior to this over the period 1972–2011 had remained stable (Redmore *et al.* 2016).

As many as 30 per cent of adolescents who self-harm report previous episodes, many of which have not come to medical attention. At least 10 per cent will repeat self-harm during the following year, with repeats being especially likely in the first two or three months (Hawton and James 2005). Later research has found that as many as many as 20 per cent of adolescents may re-present with repeat self-harm to the same hospital within one year (Bergen *et al.* 2010).

As well as apparent increases in self-harm, in some circles it is seen as an appropriate response to stress. Sometimes groups of young people self-harm together and having a friend who self-harms may increase a young person's chances of doing it as well.

Suicidal ideation is relatively common among adolescents; precipitating events may be non-specific; acts of self-harm are often impulsive; and secrecy and denial are common, making prevention more difficult. Self-harm is not usually a disorder in itself, but indicative of other problems that may or may not be related to mental health.

Presentation

Self-harm includes actions such as:

- taking an overdose (the usual method of self-harm, analgesics being most commonly used)
- scratching or cutting the skin
- self-burning
- banging the head and/or self-punching
- self-strangulation

- hair-pulling

- biting

- becoming involved in risky or dangerous behaviour (such as involvement in joy-riding, substance use, criminal activity)

- dangerous or unwanted sexual relations.

Other presentations and associated features may include:

- verbalising intent to self-harm

- evidence of ideas or plans about self-harm (e.g. school essays, shared diary)

- using self-harm as a means of dealing with feelings, as it often provides a release from difficult thoughts

- acute distress

- hostility and lack of communication

- poor skills in dealing with problems (especially social problems)

- a sense that self-harm brings about a degree of control for the young person.

Sometimes self-harming may be seen as a 'cry for help', and it is essential not to dismiss a young person's distress, as they may be dealing with some difficult feelings, such as depression, anxiety, anger, grief or hopelessness, and presentation may be related directly to the escalation or arrival of a social problem (such as bullying or family discord).

Risk factors

Factors associated with self-harm include:

- previous self-harm

- substance use

- presence of a mental health problem such as depression or anxiety

- being in a vulnerable high-risk group

- experience of physical, emotional or sexual abuse
- being lesbian, gay, bisexual, or transgender
- loss of a relationship
- poor or inadequate coping skills
- family history of self-harm and suicidal behaviour
- availability of means (access to, for example, medication, sharp objects; the availability of firearms increases the likelihood of completed suicide and should be enquired about)
- family discord
- parental mental illness and/or parental substance use
- intercultural stressors, especially for South Asian females
- school and peer problems
- insomnia
- unemployment
- poverty/homelessness.

Young people who self-harm typically exhibit or have:

- negative feelings and traits
- feelings of being inadequate and low self-esteem
- distrust of others
- lack of control
- lack of supportive relationships and low family cohesion
- cognitive distortions and attribution styles
- maladaptive cognitive strategies relating to expectations, problems, commitments and explanations for events.

The physical severity of the self-harm is not a good indicator of suicidal intent because adolescents are often unaware of the relative toxicity of substances such as paracetamol, which people may incorrectly assume to be harmless. Many episodes of self-harm are impulsive and not repeated.

It can be difficult for families and professionals to understand why young people self-harm. Self-harm for some is a strategy for coping with acute distress. It can also be a form of self-punishment. Young people can perceive self-harm as an effective method of ensuring they are heard. It is important to try not to panic and instead to focus on listening to the young person's account of experiences without being judgemental or critical. Unless you have the necessary skills, it is probably more appropriate to refer to someone who is able to assess and manage risk. However, depending on your role it may also be relevant to undergo appropriate training in order to be able to manage some aspects of self-harm, such as support within school. It is also helpful to undertake some preventative awareness-raising with young people, to enable them to seek help should they feel they might start to self-harm, or if they are already doing so.

It may be useful to encourage the young person think of self-harm as something that may be unhelpful longer term and that needs addressing. However, it is also important to be sensitive in how this is approached because self-harm may at that point in the young person's life be the only way in which they have found relief from unbearable or overwhelming feelings and thoughts. So, careful consideration should be given to the timing of this; such approaches can be made once the young person is engaged and beginning to acknowledge possible benefits to exploring alternative approaches to managing such feelings. For many young people, this discussion can occur during the first occasion of discussing self-harm if they have shown openness to these concepts. Otherwise, it can lead to disengagement. It is counterproductive to promise that the self-harm will not be disclosed to other people in the young person's life, as this may become necessary if there is increased risk.

A further concern is that self-harm is a risk factor for completed suicide, or can result in unintended serious injury or fatality. Among adolescents who harm themselves, the factors that are most likely to be associated with a higher risk of later suicide include:

- male gender
- older age
- social isolation
- high suicidal intent (e.g. using a dangerous and/or violent method)

- psychosis

- depression

- feelings of hopelessness.

The risk of suicide after self-harm lies between 0.24 per cent and 4.30 per cent (depending on the population and type of study). Psychological post-mortem studies of suicides show that a psychiatric disorder (usually depression, rarely psychosis) is present at the time of death in most adolescents who die by suicide. A history of behavioural disturbance, substance misuse, and family, social and psychological problems is common. There are strong links between suicide and previous self-harm: between one quarter and one half of those completing suicide have previously carried out a non-fatal act (Hawton and James 2005). It can be difficult to identify young people at risk of self-harm, even though many older adolescents who are at risk consult their general practitioners before they self-harm.

Assessment

The National Institute for Health and Care Excellence (NICE) and the National Collaborating Centre for Mental Health (NCCMH) have published a guideline for the NHS in England and Wales on the care of people who self-harm (NICE 2013). The guideline makes recommendations for the physical, psychological and social assessment and treatment by primary and secondary services of people in the first 48 hours after an episode of self-harm. It covers acts of self-harm that are an expression of personal distress and where the person directly intends to injure him/herself, for example through cutting or poisoning (overdosing). Similar guidelines are available in other countries (e.g. see Carter et al. 2016). Following a serious self-harm episode, attendance at an Emergency Department should be considered to ensure that any immediate medical concerns are addressed. All events of self-harm should be taken seriously, even if they seem to be superficial, although superficial cutting rarely requires immediate medical attention.

A risk assessment must be undertaken that can inform the development of a safety management plan, which should then be reviewed at regular intervals. A risk assessment includes clarification of whether the episode was impulsive or planned, whether a note was left, whether alcohol or other drugs were also ingested, what the young person expected might happen, and how the young person feels about the overdose, as well as assessment of strengths such as personal attributes, what supports are in place for the young person, and what is likely to prevent the young person repeating the attempt. The guidelines recommend paying special attention to: confidentiality, young person's consent (including Gillick competence), parental consent, child protection issues and use of the Mental Health Act and the Children Act.

Management

Admission to a medical ward of any young person who has self-harmed is recommended (NICE 2013) and they should be assessed by a specialist the next day. All young people who have self-harmed should as a minimum be discussed by the assessing medical team with a child and adolescent psychiatrist or specialist mental health nurse. Treatment goals should, depending on individual need, include management of any associated mental illness, reduced distress, increased coping skills, and prevention or decreased frequency and severity of self-harm episodes.

If the self-harm has occurred in the context of a disorder such as depression, poor self-esteem or poor social skills, then those issues will need to be addressed. For all children and young people, caregivers should be advised to remove all means of self-harm as is practicable, including medication, before the child or young person goes home, as a means of reducing further risk.

For those young people who do not have a mental health problem, there may still be benefits in exploring more appropriate coping strategies with them. Cognitive behaviour therapy (CBT), problem solving therapy (PST), dialectical behaviour therapy (DBT), motivational interviewing (MI), and interpersonal therapy (IPT) are all forms of psychological treatment with proven effectiveness for helping people with depression, anxiety disorders and other mental health problems. There are no physical side-effects to these therapies. There is relatively good evidence for the effectiveness of DBT (Linehan 1993; and see Chapter 15 for more details), which acknowledges the importance of both managing problematic emotions and situations when they arise, by using a wide range of techniques derived from CBT, and understanding why it is that self-harm and other behaviours that may be considered impulsive are used by people with a history of trauma.

For young people who have self-harmed several times, consider offering developmental group psychotherapy with other young people. This should include at least six sessions but can be extended by mutual agreement (NICE 2004).

Depending on what is found at assessment, family therapy may also be indicated as a way of improving specific cognitive and social skills to promote the sharing of feelings, emotional control, and negotiation between family members.

The situation is more complex when there are chronic problems relating to the young person's environment, such as placement issues, schooling problems, and family discord, irrespective of whether these are further complicated by personal or family mental health issues. In these circumstances, the young person and the family may have expectations that mental health professionals can bring about change in these areas, when this may not be the case. If school problems, particularly bullying, are prominent, liaison with the school is important. Further help may be provided by a school counsellor. In the case of Intellectual Disability, an assessment by an educational psychologist may be helpful in devising suitable educational options.

When the self-harm occurs alongside substance and alcohol misuse or violence, specific treatments for these conditions may be indicated. For older adolescents, referral to a self-help agency or walk-in counselling service may be appropriate and more readily accepted (Hawton and James 2005).

Key points about self-harm

- Self-harm is a behaviour that can occur in many different disorders and situations.

- All self-harm needs assessment.

- Self-harm in young people usually reflects acute distress and is usually not indicative of mental illness, in which case social, behavioural, and psychotherapeutic approaches are advised.

- Where there is an underlying mental illness, this should be appropriately treated, as it will help reduce risk of further self-harm.

References

Bergen, H., Hawton, K., Waters, K., Cooper, J., Kapur, N. (2010) 'Epidemiology and trends in non-fatal self-harm in three centres in England: 2000–2007'. *British Journal of Psychiatry, 197*, 6, 493–498.

Carter, G., Page, A., Large, M., Hetrick, S. *et al.* (2016) 'Royal Australian and New Zealand College of Psychiatrists clinical practice guideline for the management of deliberate self-harm.' *Australian and New Zealand Journal of Psychiatry 50*, 10, 939–1000.

Centers for Disease Control (1990) 'Attempted suicide among high school students – United States.' *Journal of the American Medical Association 266*, 14, 1911–1912.

Hawton, K., Bergen, H., Casey, D., Simkin, S. *et al.* (2007) 'Self-harm in England: a tale of three cities. Multicentre study of self-harm'. *Social Psychiatry and Psychiatric Epidemiology 42*, 513–521.

Hawton, K., Fagg, J. and Simkin, S. (1996) 'Deliberate self-poisoning and self-injury in children and adolescents under 16 years of age in Oxford, 1976–1993.' *British Journal of Psychiatry 169*, 202–208.

Hawton, K. and James, A. (2005) 'Suicide and deliberate self-harm in young people.' *British Medical Journal 330*, 891–894.

Hawton, K., Rodham, K., Evans, E. and Weatherall, R. (2002) 'Deliberate self-harm in adolescents: Self-report survey in schools in England.' *British Medical Journal 325*, 1207–1211.

Inchley, J., Currie, D., Young, T., Samdal, O. *et al.* (2016) 'Growing Up Unequal: A Health Behaviour in School-aged Children (HBSC) study.' *World Health Organization: Health Policy for Children and Adolescents, No. 7.* ISBN 978 92 890 5136 1

Linehan, M. (1993) *Cognitive-Behavior Therapy for Borderline Personality Disorder.* New York: Guilford Press.

NICE (National Institute for Health and Clinical Excellence) (2004) *Self-harm – The short-term physical and psychological management and secondary prevention of self-harm in primary and secondary care.* Clinical guideline [CG16].

NICE (National Institute for Health and Clinical Excellence) (2013) *Self-harm.* London: National Institute of Clinical Excellence. Available at http://pathways.nice.org.uk/pathways/self-harm.

Owens, C., Hansford, L., Sharkey, S. and Ford, T. (2016) 'Needs and fears of young people presenting at accident and emergency department following an act of self-harm: Secondary analysis of qualitative data.' *British Journal of Psychiatry 208*, 3, 286–291.

Redmore, J., Kipping, R., Trickey, A., May, M.T. and Gunnell, D. (2016) 'Analysis of trends in adolescent suicides and accidental deaths in England and Wales, 1972–2011.' *British Journal of Psychiatry 209*, 4, 327–333.

Websites

www.focusas.org (Focus Adolescent Services)

www.themix.org.uk/mental-health/self-harm (Young People and Self-Harm)

www.nshn.co.uk (National Self-Harm Network)

www.suicidology.org (American Association of Suicidology)

www.afsp.org (American Foundation for Suicide Prevention)

CHAPTER 13

Mental Health Disorders

The focus in this chapter is on mental health disorders that can present in childhood or adolescence not covered in previous chapters. These include mood disorders (depression and bipolar disorder), schizophrenia, eating disorders, and problem substance use.

Depression

Depression in children and young people can be seen as a spectrum of presentations that range from mild to severe. Figures are variable, but a range of studies suggest that severe depression has a prevalence of 2–3 per cent in adolescence, whilst the prevalence is between 5 and 15 per cent for moderate depression (Moffitt *et al.* 2010). The prevalence of depression in childhood is lower than for adolescence with rates around 2.5 per cent, although twice that number may be significantly distressed (Birmaher, Ryan and Williamson 1996; Fombonne 1994; Kashani *et al.* 1987; Office for National Statistics 2000, 2005). The prevalence rates in prepubertal boys and girls are equal, with rates rising relatively higher in girls across adolescence.

Presentation

Young people may present with low mood as the primary complaint (this must be mostly pervasive over time for depression to be diagnosed) or they may present with irritability instead, as well as a range of biological, affective and cognitive symptoms of depression including:

- changes in behaviour

- self-harm or thoughts about self-harm

- suicidal thinking and behaviour

- feelings of hopelessness

- negative self-image and low self-esteem

- losing interest and enjoyment in usual hobbies

- reduced motivation or enthusiasm

- reduced energy and readily fatigued

- poor concentration

- sleep problems (e.g. waking early, usually unrefreshed)

- reduced appetite

- weight loss or failure to achieve expected weight gain

- inability to keep up at school or a drop in academic performance

- frequent vague, non-specific physical symptoms, such as headache or tiredness

- an increase in moody, irritable, snappy, aggressive and hostile behaviour (often noted by parents)

- reduced emotional reactivity

- substance use (which may have been a precipitating factor or may be used to some extent as self medication).

They may also present with features of disorders that are commonly comorbid with depression, such as anxiety, compulsive behaviour, and oppositionality. It is less common for young people to present with biological features. In severe depression the young person may additionally present with psychosis and have delusions (which are fixed false beliefs; see 'Psychosis' section below) of a nihilistic, self-derogatory or persecutory nature, or hallucinations (which are the experience of a sensation in the absence of a stimulus; see 'Psychosis' section), usually auditory and in the form of voices telling the young person that they are worthless, useless, hopeless and which may reinforce other negative self-perceptions. The voices may also command them to do things, including self-harm or suicidal actions, or cause harm to others.

Whilst many young people report low mood, it is less clear how many have a mood disorder. Younger children may not have the vocabulary to articulate their feelings and they may choose to describe low mood when they are bored or under-stimulated or vice versa. Low mood is common in young people, but depression or a depressive illness is much less common. Signs of depression may be missed or incorrectly attributed to the perceived normal turmoil of adolescence. Outbursts, hostility and irritability may be interpreted as conduct disorder or disobedience. There needs to be a balance between not giving young people an inappropriate diagnosis and making sure a thorough assessment is undertaken to ensure that a treatable disorder is not missed.

Risk factors
It is usually the interaction of several of the following risk factors that leads to depression.

Gender
Prior to age 12, boys and girls have equal rates of depression, following which there is a relatively higher prevalence in females. There is speculation that females may internalise their distress and report depression, whereas males externalise their distress, showing conduct disorder or substance use.

Self-image
Poor self-esteem and negative body image are more common in females and may be antecedents of depression. There is currently no evidence to suggest that there is a neurochemical or hormonal basis that would explain the increased rate of depression in females.

Family history
There is a significantly increased risk of depression if one or both parents, multiple siblings or second-degree relatives have a history of affective disorder.

Family relationships
Marital and familial discord may increase the risk. Mother–child, father–child, parental and sibling relationships may also be factors in depression. Warm, communicative and caring parents instil confidence and high self-esteem in their children. Over-protective or rejecting

parenting also appears to be related to low levels of mastery and higher levels of depression.

Attributional styles

Social self-appraisal and self-esteem are important. Depressed young people tend to formulate faulty strategies to deal with social problems, and these are then aggravated by low self-esteem and low social confidence, rendering them socially dysfunctional. Adolescents differentiate various domains of self-esteem and their evaluation of these appears to be linked to depression. Low self-perception about attractiveness and potential mates is linked to depression but not to scholastic, athletic or job domains. Stress may also be linked to depression.

Development and transitions

Adolescents are susceptible to various stressors, such as biological changes, social changes (e.g. relocation), school transitions, parental separation, divorce or reconstitution of the family, and gender-role expectations.

Life events

This could include accidents, bereavement, trauma, abuse and loss of romantic relationships.

Physical illness

Physical illness is a risk factor, especially chronic illness, such as diabetes and cystic fibrosis.

Consequences of depression in adolescence

The most alarming consequence is suicide; however, depression alone is rarely the cause of suicide in adolescence. Another major consequence of depression in adolescence can be the interruption of the completion of developmental tasks in the educational, social and psychological spheres. Impairment in relationships with family and friends is a frequent feature of depression. The subsequent lack of social support may generate a negative feedback loop in which the consequences of the initial low mood may serve to maintain the depressive episode. Untreated depression also carries a higher risk of poor physical and other mental health outcomes.

Assessment

If a young person is thought to be moderately to severely depressed, they need to be assessed by a specialist service or professional. Some primary care staff may be very good at recognising depression, but the majority is unlikely to have much experience of this. It is critical that a risk assessment is undertaken as part of the assessment.

Management

Mild depression may be best treated by addressing factors that might be implicated in its onset, general supportive measures, and in some instances, psychological therapy, such as cognitive behaviour therapy or interpersonal psychotherapy. Counselling to address issues of self-esteem, social confidence, effective problem solving and managing relationships should be undertaken. If this is not effective after three sessions, then medication should be considered if criteria are met for a moderate or severe disorder. This should be done in conjunction with cognitive behaviour therapy to address negative cognitions.

Moderate to severe depression is likely to need a combination of these interventions plus medication. However, combining CBT with SSRI (Selective Serotonin Reuptake Inhibitor) medication may not provide additional benefit over and above an SSRI alone beyond the first 12 weeks (Dubicka et al. 2010). SSRI medication is the most effective in treating adolescent depression and associated with fewer side-effects in adolescence than other groups of antidepressants. Fluoxetine is recommended as a medication to use in the first instance. NICE guidelines provide a more detailed review (NICE 2005, updated 2015). Most SSRIs are safe in adolescence, except paroxetine, which should not be prescribed due to much higher rates of suicidal ideation associated with it. Please refer to Chapter 15 for more detail on medication and therapy options.

Most young people can be managed in the community. However, if a young person is expressing thoughts about self-harm and there is a high risk, then inpatient management may be necessary until this risk has subsided and the young person and their family are more able to manage this risk. If psychosis is present, this may respond to antipsychotic medication, which can be prescribed in addition to antidepressant medication. Some adolescents with psychotic depresson may need admission irrespective of suicide risk due to increased vulnerability and inability to manage self care.

Depression may be related to past experiences, in which case the issues around these experiences (such as abuse) may need to be addressed. Individual or group work to address issues of self-esteem, social confidence, effective problem solving and managing relationships may also be undertaken. The family will also need to be educated about the illness. Outcomes are usually good but there is a significant likelihood of a recurrence.

CASE STUDY: Tim

Tim is a 15-year-old boy with a three-month history of low mood (feeling sad), poor concentration, poor sleep, tiredness, lack of interest in playing football (he had been on his school team), with deterioration of his schoolwork. His parents felt he was also irritable and argumentative, which he had not been previously. They were also concerned with ideas of hopelessness although he had not considered self-harm. Tim eventually agrees to a referral to CAMHS.

– What should the management plan include?

Psychosis

Psychosis is not a diagnosis in itself but a collection of signs that constitute a current mental state. Someone who is experiencing psychosis may have a range of signs or symptoms and these include:

- hallucinations – the experience of sensing something when there is no stimulus to that sensation; these may be auditory (e.g. hearing voices), visual (seeing things), olfactory (smell), gustatory (taste), tactile or haptic (touch), or somatic (internal)

- delusions – firmly fixed, false beliefs that are not culturally contextual; these can be persecutory, nihilistic, religious, self-denigratory or grandiose in content, or the young person may experience delusions of passivity, when they believe themselves to be controlled by others or outside forces

- thought disorder – sometimes known as formal thought disorder, this refers to changes in thought processes, whereby thoughts become disorganised and lack the usual logical connection and flow. Specific thought disorders include thought withdrawal (experienced as one's own thoughts being taken away, which may also be observed by others), thought insertion (experienced as thoughts that are not one's own being put in to one's mind), thought blocking (sudden interruption to the flow of thoughts), derailment (sudden switches of topic, sometimes likened to repeatedly moving between radio stations), poverty of speech, tangentiality, illogicality, perseveration (the repetition of a word or phrase without apparent purpose), and neologism ('making up' new words that only have meaning to the patient).

Another way that concern may be raised is if the young person shows a change in behaviour suggestive of persecutory beliefs, such as refusing to eat food prepared by someone in particular, hiding behind drawn curtains, or extreme responses to minor stimuli. These behaviours may be directly related to the perceptual abnormalities and thought disorder being experienced. The young person themselves may be very suspicious of interventions and often does not share everyone's concerns.

Causes of psychosis in young people include substance use, a medical cause (such as fever, trauma, epilepsy, and rare neurological disorders) or side-effects of prescribed medication. Psychosis may be associated with a mood disorder (depression or bipolar disorder), schizophrenia or other functional mental health disorders. All potential common causes should be assessed as early as is practicable.

It may be difficult to differentiate between a true psychosis and a marked episode of derealisation or depersonalisation associated with acute anxiety or distress, particularly in children (Garralda 2017). A single short episode of psychosis does not necessarily mean that the young person has either an affective disorder or schizophrenia. Simple hallucinations in children do not predict a psychotic illness (Garralda 2017). The diagnosis of psychosis is highly complex in young people with an Intellectual Disability due to the difficulties young people in this group have with accurately reporting symptoms.

Assessment

Someone who is acutely psychotic needs urgent assessment and treatment. A risk assessment is important. Someone who has paranoid delusions may be at risk of harming others (believing they need to protect themselves), but they may also be a significant risk to themselves. This also applies to someone who is experiencing auditory hallucinations that may command them to harm themselves. As the person is unable to differentiate these perceptions from their normal ones, they may obey the hallucinations.

Assessment is required to establish whether the young person is psychotic, and this needs to be undertaken by specialist CAMHS. Assessment will also help identify the potential causes of the psychosis, including medical causes. The young person may be unable to give a competent history because of their mental state, so corroborative histories from other informants, such as family members or teachers, are important. It can be difficult to identify substance use, but it is important to explore this as a reason for the presentation of psychosis in adolescence. Urine and blood tests to detect substances may be appropriate. However, consent is required for this. A full assessment may thus take place over a period of days or weeks.

Management

Early intervention is essential and may comprise medication, specialist nursing, psychoeducation, provision of specialist milieu in the form of day hospital or inpatient care, and rehabilitation. As well as addressing associated risk, early intervention may improve prognosis (Lehman 2007). A person who is acutely psychotic is likely to need admission, particularly where there is marked distress or risk or when the clinic situation requires a relatively rapid titration of antipsychotic medication to a high dose that could be more safely monitored in hospital. Unfortunately, the facilities to admit acutely psychotic young people to specialist adolescent units may be very limited. Adult wards, which should be avoided where possible, may sometimes be the only viable option, in which case it is crucial that young people receive appropriate support from child and adolescent mental health specialists.

Antipsychotic medication is described in more detail in Chapter 15. Young people can experience significant side-effects that can last beyond the course of treatment, and the medication may need to be given under supervision. However, specialist community-based early psychosis intervention teams can deliver safe and effective treatment without the need for admission (McGorry and Jackson 1999). Early management needs to include investigation to establish a diagnosis so the underlying problem can be appropriately addressed.

Nursing care in the community or hospital plays an important part in supporting young people with psychoses: key features include engaging with the young person, reality orientation (in time, place and person) and provision of a calm, comfortable, secure, predictable and low-stimulus environment.

Psychosis can be frightening for the young person and their family, so sensitive support is essential, which should include the provision of information about psychosis and its treatment. Irrespective of the cause of the psychosis, assessment should be made, early on during treatment, of the young person's needs following recovery. This will lead to the development of an agreed rehabilitation programme, which may include ongoing family and community support or alternative accommodation, clinical reviews, support in activities of daily living, and an individualised education programme or, in older teenagers, retraining and sheltered work experience. Rehabilitation depends on close cross-agency working between the mental health team and front-line professionals.

Bipolar affective disorder (manic-depressive disorder)

Bipolar affective disorder is rare in early adolescence or prepubertally (exact prevalence figures are generally not available) but can be very difficult to manage when it does occur. It is also commonly known as manic-depressive illness, indicating each end of the bipolar spectrum. Its prevalence increases throughout adolescence, rising to that of adult rates of 2–4 per cent. Some researchers in the US have proposed a broadening of diagnostic criteria in children and adolescents, which has been controversial, particularly when this leads to the use of medication that would not otherwise be prescribed. The picture is complicated because bipolar (hypomanic) symptoms are common in adolescence, but do not predict the onset of bipolar disorder (Tijssen et al. 2010).

Presentation

A young person who has bipolar affective disorder is usually likely to first present with a depressive episode. A manic or hypomanic (i.e. less than manic) episode may arise at any time and precede or follow a depressive episode. Hypomania is characterised by:

- elated mood or irritability, although the mood may be very labile (changeable)

- expansive and elated behaviour

- apparent boundless energy

- taking on a number of tasks, most of which will be left uncompleted

- poor concentration and attention

- little continuity of thought

- expression of a number of disconnected or tenuously connected ideas

- rapid speech and frustration at other people's inability to keep up

- expression of grandiose ideas and schemes

- making unrealistic and over-ambitious plans

- reduced amount of sleep (though without fatigue)

- disinhibition

- socially and sexually inappropriate behaviour

- risk of engaging in unprotected and otherwise unwanted sexual activity

- risk of abuse because of increased vulnerability

- reduced likelihood of making competent decisions.

Manic episodes present with the same features, though usually at a severity that would increase risk to self and others to the extent that hospital admission, usually involuntary, is indicated. There may be psychotic features associated with mania. It can be clinically difficult to differentiate bipolar affective disorder from schizophrenia at the time of the first episode because of the nature of the presentation.

Risk factors

Family history of the disorder is the major risk factor and, whilst stress may trigger episodes, it does not cause bipolar affective disorder.

Assessment

Urgent assessment may be required, depending on the presentation. It is important to undertake a risk assessment, including issues of self-harm ideation and child protection, which may be a priority as some of the behaviours associated with bipolar affective disorder (e.g. disinhibition, hypersexuality) may put the young person, their siblings, or peers at considerable risk.

Management

The acute phase of mania or hypomania needs to be treated, and depending on social supports this may be managed at home. If the mania is moderate or severe, inpatient care is likely to be the most appropriate option. Young people can be very difficult to manage when they are acutely manic and often do not receive therapeutic doses of appropriate medication. Atypical antipsychotic medication is increasingly used to manage acute psychosis, although older medications may still be used. Mood stabilisers (such as lithium or sodium valproate) may be used in the acute phase together with antipsychotic medication and then continued as maintenance medication. These medications are described in further detail in Chapter 15. Rehabilitation should be considered as described under psychosis above.

There is increasing, though still limited, evidence to support the use of psychotherapeutic approaches in the management of bipolar disorder in children and adolescents (West and Pavuluri 2009; Young and Fristad 2007). These include family-focused treatment (FFT), child and family-focused cognitive behaviour therapy (CFF-CBT), the RAINBOW Program, multi-family psychoeducation groups (MFPG), dialectical behaviour therapy (DBT), interpersonal and social rhythm therapy (IPSRT), and individual family psychoeducation (IFP). These therapies are to be used as an adjunct to, rather than to replace, medication.

The UK National Institute for Health and Care Excellence provides detailed guidance on the management of bipolar disorder in children and adolescents (NICE 2014, updated 2016).

Schizophrenia

Schizophrenia may be seen as a collection of several disorders rather than one single disease or illness. All the disorders have a degree of psychosis but some will have a greater degree of what are called 'negative' signs and symptoms of the disorder, as described below. It is important to understand that schizophrenia is not a 'split personality' as is sometimes thought. Confusingly, the term 'childhood schizophrenia' was once used to refer to autism, which should be borne in mind when reading some older texts.

Schizophrenia is uncommon in early adolescence, but prevalence increases by late adolescence, especially in males (Torrey 1987). It may be that some of the 'odd' young people seen in early or mid adolescence are in a pre-illness or prodromal phase. In adults, the prevalence of schizophrenia is 1 per cent internationally. It is significantly less than this in children and adolescents. However, most people with schizophrenia develop symptoms in adolescence or early adulthood, and the continuity of symptoms from the time of assessment in adolescence through to adulthood is high (Hollis 2000). Although more common in adult males than females, prevalence studies in adolescents have been contradictory with some replicating this and others finding equal sex ratios.

Presentation

Most adolescents present with an insidious onset, making early recognition difficult. There is typically a prodromal period, characterised by some apparent decrease in functioning, though without detectable symptoms. This period of ambiguous and non-specific changes in behaviour may last several months, or even years, and then be followed by the presentation of psychotic symptoms and sometimes an acute presentation. These early signs might be observed by family, school and peers, though their significance may go unrecognised at this stage and indeed may cause the young person or those around them some distress because they are without explanation, possibly out of character for that person, and not responsive to attempts to manage these changes in behaviour. There is a range of ways in which young people may present:

- acutely, in a psychotic state

- less acutely, with delusions, thought disorder or hallucinations

- gradually, with subtle changes in personality

- with a significant reduction in social contacts

- with a reduction in personal care and hygiene.

Some young people present with what are called 'negative signs' such as:

- decreased functioning in multiple areas (e.g. socially, academically)

- blunted or flat affect, or inappropriate responses of emotion

- reduced energy or spontaneity (avolition)

- lack of enjoyment (anhedonia).

Young people may not understand or agree with their parents that there is anything wrong and may be very suspicious and dismissive of efforts made to engage them. They may appear to present with other conditions, such as depression and anxiety. This highlights the importance of completing a full mental state examination in all young people, irrespective of what they present with.

Risk factors and associated findings

Risk factors in adolescent-onset schizophrenia include:

- a family history of schizophrenia – there is increased risk if there is a diagnosis in a first-degree relative (i.e. parent, sibling) or in multiple second- and third-degree relatives

- complications during pregnancy and birth, such as malnutrition, or prenatal exposure to toxins (including drugs) or certain viruses

- use of psychoactive drugs, particularly and most commonly cannabis, in early teen years (and on in to young adulthood), when the brain is particularly susceptible and vulnerable

- over-activation of the immune system, such as occurs in autoimmune diseases or some inflammatory processes

- having a father who is much older than most.

Other factors associated with the development of schizophrenia in adolescence include:

- biochemical factors – individuals with schizophrenia appear to have a neurochemical imbalance of some neurotransmitters, which are chemicals in the brain that are involved in the communication between neurons (brain cells)

- altered brain structure and function – for example, people with schizophrenia appear to have difficulty coordinating activity between different areas of the brain, shown by using positron emission tomography (PET) scans (Manaa, Paillère Martinot and Martinot 2010), and the ventricles of people with schizophrenia are often enlarged, shown by using magnetic resonance imaging (MRI) scans (Brent *et al.* 2013; Rapoport *et al.* 1999; Reig *et al.* 2008).

Some factors, whilst not necessarily causing schizophrenia, can perpetuate an episode or trigger relapse:

- stress

- substance use – there is increasing evidence of a causal link between cannabis use and schizophrenia

- family communication – family-based interventions can reduce relapse in families that express high levels of emotion (Kavanagh 1992; Vaughn and Leff 1976).

Assessment

Any young person presenting with acute psychosis needs urgent assessment as discussed above. However, the presentation in young people is often more gradual and less clear. There may be non-specific concerns about the young person being odd (e.g. inappropriate social responses), a loner or beginning to withdraw socially. If the presentation is unclear, the assessment may need to be completed over a few months and any changes carefully monitored. Schizophrenia may also coexist with a mood disorder, when the term schizo-affective disorder is used. Schizophrenia is associated with significant cognitive impairment; neuropsychological testing can be useful in determining the need for specific interventions to address this, such as cognitive remediation therapy (described below) and environmental support tailored to the individual to assist functioning in school or vocational training and at home.

Management

In addition to the general management of psychosis described in the 'Psychosis' section above, there are several areas that need to be addressed in a young person with schizophrenia (NICE 2013):

Longer-term management of psychosis and the maintenance of medication

This also needs to include strategies to reduce the distress that is often associated with hallucinations, for example diversionary tactics, relaxation techniques and recreational activities.

Individual cognitive behaviour therapy

This is needed to help develop skills and appropriate coping strategies. There is some recent research (in adults) that suggests that the positive changes associated with CBT in patients already on medication are accompanied by changes in brain function and connectivity (Mason *et al.* 2017).

Education of the young person and their family about the disorder

It may also be helpful to consider the impact of the illness on the family and the range of emotions the family members may experience once a diagnosis has been made. Feelings may include anger, guilt, shame, sadness, a sense of loss, isolation and ambivalence. The family may find itself under considerable stress and need support in its own right. Self-help and family support groups through national or local organisations may be the most useful way of addressing this. The family may also need to be educated about possible relapses and the need for early interventions.

Support in school

Adolescents with schizophrenia may need specific supports afforded to them in order to maintain their schooling. This might entail an assessment of special educational needs and ongoing liaison between the treating health team, school and family.

Cognitive remediation therapy (CRT)

CRT is specifically focused on cognitive processes (such as attention, working memory and executive functioning), and/or social cognition, in order to improve daily living, social, educational or vocational skills (Wykes and Reeder 2005).

Social support and rehabilitation

This may be through group or individual work. It also needs to address the issues of rehabilitating the young person into society, especially if they have had a lengthy period of illness. They may lack confidence and may have lost some skills, as well as possibly facing considerable prejudice. Recreational opportunities are also important. Peer support may be especially important for young people.

Medication use is described in more detail in Chapter 15. Unfortunately, the side-effects of some of the medications used to manage psychotic illnesses are more marked in young people and are significantly distressing, making compliance difficult. These issues need to be sensitively and carefully addressed with the young person.

Studies looking at intervention in the prodromal period (i.e. before definitive symptoms present) or individuals at 'ultra high risk' of developing schizophrenia have shown some promising results (Yung et al. 2007). Specific psychological intervention may be beneficial (Bechdolf et al. 2012). There is some early evidence that high dose omega-3 in the form of fish oils may be beneficial (Amminger et al. 2015), though these studies need to be replicated. The use of antipsychotic medication at this early stage is not supported on current evidence.

Evidence for the effectiveness of a specialist team approach to early psychosis intervention has supported the development of early intervention teams in countries across Europe, North America, Australasia, and Asia (McGorry 2015).

CASE STUDY: Simon

Simon is a 16-year-old boy coming up to doing his GCSEs. Until six months ago he had been making plans enthusiastically for a career in business and had decided which A-levels he wanted to take. However, over the last six months there has been a gradual deterioration in his socialisation. His mother notes that he appears to have become particularly selfish, not being interested in what other members of the family want or need. He will often insist on watching a television programme and get very angry if he is not allowed to watch what he wants. The family has found that they have tended to give in to this because it avoids a confrontation. However, they have noted that even when he is watching television he will sometimes look quite blank, while at other times he can appear quite agitated. He will often not participate in family conversations although will misinterpret what is said.

– Simon's parents come and meet with you to express their concerns. How would you manage this?

– After some persuasion, Simon agrees to meet with you. What are the key areas that you would need to ask Simon about?

Simon is subsequently seen at a CAMHS. After a time, a diagnosis of schizophrenia is made on the basis of the history and mental state examinations. The assessment is completed by a brief admission to hospital. Simon is started on risperidone (antipsychotic medication) and after a couple of weeks' hospitalisation is discharged from hospital.

– What roles do the school and the GP have in supporting Simon's rehabilitation?

– What cultural issues might there be?

Eating disorders in older children and adolescents

Young people are often dissatisfied with their appearance and their attempt to change it can result in an eating disorder. Worries about weight, shape, food and dieting are especially common amongst teenage girls. The majority of problems occur in young people between the ages of 14 and 19 years. Eating disorders, such as anorexia nervosa and bulimia nervosa, occur more frequently in girls but have more recently started to increase in boys. These disorders are ten times more common in girls than boys with the prevalence rate for girls between 15 and 19 years being around 1 per cent (Crisp, Palmer and Kalucy 1976); however, rates are variable across different populations. Studies in Western countries show rates of 0.7–0.8 per cent (Morande, Celada and Casas 1999; Rastam, Gillberg and Garton 1989; Steinhausen, Winkler and Meier 1997). In non-Western populations it may be that there are different variants of the disorder (Srinivasan, Suresh and Jayaram 1998) although one Iranian study found rates that were comparable to Western populations (Nobakht and Dezhkam 2000). Rates are often higher in private educational facilities (Rastam *et al.* 1989), ballet dancers and models.

Anorexia nervosa

A young person with anorexia nervosa nearly always starts by restricting dietary intake ('dieting'). Around one third have been overweight before starting to diet. Although 'anorexia' literally means 'loss of appetite', the appetite is usually normal but instead the usual hunger cues misinterpreted.

Presentation

The young person may present at school, home, or health services, including dental and emergency departments, with the following:

- marked distortion of body image such that the person believes themselves to be overweight when they are not

- marked weight loss

- a preoccupation with thinness or dieting

- an intense fear of being fat or of calories

- preoccupation with food, for example often prepares food for others

- continuing to diet when thin

- compulsive exercising

- lying about food

- self-induced vomiting or use of laxatives

- physical development interrupted or hindered

- irregularities or cessation of menstrual cycle (three missed cycles if menstruation was established)

- hair loss

- cold extremities

- growth of a fine, downy hair all over the body (lanugo)

- dental decay

- depression

- anxiety.

Risk factors

Young people may feel under considerable social pressure to conform to current fashion trends, media images of attractiveness and peer pressures. However, the risk of developing anorexia is more likely in the presence of the following factors:

- feeling of not being in control in one or many aspects of their lives; dieting can be a tangible way of showing self-control

- fear of growing up or developing (puberty)

- poor communication or self expression in the family or over-protectiveness or criticism within the family

- personality characteristics of over-compliance, perfectionism, and dependence

- family history of anorexia nervosa (though some research findings are conflicting)

- stressful life events (including loss, threats to self-integrity, and physical illness).

Assessment

It is usually parents or friends who become concerned, and assessment can be difficult as the young person is often resistant to hearing that there are valid concerns for their safety. It is important to undertake a full mental health and physical health history. The impact of starvation has physical implications, which if not recognised or managed may have serious consequences. Vital signs (temperature, blood pressure and pulse) should be recorded at first interview.

Diagnosis is made on the basis of restricted dietary intake relative to that needed, leading to significantly low weight (which may be defined as consistently less than 15 per cent below expected weight for height and age) or failure to show expected weight gain in prepubertal children and young adolescents, plus an intense fear of gaining weight and disturbed body image.

Complications of the disorder include muscle weakness, heart murmurs and arrhythmias, tooth decay, bowel damage, kidney damage, seizures, loss of bone density, gastric ulcers, coma and death. Studies on the mortality rate of young people with anorexia suggest that it is high: between 5 per cent and 10 per cent (Neumaker 1997; Sullivan 1995). If there is rapid weight loss, then urgent medical assessment and treatment is necessary. If onset is prepubertal, puberty may be delayed or arrested.

Management

It is easier to help young people if the problem is noticed and dealt with early. The more entrenched the problem the more difficult it is to manage. Problems are usually recognised by the family, so they can be important in the assessment and treatment of the problem. The first step to treating an eating disorder is recognising it.

CASE STUDY: Nasreen

Nasreen is a 15-year-old girl who has a four-month history of weight loss and changing body image. She has been exercising excessively as she feels that she remains too fat despite the recent weight loss. As her schoolteacher, you have become increasingly concerned as she is looking thinner. She is often cold and unable to concentrate. You are worried that Nasreen may have anorexia nervosa and encourage her to seek help. Nasreen insists that there is nothing wrong.

– How would you manage the situation?

– Can the school use the Mental Health Act to get Nasreen to see a mental health professional?

Nasreen is taken to the GP by her mother and referred to CAMHS, where a diagnosis of anorexia nervosa is confirmed.

– What might be the specific cultural issues that need to be considered in this case?

Once the problem is suspected or recognised, referral to CAMHS is necessary. Depending on the severity of the condition, there may be a need for the intervention to take place in an inpatient setting. Eating disorders such as anorexia can often make it difficult for the young person to take part in regular family life; therefore, it is important to support the family through the intervention as well.

If there are several different professionals involved in the care, it is imperative that there be a single cohesive management plan that addresses all components of the young person's health. The very nature of the problem means that the young person has distorted cognitions, so they can present as hostile and uncooperative. It may be useful to see this as an expression of their difficulty in managing the situation. It is crucial to involve the family collaboratively in the management to minimise the possibility of miscommunication and ensure the parents continue to take responsibility as appropriate. The general principles of management and treatment include:

• encouraging regular, balanced meals in consultation with a dietician

- directing therapies at the young person's self-image, including body image and self-esteem, and helping to cope with peer influence

- achieving a balanced exercise regime

- ensuring sufficient sleep and rest

- encouraging the young person not to be influenced by other people skipping meals or commenting on weight

- achieving gradual weight gain

- engaging in concurrent individual and/or family therapy, depending on underlying issues; family therapy is the treatment of choice for young people with anorexia nervosa under 16 years of age.

An intensive community-based family therapy approach developed at the Maudsley Hospital, London (known as the Maudsley Approach) has been shown to be particularly effective and is employed internationally. This is described further in Chapter 15.

Bulimia nervosa

Bulimia involves binge eating, which is the consumption of excessive amounts of high-calorie food over a short period of time. Purging often follows this, which is associated with immense feelings of guilt for having consumed 'restricted' foods. This disorder is seen in older adolescents and adults, and is uncommon in younger children.

Presentation

Bulimia is characterised by:

- a fear of fatness

- binge eating: there is a persistent preoccupation with eating and the overwhelming desire for food leads to episodes of consuming large amounts of food in short time periods

- maintenance of normal weight

- purging by induction of vomiting and/or excessive use of laxatives

- alternating episodes of calorie restriction and using appetite suppressants, or diuretics

- feeling out of control

- depression or mood swings.

Complications of bulimia can include swollen glands in the face and neck or (rarely) a ruptured oesophagus from vomiting, weakness and exhaustion, damage to bowels from taking laxatives, and stomach acid possibly dissolving the enamel on teeth.

In many cases, the bulimia follows an episode of anorexia nervosa, although the period of time between the two disorders may vary considerably.

Management

As with anorexia nervosa the following are useful:

- encouraging regular, balanced meals in consultation with a dietician

- directing therapies at the young person's self-image, including body image and self-esteem, and helping to cope with peer influence

- achieving a balanced exercise regime

- psychoeducation about healthy eating.

Cognitive behaviour techniques (including diary-keeping) are particularly useful. The outcome for bulimia is generally good in the absence of other problems.

Substance use and problem substance use (PSU)

Substance misuse can be harmful to young people in a number of ways. It can threaten their health and welfare, and prevent them from reaching their full potential across a number of domains. Substance misuse in young people is widespread, but can be preventable (McKay, Hatton and McDougall 2006). For most people who use psychoactive ('mind-altering') drugs, their first experience was in adolescence. There is generally positive promotion of alcohol and tobacco in Western society, with a cultural ambivalence towards other drugs. It is difficult to be precise about the prevalence of substance use, as much of the information is usually self-reported by young people. However, in the UK, it has been estimated that one in ten young people between the ages of 11 and 15 years uses drugs at some point (HAS 2001). In recent years there has been an escalation of use in many countries, including the UK and Australia (Miller and Plant 1996; National Statistics 2000; Success Works 1998; Sutherland and Willner 1998). These studies also show that over the years the gender divide has decreased, as has the age at first use. Miller and Plant (1996) found cigarette smoking to be more common among girls than boys.

A follow-up study by Miller and Plant (2001) found that whilst alcohol and cigarette use remained stable, illicit drug use had fallen, suggesting that this may have reached a temporary saturation point. A detailed community survey of 29,447 adolescents in Australia aged 12–17 years (Lynskey *et al.* 1999) found that 44.1% of males and 35.9% of females reported having used at least one illicit drug in their lifetime. Cannabis was most widely used (36.4%), with other psychoactive drugs ranging 3.6–8.6 per cent. One point eight per cent had at some point misused anabolic steroids. Although most had used drugs relatively infrequently, a small minority reported more frequent use. There were strong associations between regular cannabis use and the use of other drugs, and moderate associations between tobacco and alcohol use and the use of other drugs. Although problematic use of legal highs is not prevalent in adolescence, it attracts much media attention.

Whilst use during adolescence may not be seen as problematic at the time, it may lead to tangible problems in the future. Young people who use substances are more likely to:

- be involved in road traffic and other accidents

- find their psychological and emotional development impaired

- have coexisting mental health problems

- self-harm and attempt or complete suicide

- be involved in crime, including murder (as victims and perpetrators)

- contract sexually transmitted diseases (through unprotected sex as they may be disinhibited and less cognitively aware, or may also be sexually active to fund drug-taking)

- be homeless
- be at increased risk of contracting HIV through shared needle use.

A wider range of drugs is now available for use. There is also increased polydrug use (i.e. the use of more than one drug).

Risk factors

Risk factors for problem substance use fall into three categories: environmental, individual and family.

Environmental factors

- Access and drug availability
- Peer influence and social acceptance
- Social status (any marginalised group may be at increased risk)
- Poor community networks.

Individual factors

- Psychiatric comorbidity (depression, anxiety, conduct disorder, psychosis and ADHD)
- Genetic/biological predisposition
- Psychological factors such as personality characteristics, ability to cope.

Family factors

- Chaotic families
- Families with mental health problems
- Families that have a substance use history
- Abuse
- How the family handles adolescence and the issues that it brings
- Families with relationship problems.

Types of drugs used

The same drug will often have a wide variety of names, and just as professionals become streetwise with the current names, so they keep changing. Professionals need to keep themselves updated if they work in this area. Within local groups and contexts there may also be different names used. Many substances have more than one effect and may be used for any of the effects. Commonly used substances are shown in Figure 13.1. Although not used for psychoactive purposes, anabolic steroids can also impact on mental health.

Management

Brief intervention may be appropriate for young people with less serious problem substance use. However, it can be a mistake to assume that young people cannot have serious PSU as the major issue. Interventions aimed at risk reduction have been found to be the most effective in improving morbidity. This can include abstinence, though this does not need to be a goal, except for high-risk substance use such as solvent and petrol sniffing. Whilst young people should not be given the impression that professionals condone their substance use, they also should not feel criticised or judged as this is unlikely to engage them. If they remain engaged, they are more likely to attend or (if they disengage then) to return and seek help at a later stage.

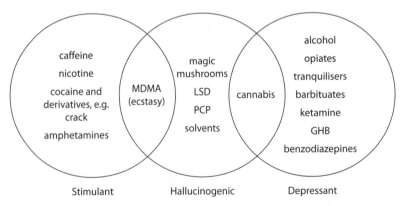

Figure 13.1 The psychoactive effects of commonly used drugs

Education

Providing accurate information on substances and how to use them safely may help to minimise harm. This can be very controversial, as some feel that giving young people information and not judging their substance use condones such behaviour. Young people are likely to use drugs if that is what they have decided, and minimising further risks such as pregnancy and sexually transmitted diseases (through unprotected sex if uninhibited and judgement impaired) may be the best, if not the only, option. Most individuals are ambivalent about change, and young substance users are no exception.

Motivational Interviewing (MI)

Motivational Interviewing techniques (a brief psychotherapeutic intervention), which use focused and goal-directed approaches to bring about change in the person, have proven successful in working with young people who misuse drugs and alcohol. Over a period of time, it can help to instigate a desire to change any negative behaviours, and help the young person to explore any feelings of ambivalence they may have (NICE 2007).

Family-based interventions

Family-based interventions can also be highly effective in offering structured support to young people who are involved in substance misuse (NICE 2007). Engagement of a family member in the delivery of any intervention is the single most positive prognostic factor. Such interventions would include:

1. at least three motivational interview sessions with parents/ carers

2. assessment of family interaction

3. parenting skills training

4. encouraging parents to monitor their child's behaviour and academic performance

5. offering feedback to the family on progress

6. more intensive support offered to families who are found to need it.

Monitoring

If, through monitoring, the young person is able to see their substance use increasing, and see problems arising from it, they may be more motivated to begin to change their life.

Medically assisted withdrawal

Medically assisted withdrawal is usually best done in a safe and supportive environment, although increasingly home-based withdrawal may be considered. During withdrawal, as well as medication, relaxation techniques, massage, exercise, and emotional support may be of help.

Rehabilitation

Rehabilitation may include maintenance drug programmes (again these can be very controversial for young people) and recreational activities, as well as other components of rehabilitation listed under psychosis above. This can prove difficult in economically and socially disadvantaged areas.

References

Amminger, G.P., Mechelli, A., Rice, S., Kim, S-W. *et al.* (2015) 'Predictors of treatment response in young people at ultra-high risk for psychosis who received long-chain omega-3 fatty acids.' *Translational Psychiatry 5*, January, e495.

Bechdolf, A., Wagner, M., Ruhrmann, S., Harrigan, S. *et al.* (2012) 'Preventing progression to first-episode psychosis in early initial prodromal states.' *British Journal of Psychiatry 200*, 22–29.

Birmaher, B., Ryan, N.D. and Williamson, D.E. (1996) 'Childhood and adolescent depression: A review of the past ten years. Part 1.' *Journal of the American Academy of Child and Adolescent Psychiatry 35*, 11, 1427–1439.

Brent, B.K., Thermenos, H.W., Keshavan, M.S. and Seidman, L.J. (2013) 'Gray matter alterations in schizophrenia high-risk youth and early-onset schizophrenia: A review of structural MRI findings.' *Child & Adolescent Psychiatry Clinics 22*, 4, 689–714.

Crisp, A.H., Palmer, R.L. and Kalucy, R.S. (1976) 'How common is anorexia? A prevalence study.' *British Journal of Psychiatry 128*, 549–554.

Dubicka, B., Elvins, R., Roberts, C., Chick, G., Wilkinson, P. and Goodyer, I.M. (2010) 'Combined treatment with cognitive–behavioural therapy in adolescent depression: Meta-analysis.' *British Journal of Psychiatry 197*, 6, 433–440.

Fombonne, E. (1994) 'Increased rates of depression: Update of epidemiological findings and analytical problems.' *Acta Psychiatrica Scandinavica 90*, 3, 145–156.

Garralda, M.E. (2017) 'Hallucinations and mental health in children.' *CNS Journal 2*, 2, 32–36. Available at www.oruen.com/cns/wp-content/uploads/2017/01/Hallucinations-print.pdf, accessed on 17 July 2017.

Health Advisory Service (HAS) (2001) *The Substance of Young Needs: A Review.* London: Health Advisory Service.

Hollis C. (2000) 'Adolescent schizophrenia.' *Advances in Psychiatric Treatment 6,* 2, 83–92

Kashani, J.H., Beck, N.C., Hoeper, E.W., Fallahi, C. *et al.* (1987) 'Psychiatric disorders in a community sample of adolescents.' *American Journal of Psychiatry 144,* 584–589.

Kavanagh, D.J. (1992) 'Recent Developments in Expressed Emotion and Schizophrenia.' In J. Jenkins, K. Oatley and N. Stein (eds) (1998) *Human Emotions – A Reader.* London: Blackwell Publications.

Lehman, A.F. (2007) 'Early intervention for psychosis and schizophrenia.' *Journal of Nervous and Mental Disease 195,* 12, 965–967.

Lynskey, M., White, V., Hill, D., Letcher, T. and Hall, W. (1999) 'Prevalence of illicit drug use among youth: results from the Australian School Students' Alcohol and Drugs Survey.' *Australian and New Zealand Journal of Public Health 23,* 5, 519–524.

Manaa, S., Paillère Martinot, M.L., Martinot, J.L. (2010) 'Brain imaging findings in children and adolescents with mental disorders: A cross-sectional review.' *European Psychiatry 25,* 6, 345–354.

Mason, L., Peters, E., Williams, S.C. and Kumari, V. (2017) 'Brain connectivity changes occurring following cognitive behavioural therapy for psychosis predict long-term recovery.' *Translational Psychiatry 7,* e1001.

McGorry, P.D. (2015) 'Early intervention in psychosis: Obvious, effective, overdue.' *Journal of Nervous and Mental Disorders 203,* 5, 310–318.

McGorry, P.D. and Jackson, H.J. (1999) *The Recognition and Management of Early Psychosis: A Preventative Approach.* Cambridge: Cambridge University Press.

McKay, D., Hatton, T. and McDougall, T. (2006) 'Substance Misuse, Young People and Nursing.' In T. McDougall (ed.) *Child and Adolescent Mental Health Nursing.* London: Blackwell Publications.

Miller, P. and Plant, M.A. (1996) 'Drinking, smoking, and illicit drug use among 15- and 16-year-olds in the United Kingdom.' *British Medical Journal 313,* 394–397.

Miller, P. and Plant, M.A. (2001) 'Drinking and smoking among 15- and 16-year-olds in the United Kingdom: A re-examination.' *Journal of Substance Use 5,* 4, 285–289.

Moffitt, T.E., Caspi, A., Taylor, A., Kokaua, J. *et al.* (2010) 'How common are common mental disorders? Evidence that lifetime prevalence rates are doubled by prospective versus retrospective ascertainment.' *Psychological Medicine 40,* 6, 899–909.

Morande, G., Celada, J. and Casas, J.J. (1999) 'Prevalence of eating disorders in a Spanish school-age population.' *Journal of Adolescent Health 24,* 3, 212–219.

National Statistics (2000) *Statistical Bulletin: Statistics on Young People and Drug Misuse: England 1998.* London: Department of Health.

Neumaker, K.J. (1997) 'Mortality and sudden death in anorexia nervosa.' *International Journal of Eating Disorders 21,* 3, 205–212.

NICE (National Institute for Health and Clinical Excellence) (2005, updated 2015) *Depression in children and young people: Identification and management.* Clinical guideline [CG28].

NICE (National Institute for Health and Clinical Excellence) (2013) *Psychosis and Schizophrenia in Children and Young People: Recognition and Management.* Clinical guideline [CG155].

NICE (National Institute for Health and Clinical Excellence) (2014, updated 2016) *Bipolar disorder: Assessment and management.* Clinical guideline [CG185].

NICE (National Institute for Health and Clinical Excellence) (2007) *Interventions to Reduce Substance Misuse among Vulnerable Young People.* London: NICE.

Nobakht, M. and Dezhkam, M. (2000) 'An epidemiological study of eating disorders in Iran.' *International Journal of Eating Disorders 28*, 3, 265–271.

Office for National Statistics (2000) *Mental Health of Children and Adolescents in Great Britain.* London: The Stationery Office.

Office for National Statistics (2005) *Mental Health of Children and Young People in Great Britain, 2004.* Basingstoke: Palgrave McMillan.

Rapoport, J.L., Giedd, J.N., Blumenthal, J., Hamburger, S. *et al.* (1999) 'Progressive cortical change during adolescence in childhood-onset schizophrenia: A longitudinal Magnetic Resonance Imaging study.' *Archives of General Psychiatry 56*, 7, 649–654.

Rastam, M., Gillberg, C. and Garton, M. (1989) 'Anorexia nervosa in a Swedish urban region: A population-based study.' *British Journal of Psychiatry 155*, 642–646.

Reig, S., Moreno, C., Moreno, D., Burdalo, M. *et al.* (2008) 'Progression of brain volume changes in adolescent-onset psychosis.' *Schizophrenia Bulletin 35*, 1, 233–243.

Srinivasan, T.N., Suresh, T.R. and Jayaram, V. (1998) 'Emergence of eating disorders in India: Study of eating distress syndrome and development of a screening questionnaire.' *International Journal of Social Psychiatry 44*, 3, 189–198.

Steinhausen, H.C., Winkler, C. and Meier, M. (1997) 'Eating disorders in adolescence in a Swiss epidemiological study.' *International Journal of Eating Disorders 22*, 2, 147–151.

Success Works Pty Ltd (1998) *Young People and Drugs: Needs Analysis.* Melbourne Department of Human Services, State Government of Victoria.

Sullivan, P.F. (1995) 'Mortality in anorexia nervosa.' *American Journal of Psychiatry 152*, 7, 1073–1074.

Sutherland, I. and Willner, P. (1998) 'Patterns of alcohol, cigarette and illicit drug use in English adolescents.' *Addiction 93*, 1199–1208.

Tijssen, M.J.A., van Os, J., Wittchen, H.-U., Lieb, R. *et al.* (2010) 'Prediction of transition from common adolescent bipolar experiences to bipolar disorder: 10-year study.' *British Journal of Psychiatry 196*, 2, 102–108.

Torrey, E.F. (1987) 'Prevalence studies in schizophrenia.' *British Journal of Psychiatry 150*, 598–608.

Vaughn, C.E. and Leff, J.P. (1976) 'Influence of family and social factors on the course of psychiatric illness.' *British Journal of Psychiatry 129*, 125.

West, A.E. and Pavuluri, M.N. (2009) 'Psychosocial treatments for childhood and adolescent bipolar disorder.' *Child and Adolescent Psychiatric Clinics of North America 18*, 2, 471–482.

Wykes, T. and Reeder, C. (2005) *Cognitive Remediation Therapy for Schizophrenia: Theory and Practice.* London: Routledge.

Young, M.E. and Fristad, M.A. (2007) 'Evidence based treatments for bipolar disorder in children and adolescents.' *Journal of Contemporary Psychotherapy 37*, 3, 157–164.

Yung, A.R., Yuen, H.P., Berger, G., Francey, S. *et al.* (2007) 'Declining transition rate in ultra high risk (prodromal) services: dilution or reduction of risk?' *Schizophrenia Bulletin 33*, 673–681.

Further reading

Bryant-Waugh, R. and Lask, B. (1999) *Eating Disorder: A Parents' Guide.* London: Penguin.

Emmett, D. and Nice, G. (2005) *Understanding Drug Issues: A Photocopiable Resource Workbook (2nd edition).* London: Jessica Kingsley Publishers.

Garner, D.M. and Garfinkel, P.E. (eds) (1997) *Handbook and Treatment of Eating Disorders (2nd edition).* London: Guilford Press.

Goodyer, I.M. (ed.) (2001) *The Depressed Child and Adolescent (2nd edition)*. Cambridge: Cambridge University Press (Cambridge Child and Adolescent Psychiatry).

Graham, P. and Hughes, C. (1995) *So Sad, So Young, So Listen*. London: Royal College of Psychiatrists and Gaskell.

McGorry, P.D., Yung, A.R., Bechdolf, A. and Amminger, P. (2008) 'Back to the future: Predicting and reshaping the course of psychotic disorder.' *Archives of General Psychiatry 65*, 25–27.

NICE (National Institute for Health and Clinical Excellence) (2002) *Self-harm: The Short Term Physical and Psychological Management and Secondary Preventions of Self-harm in Primary and Secondary Care*. London: NICE.

NICE (National Institute for Health and Clinical Excellence) (2004) *Eating Disorders: Core Interventions in the Treatment of Anorexia Nervosa, Bulimia Nervosa and Other Related Eating Disorders*. London: NICE.

NICE (National Institute for Health and Clinical Excellence) (2005) *Depression in Children and Young People: Identification and Management in Primary Care, Community and Secondary Care*. London: NICE.

Pagliaro, A.M. and Pagliaro, L.A. (1996) *Substance Use Among Children and Adolescents: Its Nature, Extent and Effects from Conception to Adulthood*. Chichester: Wiley.

Palmer, B. (2014) *Helping People with Eating Disorders: A Clinical Guide to Assessment and Treatment (2nd edition)*. London: Wiley.

Royal College of Psychiatrists (1998) *Managing Deliberate Self-Harm in Young People*. (Council Report CR 64). London: Royal College of Psychiatrists.

Torrey, E.F. (2013) *Surviving Schizophrenia: A Family Manual (6th edition)*. New York: Harper Collins.

Websites

www.mind.org.uk (Mind)

www.nimh.nih.gov (National Institute of Mental Health, US)

www.nta.nhs.uk (National Treatment Agency for Substance Misuse)

www.rcpsych.ac.uk (Royal College of Psychiatrists)

See also Royal College of Psychiatrists fact sheets, available through the Royal College on a range of mental health problems.

CHAPTER 14

Basic Interventions with Applicability in Primary Care Settings

In this chapter, we discuss a range of psychological interventions that can be used by non-specialist professionals in primary care settings. The interventions draw upon approaches and techniques from several specialist therapies. Qualified practitioners of these therapies need a high level of training and expertise to practice but we have outlined interventions which a non-specialist professional can use safely and effectively, being mindful of their limits and competence. There are sections on: planning interventions, managing complex situations, behaviour therapy, anxiety management, cognitive behaviour therapy, parenting groups, solution-focused approaches, motivational interviewing, and problem solving.

Planning interventions

Before an appropriate intervention can be planned, there should be a full and thorough assessment as described earlier. Intervention can then be discussed and agreed with the young person and the family. The first need is to decide which type of therapy is appropriate, whether this should be individual, group or family based, and whether medication and referral to a specialist is required. This needs to be written in a management plan with clear ideas of when the situation is to be reviewed and expected outcomes agreed with the parent(s), possibly other relevant professionals involved, and, where appropriate, the young person. No treatment should be unplanned or open-ended. If the treatment does not lead to resolution, first reconsider the diagnosis or formulation of the problem. It is important not to continue treatment that does not improve matters without reviewing the situation. Professionals should ensure they use the appropriate strategy for the identified problem rather than using a single strategy, technique or approach for all problems. The strategies discussed in this chapter have particular applicability in primary care; but, additionally, the usefulness of education, support and listening provided by adults should not be underestimated.

Management of complex problems

The management of mental health problems can be complicated by other health and social needs. These include serious or chronic medical disorders, such as epilepsy, and social needs, such as provision of alternative care or educational needs. Where issues of management interact, it is important for the various agencies to work closely together. It is important that those working with complex needs start to try to understand and gain knowledge surrounding young people's mental health problems, in order to identify them early. Sometimes significant mental health problems are missed, or parents are not prepared for what they may have to cope with. These difficulties can often lead to breakdown in placements.

As the nature of these young people's difficulties is often complex, the provision for their mental health problems must take place collaboratively. Some CAMHS have developed services specifically for young people at high risk of complex needs. However, for these to be effective, there still must be a great deal of planning and partnership.

Interventions can occur at a number of levels, including:

- through local networks of services meeting together to plan responsive services

- through social workers and parents accessing consultation offered by local CAMHS

- in multi-agency training initiatives

- through the development of support groups, with local CAMHS professionals involved, where parents and professionals can work together to approach problems consistently and strategically through a range of therapeutic interventions in a multi-agency setting, to meet specific needs and problems (e.g. post-abuse services, substance misuse services, youth offending teams and the voluntary sector).

Behaviour therapy

What behaviour therapy is and is not

Behaviour therapy is one application of behavioural theories and works on the principle that the frequency of a given behaviour can be increased or decreased by modifying stimuli that influence it. These stimuli can be therapeutically manipulated, either by the person showing the behaviour or by someone else, who in the case of young people may be a parent or teacher. Behaviour therapy can be used in a variety of conditions across the lifespan: anxiety disorders (such as phobia, social anxiety and separation anxiety), obsessive compulsive disorder, enuresis (wetting) and encopresis (soiling), behaviour and conduct disorders, and behavioural aspects of psychotic disorders.

Children and young people display behaviours for many reasons, some of which can be difficult to understand, particularly if the child has complex needs or problems. For a behaviour to continue it has to be 'useful' for the child and understanding the reason for a behaviour is helpful; for example, if a child screams and is given a toy, they may well use screaming to get the toy again as they have learnt that screaming gets them what they want. Behaviour therapy, however, is not an insight-directed therapy and should not be a punitive approach to exert social control. It should be used to benefit the individual whose behaviour is inappropriate. Punishment (by an individual, organisation or society) is the least effective way to bring about change, and usually has more to do with making those in control feel better or demonstrate that 'something is being done'. Criticisms of behaviour therapy are usually based on confusion between these issues, or on the notion that an individual's thoughts and feelings are ignored, which would not be good practice. These ethical considerations are particularly important in the most vulnerable, such as young people with intellectual disability.

The application of behavioural theories

Classical conditioning, operant conditioning, social learning theory and cognitive learning are described in Chapter 6. These are directly relevant to treatment. In practice, two or more models come into play in the expression of behaviour and in treatment. For instance, a child who receives little parental attention may frequently show antisocial behaviour, the consequence of which is to be told off – which, no matter how unpleasant this may be, provides the attention desired: receiving unfavourable attention provides an experience that at least acknowledges the child, which being neglected does not. This illustrates both social learning theory and operant conditioning. The treatment of a phobia by systematic desensitisation to the feared object involves both conditioning to a new stimulus (classical conditioning) and the reward of decreased anxiety while in the continued presence of the feared object (positive reinforcement of operant conditioning).

Behaviour therapy in practice

Behaviour therapy is often part of an overall management of a disorder or identified problem. It should only be considered after a comprehensive assessment has been made.

Behaviour therapy can be successfully implemented in primary care as well as in specialist services, providing the professional has had relevant training and receives appropriate supervision.

Behaviour therapy may be undertaken individually (with parents or young people), or with families, or in therapeutic groups (for parents or young people). Whatever the mode of delivery, the principles remain the same.

There are four components to its implementation, as outlined here:

- engagement

- defining goals

- assessment of the behaviour

- implementation of plans and follow-up.

Engagement

The young person and family need to fully understand the purpose of the assessment and intervention, have the resources to complete the work and be motivated to see this through a period of several weeks or months. For behaviour therapy to be successful, the family needs to be an active participant in the process.

Assessment of the family's resources is critical, as is the timing of intervention. Parents may have their own health issues or concerns, which can be a barrier to successful work. It may be appropriate to delay the start of intervention until families have additional resources, such as support from a family member. This process can also help parents understand how their own perceptions and experiences may impact on their children. They can then also be helped to appreciate their role in the behaviour being maintained.

Defining goals

Once engaged, the parents or young person, or both, should identify which behaviour(s) they wish to change. This usually concerns reducing or stopping an undesirable behaviour. Goals should be specific, definable and achievable. A parent's request that their child should 'be good and not behave badly' or a young person's request 'not to worry about things' does not meet these criteria for goals. Such requests need to be explored further and specific behaviours identified (e.g. 'to stop hitting his brother' or 'to mix with friends without feeling anxious'). It is often prudent to start with the most concerning or risky behaviour first. However, it may be more pragmatic in certain instances to start with a behaviour that would be more easily modified to demonstrate to the child or family that change is possible. The goal may have to be broken down into several achievable steps.

Reducing the frequency of an undesirable behaviour is more readily achieved and maintained if a desired behaviour with which it is incompatible is simultaneously taught and rewarded. For example, a child who is encouraged to play happily with his brother cannot be hitting him at the same time; the more he remains engaged in play, and praised for this behaviour, the less he will hit. It is therefore important to build in goals and rewards for the desired behaviour as well as trying to extinguish the undesired behaviour.

Assessment of the behaviour

The assessment of the identified behaviour(s) should include a full understanding of what is driving and maintaining the behaviour. This includes a careful history and a functional analysis, which is a detailed breakdown of antecedents, behaviour and consequences (ABC). These can be recorded on an 'ABC chart' over a period of time that would give sufficient examples to work with clinically. The chart may be completed by the young person themselves, if appropriate, or an informant, who may be a parent, carer or teacher. It may be necessary for the professional to make direct observations of the child and their environment in the same way, or use videotaped examples. The chart is usually in the form shown in Table 14.1 below, with observation of the factors described in each column.

Table 14.1 An 'ABC chart' used in the functional analysis of behaviour

Date/time	A (antecedents)	B (behaviour)	C (consequences)
	Where?	Nature/type of behaviour – described in detail	What did the child do afterwards?
	With whom?		What did others do afterwards?
	What was the child doing?	Duration?	
	What were others doing?	Severity?	Were there any changes in attention given to, and in expectations of, the child?

Adolescents with phobic disorder can use the same chart to identify the specific influences on their avoidant behaviour. Whatever the identified problem, it is sometimes helpful to have more than one person completing charts of the same events if possible. One person may observe an aspect of the situation that others do not.

Implementation and follow up

The general principal for behavioural plans is to reward the positive (desired) behaviours and ignore the negative (undesirable) behaviours.

It may be possible to avoid a trigger to the behaviour but this is not always appropriate; for example, if a request to get dressed triggers the behaviour, then you cannot stop expecting the child to dress, but you may wish to change how this request is made. Equally, with phobias, to avoid a trigger for anxiety would not be helpful, indeed would exacerbate the problem.

Positive Behaviour Support is the approach recommended for young people with intellectual disabilities and challenging behaviour and requires accurate assessment of the functions of the behaviour and then focuses on social and environmental changes, communication, clear proactive and reactive strategies, and skill building to reduce the need for the young person to use a problem behaviour. This plan would not include aversive or punishment strategies.

Common techniques to encourage the desired behaviours are summarised in Table 14.2.

Table 14.2 Glossary of common techniques or procedures

Chaining	A planned programme for the reward of sequential components of a desired behaviour in stages, e.g. used in soiling to reward sitting on toilet, followed by longer intervals there, followed by depositing faeces there.
Desensitation	Repeated exposure to an aversive stimulus while using techniques to maintain a relaxed state such as with treatment of phobias.
Graded exposure	A planned programme of desensitisation to a series of increasingly aversive stimuli, based on a hierarchy of such stimuli generated by the young person/carer.
Extinction	When a behaviour is no longer reinforced, it reduces and may stop. To be successful, this needs to be paired with a replacement behaviour.
Modelling	The demonstration of desired behaviour for the child to imitate.
Negative reinforcement	Removal of an aversive stimulus after a desired behaviour, e.g. when a child has behaved well they are excused from doing a chore they dislike.
Overcorrection	Change in frequency of behaviour beyond the required threshold, e.g. adjunct to treatment of enuresis by including additional fluid load in final stage of programme.
Positive reinforcement	Presentation of a positive stimulus (reward) after a desired behaviour. This needs to happen immediately after the behaviour to be most successful.
Progress charts	Charts used to monitor progress, e.g. a star chart where the star is used as a form of reward. These need to be individualised, achievable, specific and positive.
Time out	The planned brief withdrawal of a reinforcement (commonly social contact) following an undesired behaviour, i.e. an example of extinction and not to be confused with seclusion (the removal of a person for reasons of safety or punishment).

Some common pitfalls to avoid

Focusing on the behavioural treatment to the exclusion of other factors may lead to ineffectual implementation. This may be due to:

- the family not having the practical or emotional resources to see through the work

- an inconsistent approach by parents, which can be due to reduced communication, comprehension, ability or motivation

- failure by the professional to recognise beliefs held by the family that may block successful implementation (such as, 'he's just like his father')

- parents being unable to distinguish between styles of behaviour management, such as confusing 'firm' with 'harsh'

- emotional responses by parents that impede implementation, such as guilt, anxiety, anger

- failure by the professional to make a full assessment and therefore failure to develop a comprehensive management package, which in addition to behavioural treatment might need to address emotional or mental health issues

- failure to take into account the young person's ability, temperament, neurodevelopmental issues, skills, interests, motivation and ability to implement this aspect of the treatment.

Anxiety management

Anxiety management is not based on behavioural techniques alone, but is included here to be comprehensive. It consists of the following components, each of which can be delivered to the young person, parents or both. They may be delivered individually, or sometimes more effectively as a group therapy. The response to these techniques is highly individual and it may be the young person finds not all are useful or applicable to them.

- Education about the disorder, or 'psychoeducation'. This includes a description of the normal physiology and psychology of anxiety and guiding the parents and young person to relate this to the symptoms experienced, and to identify the maladaptive patterns that have developed.

- Inducing physical relaxation, which includes progressive muscular relaxation (focusing sequentially on relaxing muscles in an 'outward' direction from the head down) and or controlled breathing exercises. These should be practised – by the child alone, or with a parent – at times when the young person is least stressed, so that they can be used more effectively in anxiety-provoking situations.

- Mental relaxation using techniques such as guided imagery, during which the child focuses on a previously agreed visual image or memory of a favourite comfortable, safe, but non-stimulating environment.

These techniques should be explained and experienced first with the professional and then practised at home. There are many helpful websites and phone apps which reinforce the message given by the professional and help the young person practise at a time of their choosing. These sites and apps should be regularly reviewed by the professional before recommending them to ensure their suitability. It is often useful to give young people a range of sites to choose from if possible, so they can review them and find one that works for them. This approach enables children to be empowered to some extent but also enables the practitioner to take into account differing child needs and preferences. The degree to which each component is applied depends on the child's needs and presenting problem, and will usually accompany specific behavioural and cognitive interventions.

Cognitive therapy

Cognitive interventions attempt to induce change by influencing thinking. Cognitive therapy has been successfully used in three disorders in young people, mostly in adolescence, but with some effect in children: aggression, anxiety disorders and depression. There is some support for its use in ADHD, eating disorders and others, but these are not discussed here as it would not usually be a first-line approach.

Cognitive therapy implies an exclusive focus on cognitive processes. However, its application necessarily requires the integration of social, emotional and behavioural aspects with cognition. Most cognitive therapy is undertaken on an individual basis, but can also be effectively delivered in therapeutic groups and family settings. The techniques used broadly follow three steps:

1. identify distorted conceptualisations

2. test the reality of the assumptions made

3. correct the cognitive distortion.

These distortions to thinking usually occur automatically and are maladaptive. Such automatic negative thoughts result from an underlying view or belief (schema).

Cognitive therapy for aggression

Aggressive adolescents differ from their non-aggressive peers in that they:

- recall higher rates of hostile cues in social situations

- attend to fewer cues when interpreting others' behaviour

- are more likely to attribute hostile intent to ambiguous behaviour of others

- under-perceive their own level of aggressiveness

- generate fewer verbal, assertive responses to conflict

- are more likely to perceive aggression as resulting in a positive outcome, and in enhanced self-esteem

- are less likely to perceive aggression as resulting in suffering for the victim.

Such cognitive distortions and consequent maladaptive social behaviour reflect differences in information processing (see Chapter 4) and can be addressed using social problem solving approaches that include:

- self-monitoring, such as keeping a diary of cognitions, behaviour and affect

- self-instruction, such as 'stop–think–do–review'

- perspective-taking, to be more aware of the variety of non-hostile cues

- affect-labelling, to assign meaning to heightened arousal

- relaxation.

Significant reductions in aggression have been reported in the use of these techniques in adolescents, particularly in combination with interpersonal therapies and problem solving skills training, with maintenance of this effect at one-year follow-up.

Cognitive therapy for anxiety disorders

The cognitive distortions associated with anxiety in childhood and adolescence are mostly assumed from empirical work: the only definitive findings relate to thoughts of being threatened or negatively evaluated by others, and negative self-reference in a non-clinical population with high anxiety, for example statements such as 'I'm going to fail.' However, interventions have been successful with up to 50 per cent response (Kendall *et al.* 1992), and usually include a combination of:

- reappraisal of physical symptoms of anxiety, recognising that anxiety has affective, cognitive and physical components together (e.g. 'I'm feeling sick again – that means I'm anxious about something')

- self-instruction in combination with behavioural change (e.g. to treat avoidance in phobias)

- self-evaluation – re-evaluate perceived weaknesses and recognise strengths

- thought-prevention

- guided imagery, using imagined or remembered comfortable situations

- relaxation during exposure to anxiety-provoking stimulus.

Children are more amenable to using self-talk than adults, which probably reflects their use of it in play and problem solving. This may, therefore, explain why this is a particularly useful technique in young children.

Cognitive therapy for depression

Young people with depression demonstrate the same systematic negative cognitions identified in depressed adults: negative views of themselves, the world and the future. These include:

- distorted attributions, such as perceptions that events are more likely to be due to external causes

- low self-esteem, such as perceived poor academic performance

- distorted perception of past and present events.

These are mediated by cognitive processes of over-generalisation, catastrophisation (the prediction of a catastrophic result to an event or thought), selective attention to negative events and incorrectly taking personal responsibility for them. Successful interventions include:

- enhancing social skills

- developing greater self-control of cognitive processes, such as punishing self less, more self-praise, adopting less perfectionistic goals

- cognitive restructuring, such as challenging the assumed evidence supporting cognitive distortions.

The impact of cognitive therapy in depression is more variable, with, again, approximately a 50 per cent response to treatment (Lewinsohn et al. 1990), which is greater than the effect of medication. One half of responders relapse within one year, and there are no long-term follow-up studies.

Parenting programmes

There is a growing number of parenting programmes, which vary in style, structure and content but are usually based on a social learning model using modelling, rehearsal and feedback to improve parenting skills, incorporating specialised modifications of behavioural therapy. There is some evidence (NICE 2013) that properly trained non-mental health specialists can effectively deliver parenting programmes. The programmes can be undertaken with couples or with groups of parents. Programmes should consider how parents manage their child's behaviour and meet their child's emotional needs. It may be useful to develop local links to receive support from specialist services.

The rationale behind parenting programmes is an understanding that a child is presented as having behavioural problems and that on assessment these are identified as parenting issues. It is important that the parents themselves decide on the priorities and rules for their family. The professional's role is to facilitate the parental implementation of these ideas (unless this raises child protection/safeguarding concerns). Parents can sometimes request you tell them what needs doing, and whilst discussing principles with them and offering suggestions are both appropriate, it is inappropriate to over-direct them. This would not allow them to resolve the issues within the family and does not empower them to build their own skills. Parents need to be guided to take responsibility for their parenting. There are several issues that need to be addressed when considering parenting.

- The first issue is about establishing clarity of expectations and roles. This may involve exploring parental experiences during their own childhood. Parents who experienced very controlling parenting themselves may go to the other extreme and be reluctant to exercise any limits or boundaries on their own children. Parents need to be aware of the difficulties this creates for the child. Those who have very different perspectives may find themselves contradicting each other, leaving the child confused as to what is expected of them, sometimes leading to distress or frustration, which may present behaviourally.

- Parents may also need permission to be firm (and this may need to be differentiated from harsh). For example, being clear that a child is expected to go to school even if it makes them anxious and being consistent with the child about this is being firm. Not supporting them with their anxiety whilst having this expectation would be harsh.

- Parents need to ensure that their approach towards children is clear and consistent. Parents may find that they are undermined by other family members and may need to find strategies to handle this. This may be particularly true when the parents are separated. In these situations, it is helpful to see the parents together. If they find this prospect too difficult, it may be appropriate to see them separately and ensure both are given the same message. It is also worth asking parents to consider the messages the child is receiving and the position they are put in if there is ongoing hostility and acrimony between the parents. Establishing who is in charge is important, as is improving the relationship between the parents and child.

- If a child has presented with difficult behaviour, it can very easily become a defined role for that child – the child does not behave in the required way, so the child is never expected to do so, and ultimately the child will rarely do so. Parents need to take the lead in breaking the negative cycles, and a helpful way of doing this is to focus on the positives. Rewards should also be realistic and age-appropriate, and set at realistic and achievable timescales. Asking a three-year-old child to wait a week for a reward is unrealistic. Delaying dealing with undesired behaviour in young children is unhelpful, as they will often have forgotten what the behaviour was.

- Rather than punishing undesired behaviour, desired behaviour is rewarded. This is not the same as ignoring bad behaviour altogether, but is focusing on the positives. It also enables the child to move away from their assigned role within a family.

- It is also important to be explicit and specific with children about expectations. Asking a child to be good or not be bad can be very difficult for the child to understand. What might be perceived as being good one day may be perceived as not good on another day. It is more helpful to say exactly what is expected; for example, the child might be requested not to swear or hit people or to eat their meal. These are very specific and clear, whereas saying the child needs to 'be good' could be interpreted differently by each member of the family with respect to what is expected.

- Parents also need to be aware of developmental appropriateness and be realistic about their expectations. It is also important that parents select the issues that warrant concern and learn to let fewer major issues pass. It can also be helpful for the parents to learn the child's strengths and work on those and find ways of spending time with their child that is enjoyable. Parenting is not much fun for parents if they are constantly finding themselves being negative, nor is it much fun for the child. It is important not to let the behaviour define the child and become overcritical.

Counselling

The term 'counselling' has come to be used so liberally that people can often be unclear as to what it means and who should be providing such treatments. Essentially, counselling can vary from support and advice provided by informally trained staff (with no formal training) to therapy provided by highly skilled and qualified staff (who belong to professional bodies such as the BACP (British Association of Counselling and Psychotherapy) and UKCP (United Kingdom Council for Psychotherapy), which provide an ethical framework and maintain standards through revalidation).

There can sometimes be an assumption that all young people need counselling if they have had certain experiences, such as abuse or parental separation. It is important to recognise that for most of these experiences, young people do not necessarily require counselling. Often it is sufficient if the adults around them provide enough support and have an understanding of what the young person has experienced or is experiencing. The perceived need for young people to be counselled can be a reflection of the uncertainties of the adults involved. The problem with automatically suggesting counselling is that it can deprive the young person of an opportunity to deal with experiences appropriately, and can thereby inappropriately focus the problem on them. It may also inadvertently deskill a child who is able to find appropriate ways of dealing with the stressor. There will, however, be some young people who do require intervention, and although it can be difficult to identify these young people and their needs, a good indicator would be a negative change in the young person's functioning. If the counsellor is one of several professionals involved with the young person, they should ensure that they do not work in isolation. It is also important that the young person is agreeable to counselling. If a young person is insistent they do not wish to have counselling, then their view should be respected. However, one can still work with the young person, perhaps, for instance, working with him or her to explore other options or ways to manage difficulties. Young people under 16 years of age should be given confidentiality, but this has to be limited by the need to disclose information relating to safety and child protection issues. It is inappropriate for a non-specialist counsellor to continue working with a young person who is deliberately self-harming (unless appropriately supervised and/or supported by more specialist staff) or has a major mental health disorder. The primary care staff in these circumstances are probably best to focus on trying to encourage the young person to access appropriate specialist help. Primary care staff should set clear boundaries and ensure that they do not find themselves out of their depth or that the young person becomes dependent on them.

Counselling can provide the young person with an opportunity to explore their feelings and address them in ways that they find comfortable, but which are also acceptable in a wider context. Counselling should aim to improve the young person's ability to manage distress and difficult or potentially difficult situations. It can be an opportunity to enable the young person safely to explore different options. Depending on the skills, training and experience of the counsellor, several different types of techniques may be usefully employed.

Solution-focused brief therapy

De Shazer and the team at the Brief Therapy Centre in Milwaukee developed solution-focused brief therapy in the early 1980s (Evan, Iveson and Ratner 1999). It was created as a brief model of therapy that uses concepts of solution-focused thinking. The term client is used, as the model can be used with young people and their parents.

The central premise of solution-focused brief therapy is that during conversations there will be a shift from problem-domination to solution-orientation, thus enabling development in the client. This approach can produce results for the client within a few sessions.

Although this approach was intended, initially, for use as a therapy, the techniques can be utilised in many situations. Elements of the approach can be practised in conversations with young people and their parents and in work with other professionals. The approach has a number of basic assumptions:

- Attempts to comprehend the origins or causes of a problem are not necessarily a step towards its resolution. Sometimes discussing the problem can be unhelpful to developing any useful solutions.

- Successful work depends on knowing what the client wants to achieve. Once this has been established, then the aim of the approach is to find the quickest and most effective way of achieving the defined goals.

- Even if a problem seems not to have a resolution, there are always times when the client can find a solution. The most efficient use of time here is establishing 'what works' and building upon it.

The client will be able to ascertain when the problem has been resolved; sometimes small changes identified within the session can set in motion a solution to the problem, or indeed lead the system to change in other areas. The elements informing the basis of practice include:

1. Establishing a context for the work

The therapy is a collaborative approach to which the client brings knowledge of the issues and what they would like to change. Pay attention to what has been useful in the past and to how both parties will know when the process is working and what the preferred approach is for the client.

2. Identifying a preferred future

Goal-setting is central to the process. It is paramount for these to be described and explored in detail, as the therapist has no separate goal for the work other than those goals defined by the client.

3. Defining progress

The key consideration when looking at preferred future is for the client to define when they feel their work will be progressing.

The initial focus will be on when the client will know that the session has been useful. Ways of achieving this include getting the client to know what it would take to convince them that the work had been useful or asking what would be different. It can sometimes be useful to ask the client 'third person perspectives'; for example, 'What would your parents see happening if this work has been successful?' It is also important to get the client to notice or identify when small changes are being made or the identified area for change is moving forward.

4. Establishing what is working

Here the approach is to focus on what is working, either for the client or those around them, rather than focusing on what elements the client should be reducing. It is vital to encourage identification of what they could be doing more of. This involves discussing signs of progress.

5. Scaling questions

Scaling questions can be useful in allowing the client to develop a clear focus on how far they have progressed towards meeting their goals. They also allow for integration of differences in perspective between the client and their family or friends. The following types of questions can be useful:

- On a scale of 1 to 10, 10 representing the achievement of your goals and 1 being no progress, where do you feel you are?

- So, what tells you things are at…and not at 1?

- What tells you things have moved to that point?

Scaling questions can help the client to look at things like confidence and progress.

6. Identifying resources and determining a context of competence

This focuses the client on determining what is available to them in order to achieve goals; it is also important to identify the qualities they have, thus developing a context of resourcefulness and openness to change.

7. Constructive feedback

The effects of the therapeutic conversation can be amplified by giving feedback on the qualities of the client and the useful aspects of the process that has taken place during the session. It is always useful at the end of the session to see if the client needs follow-up or whether they are satisfied with the outcomes.

Motivational interviewing

Miller developed the framework for motivational interviewing in the context of addressing problem substance use. It is grounded in client-centred principles and is both practical and effective (Miller and Rollnick 1991). Its use in treatment for substance misuse is widespread; however, it can be applied in a diverse range of contexts when the young person needs to make changes in their life. Motivational interviewing uses the five recognised phases of the readiness for change model and people may move back and forth between the phases.

- *Precontemplation phase* – the user does not see their substance use as a problem, although others might.

- *Contemplation phase* – the user begins to recognise they have problems but may be unsure and ambivalent about whether change is required and how to bring about change.

- *Action stage* – the user plans and implements change.

- *Maintenance stage* – the user applies their skills to maintain the change.

- *Relapse* – substance use is resumed. This stage may be short or long before the user returns to one of the above stages.

There are five key principles to motivational interviewing:

- *express empathy* – this communicates respect for and acceptance of the young person's feelings and encourages a non-judgmental, collaborative working relationship

- *avoid argument and direct confrontation* – these tend to be counterproductive and lead to defensiveness

- *develop discrepancy* – through dialogue, help the young person focus on how their current behaviour differs from their goals or hopes for the future

- *ambivalence is normal* – acknowledge that there is always a dilemma surrounding change and that there may be good reasons not to change: resistance can be helpfully interpreted as information that the approach needs to be adjusted

- *support optimism and self-efficacy* – it is important that the young person believes change is possible and that they take responsibility for making this happen.

A discrepancy between present behaviour and important goals will motivate change.

The grounds for change should come from the client and not the professional, although it is appropriate for the professional to suggest strategies.

There is hope in the range of alternative approaches available. It is useful to prepare a 'decisions balance sheet' with the client using the above framework. There are six key steps:

Step 1

Assess readiness for change by the following types of questions (in which smoking is used as an example of a behaviour that is to be changed):

- Have you ever thought about stopping smoking? Have you ever stopped smoking before?

- Where are you in terms of your smoking? Are you interested in stopping smoking?

- What would come to mind if you thought about stopping smoking? Do you have any reason why you might want to stop smoking at some point?

Step 2

Provide a stage-specific rationale for performing a decisions balance:

- *Precontemplation* – 'So, at this point you really don't feel like your smoking is a problem for you? Is it okay if I ask a little more about your smoking so I can understand why you don't think it's a problem?'

- *Contemplation* – 'So, you're saying you have some concerns about your smoking but not sure yet whether you want to do something about that. Can I just ask a little more about that, as that may help you decide when you might be ready to make that decision for yourself?'

- *Determination* – 'It sounds like you are really determined to do something about your smoking. Can we discuss your smoking, as it may help us think about where we go next?'

Step 3

Restate your position that whatever they decide to do at this point, you will honour the decision. Acknowledge their autonomy.

Step 4

Ask the following four questions:

- What do you like about smoking? (Reflect each response and then ask what else they like about smoking.)

- What are some not-so-good things about smoking? (Again, reflect and then ask what else.)

- What concerns do you have about stopping smoking? (Again, reflect and ask what else.)

- What would be the benefit of stopping smoking? (Again, reflect and ask what else.)

Step 5

Summarise the pros and cons of not changing versus changing their behaviour.

Step 6

Explicitly leave the door open for further contact or discussion.

It can be very useful to draw up a table of the decision balance outcome as shown in Figure 14.1.

Current benefits	Current concerns
Relaxes me	Costs me too much money
Change concerns	**Change benefits**
Hard to give up because all my friends smoke	Would give me more money to spend on other things

Figure 14.1 Decision balance table

Problem solving

Problem solving therapy is an approach that seeks to develop the young person's capacity to resolve problems which are having a negative impact on their mental health and build up their long-term resilience. Although this approach may appear to be straightforward 'common sense' it follows a clear structure, and with practice it can be an effective intervention when a young person is feeling overwhelmed by a number of stressors, which can often lead to symptoms or maladaptive behaviours, such as self-harm. It is important to remember that the aim of the therapy is to empower the young person so the temptation to offer our own solutions needs to be resisted.

The therapy follows distinct steps:

1. *Explaining the treatment* – helping the young person make the link between how they are feeling and behaving with the problems they are currently experiencing in their life, at the same time normalising their reaction. It follows that if they become more adept at managing their problems their symptoms should reduce.

2. *Defining the problems* – sensitive questioning can help the young person list the problems they have been experiencing. It is important here to take plenty of time and be mindful that some may be of a highly personal nature. The language you use here is important and you might find it helpful to prompt with the types of issues many young people experience.

3. *Summarise the problems* – in your own words summarise what you have heard, listing the problems in a structured way. This helps give a different perspective on the problems, conveys that you have been listening carefully, and enables the young person to clarify and add information. The structure this gives to the interview helps the transition to the next step.

4. *Prioritising* – going through the list you have summarised, ask the young person to identify the most important or pressing problems. Here you may have to help them select one that may be likely to change in the short term and is within the young person's sphere of influence, e.g. choosing to work on a backlog of homework rather than the acrimonious relationship between their parents. Again, summarise what you have agreed.

5. *Co-creating an action plan* – think up as many solutions as you can between you (some may be ridiculous) then refine them down to a few, more pragmatic possibilities. Discuss these possible solutions, paying attention to the practicality and potential consequences of each one. Once a possible solution has been settled upon, a plan of action is developed. It is important to set measurable, realistic steps to enable progress to be monitored and experienced by the young person. It can be helpful to frame the plan as an 'experiment', which allows for any setbacks to be seen as further information to work with rather than another failure. Throughout this process, you will have to work hard to maintain the balance between helping to generate ideas and taking over with solutions of your own, even though these might be obvious to you. It is important to bear in mind that the intention of the therapy is primarily to develop the young person's problem solving skills and hence their resilience, not just to solve their problems. Summarise the plan.

6. *Review* – this is a key part of the approach and there may need to be several follow-up sessions in this stage. If there has been progress, spend some time discussing in detail how they managed to achieve this and what obstacle they had to overcome. Are they satisfied with the outcome? Do they feel ready to address another problem? If there has been little or no progress, it is important to frame this as a learning experience rather than a failure. Take some time to look at what was not working and, if necessary, create another action plan or even pick a less ambitious problem to work on.

Reframing

As well as the types of question outlined in Chapter 3 on family interviewing, a useful technique that can be used in a primary health setting is that of reframing. This is where the professional offers a different perspective on a situation, which, whilst it still fits the facts, concentrates on a family's strengths. Examples of this would be where a family member's complaints are reframed as a desire to improve a situation or where a parent's anger about an adolescent staying out overnight is reframed as concern about their safety.

The aim of reframing is to give the family the opportunity to view an impasse in a different way that may allow them to break free from an unhelpful pattern of interaction. Careful thought needs to be given about how to fit the reframe with the family's beliefs and use of language. If the reframe is presented in a way that is unacceptable to the family it will not be assimilated. However, if it is meaningful for the family it will be immediately apparent from their reaction. If the reframe does not make sense to the family or is rejected by them, it will be counterproductive to persist and the worker should put that intervention aside and consider alternative strategies. Timing of delivery is crucial: if the professional worker offers this alternative perspective too early in the session, the family will not have had time to convey their concerns and they may feel that their experiences are being dismissed.

References

Evan, G., Iveson, C. and Ratner, H. (1999) *Problem to Solution: Brief Therapy with Individuals and Families*. London: BT Press.

Kendall, P.C., Chansky, T.E., Kane, M., Kim, R. *et al.* (1992) *Anxiety Disorders in Youth: Cognitive-behavioural Interventions*. Needham, MA: Allyn and Bacon.

Lewinsohn, P.M., Clarke, G.N., Hops, H. and Andrews, J. (1990) 'Cognitive-behavioural treatment for depressed adolescents.' *Behaviour Therapy 21*, 385–401.

Miller, W.R. and Rollnick, S. (1991) *Motivational Interviewing: Preparing People to Change Addictive Behaviour*. New York: Guilford Press.

NICE (2013) Antisocial behaviour and conduct disorders in children and young people: recognition and management. Clinical guideline [CG158].

Further reading

Graham, P. (1998) *Cognitive Behaviour Therapy for Children and Families*. Cambridge: Cambridge University Press.

Green, C. (2000) *Beyond Toddlerdom: Keeping Five- to Twelve-Year-Olds on the Rails*. London: Vermilion.

Hartley-Brewer, E. (1994) *Positive Parenting: Raising Children with Self-Esteem*. London: Vermilion.

Herbert, M. (2002) 'Behavioural Therapies.' In M. Rutter and E. Taylor (eds) *Child and Adolescent Psychiatry (4th Edition)*. Oxford: Blackwell Science.

Herbert, M. (1996) *Parent, Adolescent and Child Training Skill Series*. Leicester: BPS Books.

Morris, R.J. and Kratochwill, T.R. (1983) *Treating Children's Fears and Phobias: A Behavioural Approach*. New York: Pergamon Press.

Nezu, A., Nezu, C. and D'Zurilla, T. (2013) *Problem-Solving Therapy: A Treatment Manual*. New York: Springer Publishing.

Pearce, J. (1989) *Tantrums and Tempers*. Wellingborough: Thorsons.

CHAPTER 15

Specialist Treatment Approaches

Specialist services deliver interventions that are evidenced to treat the mental health disorder with which the child or adolescent presents. There are two specific treatments available, that are best described under the broad terms of psychotherapy (treatment by psychological methods) and psychopharmacology (treatment with medication).

Psychotherapeutic approaches

Range of therapies

Psychotherapies can be described in a number of ways: by the setting or who participates (individual, group, or family therapy) and by the particular mode of therapy (e.g. cognitive behaviour therapy (CBT), interpersonal psychotherapy, systemic therapy). Many modes of therapy can be delivered in more than one setting.

Therapies directed at increasing understanding, self-awareness or insight are commonly referred to as the 'talking therapies', because they largely rely on the verbal medium. However, verbal communication can be limiting, irrespective of the person's verbal ability. Thus. additional 'vehicles' for achieving this goal, such as drama, art, and music, are used increasingly across the lifespan. Together with play, drawing and story-telling, they are regularly used in therapy with young people, who are possibly more open to such interventions, or may not have the requisite verbal skills (e.g. children with learning disability). Insight-directed therapies assist young people in addressing personal issues in the context of social relationships. They can enhance understanding, but do not necessarily provide explanation. Such therapies can be used in group or family settings as well as individually.

Evaluation of therapy

Many of the changes that take place during therapy may not be 'outwardly measurable', that is they may be other than symptomatic, behavioural or functional. Evaluation of the impact of such therapies continues to be debated. Some are more readily evaluated then others. Opinions range from using traditional experimental designs to not assessing (some of) these therapies for ethical reasons or because of pragmatic difficulties in making very individual subjective measures of internal change that are not readily compared. Research on the effectiveness of therapy is particularly dogged by issues of which specific therapy benefits which person or problem, 'dosage' (i.e. frequency, intensity and duration) and choice of outcome measures (Durlak *et al.* 1995; Hendren 1993; Weisz *et al.* 1995).

CAMHS in many countries, including the UK, now routinely measure outcome by completing instruments such as the Strengths and Difficulties Questionnaire (SDQ), including parent, teacher, and self-report forms (Goodman 1997) and the Health of the Nation Outcome Scales for Children and Adolescents (HoNOSCA), which is a questionnaire completed by the clinician (Gowers *et al.* 1999). Routine Outcome Measurement (ROM) involves the completion of these instruments at regular intervals, at least twice: before and after treatment. Findings from ROM provide a sense of the effectiveness of the various interventions delivered by CAMHS and thereby help to guide service development and policy at local, regional, and national levels.

Therapies that result in a measurable change in behaviour, symptoms or functioning are referred to as evidence-based therapies. When use of evidence-based therapies (such as CBT) is compared with treatment as usual across a range of settings, then there is a moderate chance that the therapy will provide a better outcome (Weisz *et al.* 2013). There is increasing evidence of the effectiveness of therapies that had been previously difficult to evaluate: a systematic review of studies of psychodynamic psychotherapy for children and adolescents showed effectiveness of this intervention, though many of the studies are limited by their design (Midgley and Kennedy 2011).

Setting up therapy

A trained therapist should first assess a young person who is considered potentially to benefit from such therapy. The assessment will be of the young person and the context of the therapy. This should include assessing the young person's ability to make use of the therapy, identifying goals of treatment, and assessing the support available to the child by family or other support networks during therapy. It may entail a short series of assessment sessions. The young person and parents should understand the reasons for therapy (at an age-appropriate level) and what it will entail, particularly around issues of confidentiality (as discussed in Chapter 8). It is important to be sensitive to the fact that, unlike adults, a young person may not have initiated the therapy, or fully understood the reasons for it. Young people also do not have the same control over their lives as adults, and so may have limited opportunity to apply the psychological work they have done in therapy.

A plan for the delivery of therapy should then be established and agreed, with regular reviews, particularly for therapy that may span several months or more than a year, although most interventions do not need to be long term. For most therapies, the length of each session, frequency, and time in the week of a series of sessions is agreed. These are with the same therapist in the same room. This is protected time, providing a boundary between therapy and the rest of the young person's life. Parents may also be seen at regular intervals to discuss the process of the therapy and ways in which they can support the generalisation of benefits from therapy to the rest of the child's life, but not to relate the private and confidential content of therapy sessions. They should be involved in the review meetings. Shorter-term therapy may have one review on completion. The nature of follow-up, if needed, should be discussed towards the closure of therapy. These issues remain the same for therapy delivered in the group or family setting.

Cognitive behaviour therapy (CBT)

CBT is described in the previous chapter. As well as its use in the primary care, it is employed extensively in specialist services, where it may be delivered in individual (including with young children), family and group settings.

More specialist approaches using CBT include child- and family-focused cognitive behaviour therapy (the RAINBOW programme), which is effective as an adjunct to medication in bipolar disorder (West *et al.* 2014). CBT is used in specialist clinics to treat obsessive compulsive disorder in children and adolescents, along with variations including Exposure and Response Prevention (ERP), which entails physical or mental confrontation of the anxiety-inducing stimulus (Kircanski, Peris and Piacentini 2011), and Danger Ideation Reduction Therapy (DIRT), which may be less anxiety-inducing and includes attentional focusing, cognitive restructuring, corrective information provided by the therapist, double-checking experiments, and probability of catastrophe tasks (Govender, Drummond and Menzies 2006).

Schema Therapy, which is an extension of CBT, may be used in adolescent anorexia, depression, anxiety, drug and alcohol use, sex offending, and aggression. Behavioural activation is regularly used as part of a cognitive behavioural intervention. Cognitive Behavioural Analysis System of Psychotherapy and Metacognitive Therapy are further developments that may prove to have application in child and adolescent mental health.

CBT can also be delivered to young children (Ronen 1997; Stallard 2005). Trauma-focused cognitive behaviour therapy (TF-CBT) is described under the 'Trauma-focused therapies' section below. CBT is now often combined with mindfulness (see below) as 'Mindfulness-CBT'.

Mindfulness

Developing skills in mindfulness can assist children and adolescents to achieve a state of calm awareness. This can have significant benefits for people who present with mental health disorders as well as the general population. Mindfulness is achieved by focusing awareness on the present moment. Any thoughts, feelings and bodily sensations that intrude are calmly acknowledged and accepted in a non-judgemental way before returning to the focus of the exercise. Repeated practice can lead to a general increase in self-awareness outside of the practice of mindfulness exercises. Mindfulness is practised increasingly widely and has a strong evidence base to support its use in adult practice, with over a decade of research. Results from early research in children and adolescents are promising. It may be used in a range of presentations, including depression, anxiety, emotion regulation problems, risky behaviour, and ADHD (Biegel *et al.* 2009; Broderick and Jennings 2012; Burke 2010; Thompson and Gauntlett-Gilbert 2008; van der Weijer-Bergsma *et al.* 2012). These findings are supported by a meta-analysis (Kallapiran *et al.* 2015). Mindfulness-CBT may reduce anxiety, attention and behaviour problems in children (Semple *et al.* 2010).

Mindfulness can be delivered effectively in schools too (Kuyken *et al.* 2013) and mindfulness exercises are available as apps on electronic devices,[1] which are more accessible and acceptable to young people. Anyone wishing to recommend an app like this is advised to have recently checked it and be able to talk through the current version with the young person and their family. Although mindfulness is delivered in combination with CBT, it sits more closely aligned to the principles of acceptance and commitment therapy (ACT), with which it is also often used. It is one of the four core components of dialectal behaviour therapy (DBT).

'Third wave' therapies

'Third wave psychotherapies' represent a more recent generation of psychotherapies that comprise a heterogeneous group of treatments. These include mindfulness-based cognitive therapy, behavioural activation, cognitive behavioural analysis system and metacognitive therapy and schema therapy referred to above, and acceptance and commitment therapy and dialectical behaviour therapy described in the next two sections. There is empirical evidence of the effectiveness of these modern therapies (Kahl, Winter and Schweiger 2012). This wider spectrum of therapies provides a greater choice of options in tailoring treatment to the individual and what they might benefit from, particularly for presentations previously considered difficult to treat, such as borderline personality disorder, chronic depression and generalised anxiety disorder.

Acceptance and commitment therapy (ACT)

ACT (pronounced as the word 'act') uses mindfulness and acceptance strategies, together with commitment and behaviour change strategies.

---

1   For example, www.headspace.com/headspace-meditation-app.

The central themes of this therapy are the development of skills to accept what is outside of one's personal control and commit to action that improves and enriches one's life. By doing so, the client increases psychological flexibility and clarifies what behaviours they can engage in that sit with their values. Although there has been empirical research to support its use in adults, this is still very much in its infancy for children and adolescents. Some helpful parameters to assist in delivery of this therapy in this younger population have been described (Coyne, McHugh and Martinez 2011; Greco and Hayes 2008).

Dialectical behaviour therapy (DBT)

DBT was developed in the late 1980s by Linehann for treating suicidal behaviour and Borderline Personality Disorder (BPD) in adults (Linehann 1993). It is a modified form of cognitive behaviour therapy (CBT) that is manualised and comprises four skill modules: emotion regulation, mindful awareness, distress tolerance and interpersonal effectiveness. Linehann observed that people with BPD had often experienced invalidating environments leading her to conclude that a core value in the treatment needs to be the therapist's provision of unconditional acceptance and loving kindness, which together with mindfulness are drawn from Buddhist tradition. DBT is thus based on both 'Eastern' and 'Western' concepts.

Rathus and Miller (2002) developed an adolescent version, DBT-A. This comprised a 12-week programme of twice-weekly therapy, which consisted of individual therapy and a multifamily skills training group. They found significantly fewer psychiatric hospitalisations during treatment, and a significantly higher rate of treatment completion than a comparison standard treatment group. There were significant reductions in suicidal ideation, general psychiatric symptoms, and symptoms of borderline personality. Fleischhaker *et al.* (2011) conducted a pilot study with 12 adolescents, finding reduction in features of BPD and no self-harm episodes at one year follow up. Mehlum *et al.* (2014) studied its use compared with enhanced usual care in 77 adolescents with repetitive self-harm and concluded that DBT-A may be an effective intervention to reduce self-harm, suicidal ideation, and depression in adolescents with repetitive self-harming behaviour. DBT has been adapted for adolescents with various other psychiatric disorders as well as BPD, such as mood disorders, eating disorders, disruptive behaviour disorders, and trichotillomania (MacPherson, Cheavens and Fristad 2013). A pilot study suggests benefit in adolescents with bipolar disorder (Goldstein *et al.* 2015). It has also been delivered in a range of settings: outpatient, day programme, inpatient, residential and correctional facilities.

Interpersonal psychotherapy (IPT)

IPT was originally developed by Gerald Klerman and colleagues in 1969 (Markowitz and Weissman 2012). It is based on the principle that most emotional disorders, particularly depression, for which it was first developed, occur in an interpersonal context; that is, the person's mood disorder is intimately associated with their current relationships (Markowitz and Weissman 2012). IPT is used with non-psychotic patients, usually in an outpatient setting, and may be used together with other interventions such as medication. It is delivered as a brief (12–16 session), weekly therapy and has demonstrable efficacy in depression in young people (Mufson *et al.* 1999; Stark *et al.* 1999).

There are two broad goals of IPT for the individual patient: education about the depression (i.e. symptoms, effect on function, treatment and prognosis) and enhanced understanding of the depression in the interpersonal context. The latter originally included focusing on one of four common interpersonal issues associated with the onset of depression, listed here, with the addition of a fifth in young people:

- grief – other than normal bereavement

- role disputes – the patient and one or more significant others do not share the same expectations of their relationship

- role transitions – unsuccessful attempts to deal with life changes

- interpersonal deficits – poor social skills, or inadequate, non-sustaining relationships

- single-parent families – divorce and separation, death, imprisonment or prior absence of a parent.

Psychodynamic and psychoanalytic therapies

Psychodynamic and psychoanalytic therapy in young people involves using verbal and play techniques to address issues through the relationship that develops between the young person and therapist. Links are made between current and past experiences. Sigmund Freud established the current tradition of psychodynamic and psychoanalytic therapies and first described its use in a child. Many schools of psychotherapy have since developed or departed from Freudian principles to various degrees. Klein, Anna Freud, Bion, Winnicott, and Axline have largely influenced its application in young people. Early writing focused on the process and delivery of therapy.

Young people who have experienced difficulties with life events or situations that have resulted in marked distress or confusion or a mood disorder can benefit from this approach, although it is unlikely to be a first-line intervention. Identifying which young person will specifically benefit is difficult, and the use of psychodynamic therapies is often determined by provision of resources rather than factors in the young person or presenting problems. Therapy is usually delivered individually, with regular, planned sessions and reviews that involve the parents or persons responsible for caregiving.

There are dangers in the inappropriate use of psychodynamic therapies with young people in an unsettled environment (where unmitigated threats are still present, basic needs are not met, or the immediate future of the child's care is undecided), with young people who do not have the capacity to engage in the process or to withstand the potentially powerful, painful, destructive or distressing emotions that can be aroused, or where the therapist is insufficiently supervised or trained. The assessment and planning of therapy outlined above is especially important to avoid these dangers.

Play therapy

Play therapy employs the same principles as interpersonal psychotherapy or psychodynamic therapy, using play as the primary medium. Although it can be particularly useful in young children and those with limited verbal skills, this does not in itself constitute a reason to use play therapy, and young people with good verbal skills should not be excluded. In play therapy, the child is provided with toys (including human and animal figures) and art and crafts materials. These and anything created by the child are kept safely between sessions by the therapist. The purpose of play is to provide the child with a 'vocabulary' to:

- express thoughts and feelings

- explore concepts, and conscious and subconscious fantasies

- enhance understanding.

The aim of play therapy is not to provide alternative parenting, education, opportunity for creativity, guidance, didactic counselling, or a chance to 'let off steam'. The use of toys, play and drawing provides the child with an array of means of expression, which is unavailable in verbal therapy (irrespective of verbal skills). The therapist comments and interprets the child's play, making links for the child between sessions and between what he or she presents in the session and events in the rest of his or her life. The planning, delivery and cautions are the same as described in psychodynamic therapy above.

Music therapy

Music therapy is a specific example of the use of a non-verbal communication. It is increasingly used and researched in child mental health. Music therapy can be delivered individually or in the group or family setting. It involves listening to and creating music. It can provide an opportunity to enhance certain aspects of emotional, cognitive and social development (Molyneux 2005), including:

- imitation skills

- turn-taking

- vocalisations

- appropriate use of gaze and visual fixing

- mutual exchange of feeling states.

Family therapy and family-based interventions

Working with families therapeutically is seen to be a core skill for mental health professionals working with young people, as the family is the main context in which most young people live their lives. Whilst its influence reduces as the young person develops, it is unusual to have a treatment plan that does not take the family into account as a significant factor. Although most workers do not have formal family therapy training, they draw on some of the key concepts to inform their work, which is one distinction between family-based work and family therapy undertaken by professionals with specialist training.

In recent years, family therapy has moved away from the notion that it is possible to make an objective diagnosis of what might be wrong with a family and apply an intervention to 'fix it'. The emphasis now is on working collaboratively with families to develop new perspectives, which in turn can help them find new ways of being together that provide a way out of unhelpful family patterns. The family is seen as an important resource and strength. This way of working takes into account the differing perspectives held by different members of the family and also the various contexts in which the family exists, enabling issues of social inequality to be considered in the work. Family therapy differs from other psychotherapies in that its emphasis is on the individual's interactions with the outside world rather than their inner world. A recent review of family therapy research (Carr 2014) found evidence supporting its use from a number of meta-analyses, systematic literature reviews and controlled trials. Carr reported that family therapy is an effective intervention alone or in combination with other interventions for sleep, feeding and attachment problems in infancy, child abuse and neglect, conduct problems, attention deficit hyperactivity disorder, drug misuse, anxiety, depression, grief, bipolar disorder, self-harm, eating disorders (including anorexia, bulimia and obesity), somatic problems (including enuresis, encopresis, medically unexplained symptoms and poorly controlled asthma and diabetes), and first episode psychosis.

There are many different schools of family therapy, many of which have influenced each other, and they each regard the family as the key to problem resolution. Family therapy began to establish itself during the 1940s and 1950s. Systems theory (from cybernetics and engineering) has been a significant influence on family therapy and can provide an understanding of how individual functioning and symptom development influence and are influenced by homeostatic mechanisms within families. Some of the more influential approaches include:

- strategic therapy (developed by Jay Haley, Milton Erickson, and Cloe Madanes), which focuses on interactions between family members

- structural family therapy (Salvador Minuchin), with a focus on re-organising the family

- Milan systems therapy (Mara Selvini Palazzoli), which incorporates some specific techniques to explore beliefs and how they influence family function

- intergenerational family therapy (Murray Bowen), looking at patterns of behaviour across generations

- narrative therapy (Michael White), with a range of ways to assist the family members to explore their understanding of their story.

Many other therapies can be delivered in the family context, such as cognitive behavioural, solution-focused and attachment-based therapies. As with any of the other interventions outlined in this handbook, careful thought needs to be given to when family therapy is an appropriate treatment. A series of meta-analyses in the 1980s and 1990s confirmed the benefit of family therapy. Reviews of outcome studies (e.g. Carr 2000; Asen 2002) indicate that family therapy is an effective intervention in early-onset eating disorders, depression, anxiety, psychosomatic complaints, drug and alcohol misuse in adolescents and adults, psychotic illnesses, mood disorders, oppositional behaviour problems and severe conduct disorder, marital distress, and adjustment reactions, as well as some physical health issues such as childhood asthma, enuresis and soiling amongst others. Studies suggest that family therapy is often most effective when used as part of a multi-modal approach to a particular problem. There is also evidence of that treatments work better if therapists adhere to the model.

It is unhelpful to see family therapy as a panacea for 'difficult' families and advisable to have a clear aim in mind when considering family therapy. Family therapy often falls at the first hurdle when there is insufficient clarity about the purpose of the sessions; prior discussion with the family and the therapist can reduce inappropriate referrals. A family-based psychoeducational approach seeks to empower families by giving them information and helping them develop practical strategies and problem solving skills. This has been shown to be helpful across a range of difficulties, again as part of an integrated approach to a mental health problem.

Family therapy for eating disorders

An intensive community-based family therapy approach developed at the Maudsley Hospital, London (known as the Maudsley Approach) has been shown to be particularly effective and is employed internationally. Clinicians can be trained in this treatment, which is usually delivered in the home in 15–20 sessions over 12 months. It is delivered in three phases: (1) 'Weight restoration', in which parents take control of their child's diet, during which the therapist models for the parents an uncritical stance toward the adolescent; (2) 'Returning control over eating to the adolescent', which starts once the child has accepted parental control and during which the therapist assists the parents to gradually support their child in managing and maintaining a healthy approach; and (3) 'Establishing healthy adolescent identity', when the therapist supports increasing autonomy and assists the parents to focus on issues relating to adolescent development, once a safe weight has been maintained.

Multisystemic therapy

Multisystemic therapy (MST) is an intensive community- and family-based intervention (delivered in the home and community rather than a clinic) that was developed in the US in the 1970s (Henggeler 1999). MST uses an ecological model, drawing largely from family systems theory, particularly structural and strategic family therapy principles, social learning theory, crisis intervention theory, cognitive behaviour therapy, and behavioural parent training. Intervention is across all available systems in which the young person functions, such as family, school, peer group and local community. MST is based on the premise that problem behaviours arise within systems or their interface. The delivery of MST is 'manualised' and prescriptive, the purpose of which is to retain the fidelity of the therapy.

MST is a well-validated treatment model (Kazdin and Weisz 1998). It can reduce youth re-offending (reducing long-term rates of re-arrest by 25 per cent to 70 per cent), sexual re-offending, substance use and out-of-home placements (Wolpert *et al.* 2006). It can offer an alternative to hospitalisation for a sub-group of young people with suicidal and homicidal ideation and behaviour, and psychosis.

Trauma-focused therapies

Trauma-focused cognitive behaviour therapy (TF-CBT) was developed 25 years ago by Anthony Mannarino, Judith Cohen and Esther Deblinger. There have since been refinements to it and many randomised controlled trials that demonstrate its effectiveness in children who have experienced sexual abuse, domestic violence, traumatic grief, terrorism, disasters and multiple traumas (Cohen and Mannarino 2008). TF-CBT components are summarised by the acronym PRACTICE: Psychoeducation, Parenting skills, Relaxation skills, Affective modulation skills, Cognitive coping skills, Trauma narrative and cognitive processing of the traumatic event(s), In vivo mastery of trauma reminders, Conjoint child-parent sessions, and Enhancing safety and future developmental trajectory. TF-CBT can be used with very young children (aged 3–6 years) effectively (Scheering *et al.* 2010). Specific training in this approach is available.

Eye Movement Desensitisation and Reprocessing (EMDR) has proven efficacy with adults, and studies indicate that this is a promising treatment with children and adolescents with a moderate effect for post-traumatic stress disorder and some possible benefit in disruptive behaviour disorders (Rodenburg *et al.* 2009; Wolpert *et al.* 2006).

EMDR and TF-CBT are equally efficacious (Seidler and Wagner 2006). Other promising therapies include testimonial psychotherapy and narrative exposure therapy (Ehntholt and Yule 2006). Polyvagal theory (Porges 2007), which provides a biological explanation for some aspects of a trauma response (relating this to the function of the vagal nerve and autonomic nervous system), may underpin the benefits noticed to interventions such as breathing exercises, movement-based activities (e.g. yoga, chi qong, and tae kwon do) and rhythmical activities (e.g. rocking, drumming) (Porges 2011).

Medication

A successful pharmacological intervention depends on:

- a thorough assessment (including past and current history of other prescribed and non-prescribed medication as well as any allergies)

- explanation of the reason for use to the young person and parents

- explanation of how long the young person will need medication for and why

- willingness to discuss other options available

- explanation of the side-effects and how to manage them

- baseline measures and clear goals by which progress can be measured (for which it may be useful to complete rating schedules).

Baseline investigations (height, weight, blood pressure, full blood count, etc.) may be indicated for some medications. Where a drug has a cardiotoxic profile (that is, it may impact on how the heart works), an ECG (electrocardiogram, an electrical recording of heart function) may be indicated and a review of any family history of cardiovascular disease. Medication should also be prescribed as part of a package of treatment that might include interventions such as cognitive behaviour therapy or interpersonal therapy. Rarely is medication the only component of treatment in child mental health.

Before prescribing to adolescent girls, it is important to ascertain whether there is the possibility of pregnancy, as this will influence prescribing. There can be a great reluctance to use medication in child and adolescent mental health by young people and parents, and by professionals who hold the view that their efficacy has not been sufficiently tested. This is rarely applied to psychotherapeutic interventions, which are seen as a side-effect-free intervention, though this is not always the case; there are risks in subjecting young people to any treatment that is unnecessary or inappropriate.

The most commonly used medications in child and adolescent mental health are psychostimulants (such as methylphenidate), antidepressants, anxiolytics (to manage anxiety) and antipsychotics (see Table 15.1). Non-mental health doctors are more likely to prescribe medication for sleep disorders and for behavioural control than are child psychiatrists.

A note on off-licence (or off-label) prescribing

Regulatory bodies around the world provide a list of medications that are licensed for use in particular disorders, sometimes limited by age, dosage, or duration of treatment. Pharmaceutical companies are not allowed to advertise unlicensed drugs. It is however, not illegal to prescribed an unlicensed medication, although it is advisable to inform families of this. Indeed, many medications with proven effectiveness for both physical and mental health conditions in childhood or adolescence are not licensed for those conditions in this age group. Very often this is because the pharmaceutical company has not applied for a licence in that age group, and this has been a common experience for child psychiatrists and paediatricians.

Table 15.1 Summary of commonly used medications for mental health disorders in young people

Generic drug name	Indication	Comments
Psychostimulants		
Methylphenidate	ADHD	Only approved specialist should initiate treatment. Use needs careful monitoring. Comes in several different formulations – immediate release and longer lasting forms.
Dexamphetamine	ADHD	Used if methylphenidate use limited because of side-effects or not effective.
Atomoxitine	ADHD	Not usually used as a first-line intervention.
Anxiolytics – short term use only		
Clonazepam	Anxiety disorders, OCD	Best used as short-term therapy.
Buspirone	Anxiety (generalised), treatment of self-injurious or organic-induced aggression, and in some behaviours in young people with autism	Does not cause withdrawal reactions, memory or psychomotor impairment and has no demonstrable potential for abuse.

cont.

Generic drug name	Indication	Comments
Antidepressants (also used for anxiety)		
SSRIs		
Fluoxetine	Depression, bulimia, OCD	Also used in social anxiety and panic disorder.
Fluvoxamine	OCD	Licensed for use in younger children with OCD.
Paroxetine	OCD, panic disorder and social phobia	Can be more sedating than the others, which may make it more appropriate where this side-effect is desired (e.g. poor sleep); withdrawal can be a problem.
Sertraline	OCD	
Citalopram	Panic disorder	May be used as second-line treatment for depression under close specialist supervision.
SNRIs		
Venlafaxine		There is not yet sufficient evidence to warrant the routine use of SNRI medication in adolescents for depression and anxiety, though these may be considered in a specialist setting after two failed trials of SSRI medication.
Desvenlafaxine		
Duloxetine		
Tricyclic antidepressants		Not used in depression as no efficacy in children and adolescents, high risk if taken as overdose, and many unpleasant side-effects
Imipramine	Enuresis (bedwetting)	
Mood stabilisers		
Lithium carbonate	Treatment of mania, prevention of relapse of manic-depressive psychosis	Regular blood tests required.

Sodium valproate		Contraindicated in girls due to the risk of polycystic ovarian syndrome and foetal abnormalities.
Lamotrigine		Need to warn the patient and parents of risks associated with Stevens-Johnson syndrome.
Carbamazepine	Second-line treatment	Particularly effective in patients with rapid cycling bipolar affective disorder.
Antipsychotics		
Atypical antipsychotics		These have fewer side-effects than the typical antipsychotics but weight gain, sometimes associated with increased blood pressure and risk of diabetes, and other possible side-effects such as sexual dysfunction, may be problematic.
Risperidone	Treatment of psychosis, schizophrenia and disruptive behaviour in children and adolescents with autism spectrum disorder	First-line treatment, and there are studies underway to investigate early intervention with lower doses. Minimal side-effects at maintenance doses. Particularly useful in those who are resistant to treatment by other antipsychotics or who have tardive dyskinesia. However, with a 1% risk of causing leucopoenia (decrease in white blood cells), people on clozapine need regular full blood counts.
Quetiapine	Treatment of psychosis, schizophrenia	High rates of efficacy and a low side-effect profile.
Olanzapine	Treatment of psychosis, schizophrenia	High rates of efficacy and a low side-effect profile, except weight gain.
Clozapine	Treatment-resistant schizophrenia, i.e. two failed trials of other antipsychotic medication	

cont.

Generic drug name	Indication	Comments
Typical antipsychotics		
Chlorpromazine	Treatment of psychosis	Considerably cheaper than the atypical antipsychotics. Marked sedating effect so can be useful with violent patients. Can be given orally or by intramuscular injection. In young people it can have marked extrapyramidal side-effects. Neuroleptic malignant syndrome is a rare but potentially fatal side-effect.
Haloperidol	Treatment of psychosis, schizophrenia	As for chloromazine but more likely to cause extrapyramidal side-effects. Only available as an injection. Not recommended for use in children.

Medication for sleep

There is little, if any, justification to use medications to sedate children. Medication for sleep disorders is usually not helpful in the long term, although it may have a specific short-term role in preventing exacerbation of an acute situation by providing brief respite. An antihistamine such as trimeprazine (Vallergan) or promethazine (Phergan) is commonly used for its side-effect of drowsiness. Alternatively, melatonin can be used, or an antidepressant or antipsychotic medication for their sedating effects.

Psychostimulants

The most commonly used psychostimulants are methylphenidate and dexamphetamine, which are amphetamines. These are usually the drug treatment of choice for ADHD with a strong evidence base for their use. Methylphenidate is available in a few preparations: short-acting (e.g. Ritalin), i.e. 2–4 hours; long-acting (Ritalin LA), i.e. 3–8 hours; and extended release (Concerta), i.e. 8–12 hours. Dexamphetime is now also available in a long acting preparation as its precursor, lisdexamfetamine (Vyvanse).

Stimulant medication increases frontal lobe function, with effects on vigilance, concentration and motor control in children. It is usually inappropriate to use it without other treatments to manage all aspects of ADHD. Methylphenidate is effective in 70 per cent of cases of ADHD. It can have significant side-effects, so its use needs to be carefully monitored. These include insomnia, decreased appetite (which might be associated with weight loss or failure to grow), mood changes, gastrointestinal symptoms, convulsions and cardiac symptoms. Medication-free periods should be considered at intervals over the child's life to determine whether it is still needed, although the need for so-called 'drug holidays' (i.e. breaks from treatment) has been questioned. Height and weight should be monitored, as there is a small risk of growth retardation, and a full blood count taken every six months to a year. Atomoxetine (Strattera) is now also available and may be effective where methylphenidate has been less useful. It tends to be given as a once-only dose, and is not a controlled drug so may be appropriate for some families.

Antidepressants

This is the most commonly used type of medication in adolescents. There are several types of antidepressant and the most commonly used are the selective serotonin reuptake inhibitors (SSRIs), such as fluoxetine. There was concern that the use of antidepressant medications themselves may induce suicidal behaviour in youths. Following a thorough and comprehensive review of all the available published and unpublished controlled clinical trials of antidepressants in children and adolescents, the US Food and Drug Administration (FDA) issued a public warning in October 2004 about an increased risk of suicidal thoughts or behaviour (suicidality) in children and adolescents treated with SSRI antidepressant medications. Similar action followed in the UK and only fluoxetine is licensed for use as an antidepressant for young people under the age of 16 years. The other SSRIs remain licensed for other conditions, but may only be used off licence for depression. Prescribing of antidepressants reduced internationally in the decade following these warnings, with evidence of a subsequent rise in completed suicides, presumably resulting from untreated depression. However, antidepressants are usually best prescribed by child psychiatrists or after discussion with a child psychiatrist, as depression severe enough to warrant their use should probably be managed by a specialist CAMHS. In psychotic depression, the psychosis should also be treated.

The efficacy of antidepressants in young people is debatable and certainly cognitive behaviour therapy, individual counselling or family work are usually essential components of overall management. One major clinical trial (Treatment for Adolescents with Depression Study Team 2004) has indicated that a combination of medication and psychotherapy is the most effective treatment for adolescents with depression. The clinical trial of 439 adolescents aged 12 to 17 with moderate depressive disorder compared four treatment groups – one that received a combination of fluoxetine and CBT, one that received fluoxetine only, one that received CBT only, and one that received a placebo only. After the first 12 weeks, 71 per cent responded to the combination treatment of fluoxetine and CBT, 61 per cent responded to the fluoxetine only treatment, 43 per cent responded to the CBT only treatment, and 35 per cent responded to the placebo treatment. It is worth noting that a comprehensive review of paediatric trials conducted between 1988 and 2006 suggested that the benefits of antidepressant medications likely outweigh their risks to children and adolescents with major depression and anxiety disorders (Bridge *et al.* 2007). SSRIs differ in their side-effect profiles and can affect individuals in different ways, so finding the right medication for an individual can be a case of trial and error. Some SSRIs can cause sleep disturbance and should therefore be taken in the morning. Progress needs regular review, especially if side-effects have been problematic. There may be benefits to maintaining treatment after remission of symptoms as a prophylaxis against relapse. A family history and the frequency of episodes guide the use of the maintenance phase, which is usually 6–12 months duration from the time of remission. In practice, many adolescents discontinue treatment before then. Antidepressants should be tailed off gradually over 1–3 weeks, depending on the dose reached.

SNRI (serotonin and noradrenalin reuptake inhibitor) medication has become available over the last two decades, though current research findings do not support their use in children and adolescents. However, SNRI medication may be considered for some adolescents who have not responded to at least two trials of SSRI medication.

Use of tricyclic antidepressants is not justified, given their lack of efficacy, problematic side-effect profile, and toxicity in overdose, although low-dose imipramine may be used as part of the management of enuresis (for its anticholinergic side-effect). St John's Wort is marketed as a herbal remedy and is available without prescription. However, its side-effect profile is similar to that of the older antidepressants and therefore needs monitoring in the same way as other medications. Its use is strictly contraindicated when antidepressants are prescribed and families should be made aware of this.

Anxiolytics (anti-anxiety medication, aka minor tranquillisers)

SSRI medication can also be useful in obsessive compulsive disorder, social phobia and panic disorder. They are the first-line choice if medication is to be used.

Buspirone has been shown to be an effective anxiolytic and has potential as an antidepressant; it may also be useful in the treatment of self-injurious or organic-induced aggression and in some behaviours in young people with autism. It does not cause withdrawal reactions, memory or psychomotor impairment and has no demonstrable potential for abuse.

Benzodiazepines (e.g. diazepam, lorazepam, clonazepam) are highly effective anxiolytic agents with a relatively rapid onset of effect. The particular characteristics of clonazepam make it a reasonable first choice. However, if using any benzodiazepines, there is a need to be aware of their side-effects, especially in children. These include sedation and behavioural disinhibition, but if they are used in the short term (that is, for a few days only) there should be few withdrawal problems. Longer-term use, sometimes more than a few days, can be associated with dependence.

Mood stabilisers

These are used to control mania and prevent recurrences of mania and depression in bipolar affective disorder. The most commonly used medication is lithium carbonate. Blood levels have to be carefully and regularly monitored to ensure they are therapeutic but not so high as to cause potentially life-threatening toxic effects. Sodium valproate, lamotrigine, and carbamazepine may be used when lithium cannot, or sometimes as first-line treatment. Some antipsychotic medication can also be used as mood stabilisers in the maintenance phases of bipolar disorder as well as anti-manic agents in acute mania.

Antipsychotics (also known as neuroleptics or major tranquillisers)

Antipsychotics are used to manage acute psychosis and schizophrenia and also have mood stabilising qualities. There is a range of new atypical antipsychotics with fewer side-effects than previous (typical) antipsychotics. Atypical antipsychotics are thought to improve cognitive symptoms as well as social withdrawal and include risperidone, clozapine, olanzapine and quetiapine as well as third-generation antipsychotics, such as aripiprazole. Whilst they have fewer side-effects, these can still be significant, and include weight gain and sexual dysfunction.

Typical antipsychotics are still widely used, as they are much cheaper than the atypical group. However, as young people are particularly susceptible to the extrapyramidal side-effects (see below) of the typical group, the atypical ones are preferred. The typical ones are more likely to have been licensed for use in young people. They have a rapid effect on the symptoms of acute psychosis, such as hallucinations and delusions. Typical antipsychotics include chlorpromazine, haloperidol and fluphenazine. They come in preparations suitable for daily doses or in injectable forms for depot administration (giving a steady release over several weeks).

Neuroleptic malignant syndrome is a rare but potentially fatal side-effect of antipsychotics, presenting with restlessness, muscular rigidity, pyrexia (fever), and autonomic nervous system changes (raised blood pressure, rapid pulse and breathing, sweating). This needs urgent treatment. Side-effects of typical antipsychotics include:

- extrapyramidal symptoms
  - akinesia (slowed movement)
  - akathasia (restlessness of limbs)
  - tardive dyskinesia (permanent movement disorder)
  - dystonia (spasms and stiffness of joints)
  - Parkinsonian-type signs including tremors, shuffling gait, difficulty swallowing and lack of facial expression (mask-like face)
- anticholinergic side-effects (can be very uncomfortable)
  - dry mouth

- — blurred vision

- — constipation

- — nausea

- cardiovascular

  - — hypotension (low blood pressure)

  - — fainting

  - — dizziness

- others

  - — decrease in white cell count

  - — various rashes

  - — increased sensitivity to sun, and therefore increased risk of sunburn

  - — endocrine (hormonal) side-effects, such as weight gain, gynaecomastia (breast enlargement, which may be particularly embarrassing for adolescent boys).

The use of other psychotropics (drugs that affect the brain) should be limited to specialists in specific situations.

'Third generation' antipsychotic medications are becoming available, heralded by aripiprazole, which have interesting differences in the mechanism of action in that they might, in some neural circuitry, be partially agonistic, and in others antagonistic at particular receptors. This may explain their improved side-effect profile and research on their effectiveness is very promising.

Electroconvulsive therapy and other physical treatments

Electroconvulsive therapy is very rarely used in the UK for young people under the age of 16. It is a very specialist treatment and should not be carried out without a thorough exploration of all relevant issues. There can be exceptional clinical circumstances, such as marked dehydration as a medical complication of psychomotor retardation in severe depression, and catatonia (a stupor rarely found in schizophrenia) when ECT may be the treatment of choice.

Early evidence of the benefits of repetitive Transcranial Magnetic Stimulation (rTMS) have been demonstrated in adolescent depression (Loo, McFarquhar and Watter 2006), though there is more research needed before this can be considered as part of a treatment protocol.

Residential programmes

Following the acute management of a psychotic illness or withdrawal from substance use, the young person may benefit from a residential inpatient programme, such as a therapeutic community. This enables them to access appropriate counselling, self-help groups and/or family therapy in a more structured, stable, consistent and perhaps also more emotionally safe environment. They may also need help integrating back into school and their local community as they may have lost contact either through their illness or through admission to a residential unit. Long-term admissions to residential facilities may be disadvantageous as the young person may lose opportunities to engage in the usual activities of adolescence at the same time as their peers. However, admission may be an opportunity to begin therapeutic work that can continue in an outpatient setting.

References

Asen, E. (2002) 'Outcome research in family therapy.' *Advances in Psychiatric Treatment 8*, 3, 230-238.

Biegel, G.M., Brown, K.W., Shapiro, S.L. and Schubert, C.M. (2009) 'Mindfulness-based stress reduction for the treatment of adolescent psychiatric outpatients: A randomized clinical trial.' *Journal of Consulting and Clinical Psychology 77*, 5, 855–866.

Bridge, J.A., Iyengar, S., Salary, C.B., Barbe, R.P. *et al.* (2007) 'Clinical response and risk for reported suicidal ideation and suicide attempts in pediatric antidepressant treatment: A meta-analysis of randomized controlled trials.' *Journal of the American Medical Association 2007*, 297, 1683–1696.

Broderick, P.C. and Jennings, P.A. (2012) 'Mindfulness for adolescents: A promising approach to supporting emotion regulation and preventing risky behavior.' *New Directions for Student Leadership 136*, 111–126.

Burke, C.A. (2010) 'Mindfulness-based approaches with children and adolescents: A preliminary review of current research in an emergent field.' *Journal of Child and Family Studies 19*, 133–144.

Carr, A. (ed.) (2000) *What Works with Children and Adolescents*. London: Routledge.

Carr, A. (2014) 'The evidence base for family therapy and systemic interventions for child-focused problems.' *Journal of Family Therapy 36*, 107–157.

Cohen, J.A. and Mannarino, A.P. (2008) 'Trauma-Focused Cognitive Behavioural Therapy for children and parents.' *Child and Adolescent Mental Health 13*, 4, 158–162.

Coyne, L.W., McHugh, L., and Martinez, E.R. (2011) 'Acceptance and Commitment Therapy (ACT): Advances and applications with children, adolescents, and families.' *Child and Adolescent Psychiatric Clinics of North America 20*, 2, 379–399.

Durlak, J.A., Wells, A.M., Cotton, J.K. and Johnson, S. (1995) 'Analysis of selected methodological issues in child psychotherapy research.' *Journal of Clinical Child Psychology 24*, 2, 141–148.

Ehntholt, K.A. and Yule, W. (2006) 'Practitioner review: Assessment and treatment of refugee children and adolescents who have experienced war-related trauma.' *Journal of Child Psychology and Psychiatry 47*, 12, 1197–1210.

Fleischhaker, C., Böhme, R., Sixt, B., Brück, C., Schneider, C. and Schulz, E. (2011) 'Dialectical Behavioral Therapy for Adolescents (DBT-A): A clinical trial for patients with suicidal and self-injurious behavior and borderline symptoms with a one-year follow-up.' *Child and Adolescent Psychiatry and Mental Health 5*, 3.

Goldstein, T.R., Fersch-Podrat, R.K., Rivera, M, Axelson, D.A. *et al.* (2015) 'Dialectical Behavior Therapy for adolescents with bipolar disorder: Results from a pilot randomized trial.' *Journal of Child and Adolescent Psychopharmacology 25*, 2, 140–149.

Goodman, R. (1997) 'The Strengths and Difficulties Questionnaire: A research note.' *Journal of Child Psychology and Psychiatry 38*, 581–586.

Govender, S., Drummond, L.M. and Menzies, R.G. (2006) 'Danger Ideation Reduction Therapy for the treatment of severe, chronic and resistant obsessive compulsive disorder.' *Behavioural and Cognitive Psychotherapy 34*, 4, 477–480.

Gowers, S.G., Harrington, R.C., Whitton, A., Lelliott, P. *et al.* (1999) 'Brief scale for measuring the outcomes of emotional and behavioural disorders in children: Health of the Nation Outcome Scales for Children and Adolescents (HoNOSCA).' *British Journal of Psychiatry 174*, 413–416.

Greco, L.A. and Hayes S.C. (eds) (2008) *Acceptance and Mindfulness Treatments for Children and Adolescents: A Practitioner's Guide.* Oakland, CA: New Harbinger.

Hendren, R.L. (1993) 'Adolescent psychotherapy research: A practical review.' *American Journal of Psychotherapy 47*, 3, 334–343.

Henggeler, S.W. (1999) 'Multisystemic therapy: An overview of clinical procedures, outcomes, and policy implications.' *Child Psychology and Psychiatry Review 4*, 1, 2–10.

Kahl, K.G., Winter, L. and Schweiger, U. (2012) 'The third wave of cognitive behavioural therapies: what is new and what is effective?' *Current Opinion in Psychiatry 25*, 6, 522–528.

Kallapiran, K., Koo, S., Kirubakaran, R. and Hancock, K. (2015) 'Effectiveness of mindfulness in improving mental health symptoms of children and adolescents: a meta-analysis.' *Child and Adolescent Mental Health 20*, 4, 182–194.

Kazdin, A.E. and Weisz, J.R. (1998) 'Identifying and developing empirically supported child and adolescent treatments.' *Journal of Consulting and Clinical Psychology 66*, 1, 19–36.

Kircanski, K., Peris, T.S. and Piacentini, J.C. (2011) 'Cognitive-Behavioral Therapy for obsessive compulsive disorder in children and adolescents.' *Child and Adolescent Psychiatric Clinics of North America 20*, 2, 239–254.

Kuyken, W., Weare, K., Ukoumunne, O.C., Vicary, R. *et al.* (2013) 'Effectiveness of the Mindfulness in Schools Programme: non-randomised controlled feasibility study.' *British Journal of Psychiatry 203*, 2, 126–131.

Linehan, M. (1993) *Cognitive-Behavior Therapy for Borderline Personality Disorder.* New York: Guilford Press.

Loo, C., McFarquhar, T. and Walter, G. (2006) 'Transcranial magnetic stimulation in adolescent depression.' *Australasian Psychiatry 14*, 1, 81–85.

MacPherson, H.A., Cheavens, J.S., and Fristad, M.A. (2013) 'Dialectical Behavior Therapy for adolescents: Theory, treatment adaptations, and empirical outcomes.' *Clinical Child and Family Psychology Review 16*, 1, 59–80.

Markowitz, J.C. and Weissman, M.M. (2012) 'Interpersonal Psychotherapy: Past, present and future.' *Clinical Psychology and Psychotherapy 19*, 2, 99–105.

Mehlum, L., Tormoen, A.J., Ramberg, M., Haga, E. *et al.* (2014) 'Dialectical Behavior Therapy for adolescents with repeated suicidal and self-harming behavior: A randomized trial.' *Journal of the American Academy of Child and Adolescent Psychiatry 53*, 10, 1082–1091.

Midgley N. and Kennedy E. (2011) 'Psychodynamic psychotherapy for children and adolescents: A critical review of the evidence base.' *Journal of Child Psychotherapy 37*, 3, 232–260.

Molyneux, C. (2005) 'Music therapy as a short-term intervention with individuals and families in a Child and Adolescent Mental Health Service.' *British Journal of Music Therapy 19*, 2, 59–66.

Mufson, L., Weissman, M.M., Moreau, D. and Garfinkel, R. (1999) 'Efficacy of interpersonal psychotherapy for depressed adolescents.' *Archives of General Psychiatry 56*, 6, 573–579.

Porges, S.W. (2007) 'The polyvagal perspective.' *Biological Psychology 74*, 116–143.

Porges, S.W. (2011) *The Polyvagal Theory: Neurophysiological Foundations of Emotions, Attachment, Communication, and Self-Regulation.* New York: W.W. Norton.

Rathus, J.H. and Miller, A.L. (2002) 'Dialectical Behavior Therapy adapted for suicidal adolescents.' *Suicide and Life-Threatening Behaviour 32*, 2, 146–157.

Rodenburg, R., Benjamin, A., de Roos, C., Meijer, A.M. and Stams, G.J. (2009) 'Efficacy of EMDR in children: A meta-analysis.' *Clinical Psychology Review 29*, 7, 599–606.

Ronen, T. (1997) *Cognitive Developmental Therapy with Children.* Chichester: John Wiley and Sons.

Scheering, M.S., Weems, C.F., Cohen, J.A., Amaya-Jackson, L. and Guthrie, D. (2010) 'Trauma-focused cognitive behavioral therapy for post-traumatic stress disorder in three through six-year-old children: A randomized clinical trial.' *Journal of Child Psychology and Psychiatry 52*, 8, 853–860.

Seidler, G.H. and Wagner, F.E. (2006) 'Comparing the efficacy of EMDR and trauma-focused cognitive-behavioral therapy in the treatment of PTSD: A meta-analytic study.' *Psychological Medicine 36*, 11, 1515–1522.

Semple, R.J., Lee, J., Rosa, D. and Miller, L.F. (2010) 'A randomized trial of mindfulness-based cognitive therapy for children: Promoting mindful attention to enhance social-emotional resiliency in children.' *Journal of Child and Family Studies 19*, 2, 218–229.

Stark, K.D., Laurent, J., Livingston, R., Boswell, J. and Swearer, S. (1999) 'Implications of research for the treatment of depressive disorders during childhood.' *Applied and Preventive Psychology 8*, 2, 79–102.

Stallard, P. (2005) 'Cognitive Behaviour Therapy with Prepubertal Children.' In P. Graham (ed.) *Cognitive Behavior Therapy for Children and Families (2nd edition).* Cambridge: Cambridge University Press.

Thompson, M. and Gauntlett-Gilbert, J. (2008) 'Mindfulness with children and adolescents: Effective clinical application.' *Clinical Child Psychology and Psychiatry 13*, 3, 395–407.

Treatment for Adolescents with Depression Study (TADS) Team (2004) 'Fluoxetine, cognitive-behavioral therapy, and their combination for adolescents with depression: Treatment for Adolescents with Depression Study (TADS) randomized controlled trial.' *Journal of the American Medical Association 292*, 7, 807–820.

van de Weijer-Bergsma, E., Formsma, A.R., de Bruin, E.I. and Bögels, S.M. (2012) 'The effectiveness of mindfulness training on behavioral problems and attentional functioning in adolescents with ADHD.' *Journal of Child and Family Studies 21*, 5, 775–787.

Weisz, J.R., Weiss, B., Han, S.S., Granger, D.A. *et al.* (1995) 'Effects of psychotherapy with children and adolescents revisited: A meta-analysis of treatment outcome studies.' *Psychological Bulletin 117*, 3, 450–468.

Weisz, J.R., Kuppens, S., Eckshtain, D., Ugueto, A.M., Hawley, K.M., Jensen-Doss, A. (2013) 'Performance of evidence-based youth psychotherapies compared with usual clinical care: a multilevel meta-analysis.' *Journal of the American Medical Association Psychiatry 70*, 7, 750–761.

West, A.E., Weinstein, S.M., Peters, A.T., Katz, A.C. *et al.* (2014) 'Clinical guidance supplemental material child- and family-focused cognitive-behavioral therapy for pediatric bipolar disorder: A randomized clinical trial.' *Journal of the American Academy of Child and Adolescent Psychiatry 53*, 11, 1168–1178.

Wolpert, M., Fuggle, P., Cottrell, D., Fonagy, P. *et al.* (2006) *Drawing on the Evidence: Advice for Mental Health Professionals Working with Children and Adolescents.* UK: CAMHS Publications.

Further reading

Brent, D.A., Gaynor, S.T. and Weersin V.R. (2002) 'Cognitive-behavioural Approaches to the Treatment of Depression and Anxiety.' In M. Rutter and E. Taylor (eds) *Child and Adolescent Psychiatry (4th edition)*. Oxford: Blackwell Science

Buchanan, A. (1999) *What Works for Troubled Children? Family Support for Children with Emotional and Behavioural Problems.* London: Barnardo's.

Bunt, L. (1994) *Music Therapy: An Art Beyond Words.* London: Routledge.

Burnham, J. (1996) *Family Therapy: First Steps towards a Systematic Approach.* London: Routledge.

Copley, B. and Forryan, B. (1997) *Therapeutic Work with Children and Young People.* London: Continuum International.

Graham, P. (2005) *Cognitive Behavior Therapy for Chilren and Families (2nd edition).* Cambridge: Cambridge Univeristy Press.

Herbert, M. (2002) 'Behavioural Therapies.' In M. Rutter and E. Taylor (eds) *Child and Adolescent Psychiatry (4th edition)*. Oxford: Blackwell Science.

Hobday, A. and Ollier, K. (1998) *Creative Therapy: Activities with Children and Adolescents.* Leicester: BPS Books.

Jacobs, B.W. (2002) 'Individual and Group Therapy.' In M. Rutter and E. Taylor (eds) *Child and Adolescent Psychiatry (4th edition)*. Oxford: Blackwell Science.

Jones, E. (1993) *Family Systems Therapy: Developments in the Milan Sytemic Therapies.* Chichester: Wiley.

Lane, D.A. and Miller, A. (1992) *Child and Adolescent Therapy: A Handbook.* Buckingham: Open University Press.

Martin, A., Scahill, L., Charney, D.S. and Leckman, J.F. (2003) *Pediatric Psychopharmacology: Principles and Practice.* Oxford: Oxford University Press.

Ronen, T. (1997) *Cognitive Developmental Therapy with Children.* Chichester: Wiley.

Sunderland, M. and Engleheart, P. (1993) *Draw on Your Emotions.* Bicester: Winslow Press.

Vostanis, P. (2007) *Mental Health Interventions and Services for Vulnerable Children and Young People.* London: Jessica Kingsley Publishers.

Vostanis, P. (2014) *Helping Children and Young People Who Experience Trauma.* London: Radcliffe.

CHAPTER 16

Promotion and Prevention of Child Mental Health

Child mental health promotion and prevention are important because child mental health problems are common and many adult disorders have their origins in childhood risk factors. Promotion and prevention are often used interchangeably although may have very different agendas and methods of delivery. There is some evidence that promotion of mental health in childhood can have a positive impact at both the individual and community level. In this chapter we will briefly outline the terminology before exploring how children understand mental health, and the evidence to support mental health promotion.

The World Health Organization (WHO) (2016) defines mental health promotion as actions to create living conditions and environments that support mental health and allow people to adopt and maintain healthy lifestyles. These include a range of actions to increase the chances of more people experiencing better mental health.

An environment that respects and protects basic civil, political, socio-economic and cultural rights is fundamental to mental health promotion. Without the security and freedom provided by these rights, it is very difficult to maintain a high level of mental health.

They argue that national mental health policies should not be solely concerned with mental disorders, but should also recognise and address the broader issues that promote mental health. These include mainstreaming mental health promotion into policies and programmes in governmental and nongovernmental sectors. In addition to the health sector, it is essential to involve the education, labour, justice, transport, environment, housing and welfare sectors as well. There are human and economic arguments (such as better educational attainments, employability and so on) for supporting mental health promotion, which in itself is a complex process because promoting mental health depends largely on intersectoral strategies. Specific ways to promote mental health include:

- early childhood interventions (e.g. home visits for pregnant women, preschool psychosocial activities, combined nutritional and psychosocial help for disadvantaged populations)

- support for children (e.g. skills-building programmes, child and youth development programmes)

- socio-economic empowerment of women (e.g. improving access to education and microcredit schemes)

- social support for elderly populations (e.g. befriending initiatives, community and day centres for the aged)

- programmes targeted at vulnerable groups, including minorities, indigenous people, migrants and people affected by conflicts and disasters (e.g. psychosocial interventions after disasters)

- mental health promotional activities in schools (e.g. programmes supporting ecological changes in schools and ensuring child-friendly schools)

- mental health interventions at work (e.g. stress prevention programmes)

- housing policies (e.g. housing improvement)

- violence prevention programmes (e.g. reducing availability of alcohol and access to arms)

- community development programmes (e.g. integrated rural development; community asset-building)

- poverty reduction and social protection for the poor

- anti-discrimination laws and campaigns

- promotion of the rights, opportunities and care of individuals with mental disorders.

For the purposes of this book, we will focus on support offered to children through schools, given that education is a universal service.

Mental health is often not included as part of general health promotion, though it is imperative to view this as an integral part of health.

Mental health prevention

The WHO report (2016) states that mental ill health prevention aims at 'reducing incidence, prevalence, recurrence of mental disorders, and the time spent with symptoms, or the risk condition for a mental illness, preventing or delaying recurrences and also decreasing the impact of illness in the affected person, their families and the society'. It can be helpful to view prevention as targeting specific at-risk groups to prevent them from developing mental illness and reducing its impact, and promotion being aimed at promoting good mental health and strategies that support this. The focus of this chapter, given the target audience of this book, will be on mental health promotion.

How young people understand mental health

Research has indicated that many young people worldwide are not well informed about mental health (Dogra et al. 2012; Pinfold et al. 2003; Ronzoni et al. 2010; Rose et al. 2007; Sessa 2005; Stengård and Appelqvist-Schmidlechner 2010). As young people spend a significant amount of their lives in school, school-based interventions are therefore an important factor to consider regarding the promotion of mental health. Schools can have a positive impact and mitigate some of the negative impacts of other social factors. However, for some young people they can also be a considerable source of stress, worry and unhappiness (Dogra 2010). These emotions can in turn facilitate or hamper young people's learning.

In the UK, Ofsted (2013), which is responsible for monitoring quality in schools, reports that young people are interested in learning about emotional health. Of the existing school-based interventions, however, the emphasis tends to be on trying to increase mental health awareness to reduce stigmatisation (Mellor 2014), or to tackle existing problems (Tennant et al. 2007). In order to increase engagement and better understand students' needs it is also necessary to examine how young people actually understand mental health and what being mentally healthy means.

Singletary and colleagues (2015) evaluated an intervention designed to improve young people's understanding of good mental health as a key aspect of well-being and explores their perceptions of health and well-being. Two hundred and eighteen 13-year-olds participated in an interactive workshop about healthy eating, physical activity and mental health. Young people's understanding and perceptions were assessed through anonymous questionnaires at the start and end of the workshop. Common themes were identified and differences pre- and post-workshop and between girls and boys were analysed. Nearly all young people (100% before, 97% after) perceived being healthy to mean being physically healthy. A minority (8%) also considered mental health to be a component of general health, which increased to 12 per cent after the workshop. Understanding of mental health broadened after the workshop. Interestingly many mentioned physical health when asked to describe mental health, both before and after the workshop. Girls' and boys' responses were similar, except more girls included social relationships in their descriptions of mental health. Such information is useful as it can help us understand that part of promoting mental health needs to be about exploring the very concept of mental health and what it means to children. The study also shows that students' understanding of mental health and its importance to well-being can be improved through short interventions which link physical and mental health.

A recent report commissioned by Public Health England (2015) looked at various schools' practices in relation to young people's emotional health, and made key recommendations for improvements. These included listening to students' voices, developing curriculum activities with targeted support, and fostering respect for diversity. It is therefore important to consider students' own perceptions of mental health without a predefined agenda (see Spencer 2013), as well as acknowledging their different needs.

Bone and colleagues (2015) sought to understand how young people define mental health for themselves, as well as how they prefer to learn about it. A study-specific self-administered questionnaire was used at two English schools (n=980; ages 11–18), incorporating a combination of open-ended and fixed-choice statements (Bone *et al.* 2015). Overall, students understood mental health in terms of personal attributes or disorder, although older students were more likely to talk about relationships. Males were less likely than females to say they wanted to learn about mental health, believing they had no need to learn more. White students were also less interested in learning about mental health than Indian students. Overall, students said they would not use social media to learn; however, students of Indian ethnicity were most likely to want to use it. Younger students preferred school-based to online learning. Policymakers should consider targeted mental health interventions in schools and research the potential roles/barriers of the internet and social media. Long-term possible benefits relate to improved preventative strategies within schools. These findings were consistent with earlier work, which found that children in a workshop setting offered a range of ideas of what being mentally healthy meant (Svirydzenka, Bone and Dogra 2014).

It is interesting that brief training workshops appear able to produce small but positive changes in the mental health knowledge of children across different contexts as reported by Bella-Awusah and colleagues (2014). There are limited studies focusing on young people's perspectives of mental illness from non-Western contexts. Bella-Awusah et al. (2014) assessed the impact of a school-based mental health awareness programme aimed at increasing mental health literacy and reducing negative views about persons with mental illness. A total of 154 secondary school students in Ibadan, southwest Nigeria, were allocated into an intervention and a control group. Students in the intervention group received a three-hour mental health awareness session. All students completed a pre-, immediate post-, and six-month post-intervention questionnaire on their views about mental health and illness. There was a significant difference in the mean knowledge scores between the intervention and the control group post-intervention, but no significant differences in attitude and social distance scores. This led the authors to conclude that brief training workshops appear able to produce small but positive changes in the mental health knowledge of young Nigerians. These findings provide useful data for planning appropriate mental health educational programmes for young people across different contexts.

Mental health promotion and prevention in schools

Weist and Murray (2008) define school mental health promotion as:

> Providing a full continuum of mental health promotion programs and services in schools, including enhancing environments, broadly training and promoting social and emotional learning and life skills, preventing emotional and behavioural problems, identifying and intervening in these problems early on, and providing intervention for established problems. School mental health promotion programs should be available to all students, including those in general and special education, in diverse educational settings, and should reflect a shared agenda – with families and young people, school and community partners actively involved in building, continuously improving, and expanding them. (p.3)

Weist and Murray (2008) argue that quality is a key issue and that in developing mental health promotion in schools many factors, including the following, need to be taken into account:

- an inclusive approach that anticipates and sets to actively overcome barriers to promotion and intervention

- building programs that engage all stakeholders in all aspects of programme development, improvement and growth and utilise their strengths

- identifying and dealing with barriers to student learning through evidence-based student and family-friendly interventions

- building in and resourcing for systematic quality assessment and improvement and continuous evaluation

- ensuring the full promotion to intervention continuum (this may depend on resources and context)

- ensuring the staff engaged in this are the right staff and are appropriately supported with opportunities for further development

- ensuring that all efforts take into account the full range of developmental and diversity factors of students

- building interdisciplinary relationships in schools, and strong teams with clear coordination and consistency

- building strong connections and partnerships between different schools and programmes across the community.

Weist and Murray (2008) observe that if change is to happen, there needs to be a cultural shift along with training which is consistent with the definition from WHO discussed above.

The authors highlight the need to develop partnerships to support meaningful engagement and there is evidence to support this (Svirydzenka *et al.* 2016). The challenges discussed include engaging the whole school and having adequate support (in terms of willingness, but also funding), the terminology and language used (this would also need to take into consideration how mental health and illness are conceptualised), having appropriately trained staff to provide support and supervision, and engaging young people in the development of promotion. There is little said about who the partnerships should involve, but it would seem appropriate to engage with the wider community and include families as well as young people and their teachers.

The advantage of school-based programmes is that they can be particularly beneficial for children who come from disadvantaged home backgrounds or neighbourhoods. Often for such children, school is a significant protective factor.

The challenges are that most of the school-based interventions reported tend to be short-term with little long-term follow-up. They are also often evaluated immediately after the intervention. However, there is increasing evidence that some longer-term effects are emerging and that, although effects gradually decrease over time, they can still remain significant (Weare and Nind 2011).

In their systematic review, Weare and Nind (2011) identified that the characteristics of high quality programmes that were successfully implemented include:

- a sound theoretical base with specific, well defined goals that were communicated effectively

- focus on the desired outcomes

- explicit guidelines and thorough training, which is quality assured

- complete and accurate implementation.

This is consistent with high quality training interventions in any field (as outlined in Chapter 17). Weare and Nind (2011) argue that much of the evidence related to mental health work in schools would support that this is beneficial although the benefits may be small and not sustained. They also argue that even change that is small in statistical terms may translate into a significant impact on children's well-being. Although some whole-school approaches related to child mental health promotion have found fewer advantages than others, sometimes this is attributed to a lack of consistent, rigorous and faithful implementation of the programme, and it may be that the promotion is set apart so a whole-school approach is not applied. The challenge may also be how to engage the learners (that is the young people themselves) in the development and delivery of mental health promotion unless a whole-school approach is used.

References

Bella-Awusah, T., Adedokun, B., Dogra, N. and Omigbodun, O. (2014) 'The impact of a mental health teaching programme on rural and urban secondary school students' perceptions of mental illness in southwest Nigeria.' *Journal of Child and Adolescent Mental Health 26*, 3, 207–215.

Bone, C., Dugard, P., Vostanis, P. and Dogra, N. (2015) 'Students' understandings of mental health and their preferred learning platforms.' *Journal of Public Mental Health 14*, 4, 185–195.

Dogra, N. (2010) 'Social Determinants of Mental Health Disorders in Childhood.' In D. Bhugra D and C. Morgan (eds) *Principles of Social Psychiatry (2nd edition).* Oxford: Wiley-Blackwell.

Dogra, N., Omigbodun, O., Adedokun, T., Bella, T., Ronzoni, P. and Adesokan, A. (2012) 'Nigerian secondary school children's knowledge of and attitudes to mental health and illness.' *Clinical Child Psychology and Psychiatry 17*, 3, 336–353.

Mellor, C. (2014) 'School-based interventions targeting stigma of mental illness: Systematic review.' *The Psychiatrist 3*, 4, 164–171.

Ofsted (2013) *Not Yet Good Enough: Personal, Social, Health and Economic Education in Schools.* London: Ofsted. Report summary available at www.gov.uk/government/publications/not-yet-good-enough-personal-social-health-and-economic-education, accessed 17 July 2017.

Pinfold, V., Toulmin, H., Thornicroft, G., Huxley, P., Farmer, P. and Graham, T. (2003) 'Reducing psychiatric stigma and discrimination: Evaluation of educational interventions in UK secondary schools.' *British Journal of Psychiatry 182*, 4, 342–346.

Public Health England (2015) *Promoting Children and Young People's Emotional Health and Wellbeing: A Whole School and College Approach.* London: Public Health England. Available at: www.gov.uk/government/uploads/system/uploads/attachment_data/file/414908/Final_EHWB_draft_20_03_15.pdf, accessed on 22 June 2017.

Ronzoni, P., Dogra, N., Omigbodun, O., Bella, T. and Atitola, O. (2010) 'Stigmatization of mental illness among Nigerian schoolchildren.' *International Journal of Social Psychiatry* 56, 5, 507–514.

Rose, D., Thornicroft, G., Pinfold, V. and Kassam, A. (2007) '250 labels used to stigmatise people with mental illness.' *BioMedCentral Health Services Research* 7, 1, 97.

Sessa, B. (2005) 'I'll have to lie about where I've been.' *Young Minds Magazine* 76, 34–35.

Singletary, J.H., Bartle, C.L., Svirydzenka, N., Suter-Giorgini, N.M., Cashmore, A.M. and Dogra, N. (2015) 'Adolescents' perception of mental and physical health in the context of general wellbeing.' *Health Education Journal* 74, 3, 257–269.

Spencer, G. (2013), 'Young people's perspectives on health: empowerment, or risk?' *Health Education 113*, 2, 115–131.

Stengård, E. and Appelqvist-Schmidlechner, K. (2010) *Mental health promotion in young people–an investment for the future.* Geneva: World Health Organization.

Svirydzenka, N., Bone, C. and Dogra, N. (2015) 'Schoolchildren's perspectives on the meaning of mental health.' *Journal of Public Mental Health 13*, 1, 4–12.

Tennant, R., Goens, C., Barlow, J., Day, C. and Stewart-Brown, S. (2007) 'A systematic review of reviews of interventions to promote mental health and prevent mental health problems in children and young people.' *Journal of Public Mental Health 6*, 1, 25–32.

Weare, K. and Nind, M. (2011) 'Mental health promotion and problem prevention in schools: What does the evidence say.' *Health Promotion International 26*, S1, i29–i69.

Weist, M.D. and Murray, M. (2008) 'Advancing school mental health promotion globally.' *Advances in School Mental Health Promotion 1*, 2–12.

World Health Organization (WHO) (2016) 'Mental health: Strengthening our response.' Available at www.who.int/mediacentre/factsheets/fs220/en, accessed on 23 March 2017.

CHAPTER 17

Training and Child Mental Health

In this chapter, we present some skills that, in our experience as trainers and educators, are key skills that anyone who attends training in child mental health should aim to develop. We then cover training at the following levels:

1. Mental health awareness – suitable for all staff

2. Basic mental health training – suitable for staff with a particular role to attend to the needs of children; for example, special needs teaching leads, those leading mental health training in schools, and those promoting mental health in schools

3. More in-depth training for those with wider roles.

Those working directly in assessing and delivering child mental health require significantly more training.

It is beyond the scope of this chapter to cover curricula design and delivery. However, we will outline the levels of training to meet student need for different levels of service delivery. It is important that before any professional delivers any training on child mental health at any level, they should have the appropriate skills and understanding of the subject to do this without putting children at risk. Parents and young people are now often key partners in developing and delivering training – however, the scope and purpose of this needs to be clear and they need to be supported by skilled professionals to undertake this role.

As discussed in Chapter 1 most, if not all, professionals working with children, adolescents and families will come across children and adolescents who are experiencing mental health problems, given the high prevalence of these. This is irrespective of whether a professional working directly with children on the front-line considers it their role to deal with these issues. The rising prevalence of problems and an international shortage of specialist professionals in this area mean that, to ensure children's needs are met, training needs to be more widely provided. Within specialist services, child psychiatrists and child psychotherapists are often the only staff to have had specific child mental health training, with each training for three years, although the training is different for these two professions. Professionals of other disciplines may have had clinical placements in child mental health, or have undertaken additional specialist training, and these courses will vary in length and content. Training varies across different contexts. However, most child mental health care is not delivered by staff who have been specifically trained in the discipline.

Before we discuss the different levels of training we consider the skills needed by those devising and delivering such training.

Training trainers in child mental health

In this section we identify some skills required of trainers in child mental health (for example, some quality assurance mechanisms). The rationale for this is to ensure that those offering such training are skilled both in training and in child mental health. Unfortunately, a significant amount of the training available in child mental health is delivered by individuals whose expertise in child mental health is limited.

Anyone who is responsible for delivering training in child mental health should ensure that they have the necessary teaching skills. Training is available to support practitioners to be effective trainers; we have developed courses with the outcomes outlined below (Dogra 2003). The aim is to provide the principles and useful strategies to ensure that the training delivered is effective.

Learning outcomes for trainers

By the end of the training session delegates should be able to:

- describe the principles of effective training

- develop learning objectives for training in child mental health

- describe a model employed to teach basic child mental health awareness

- critically evaluate the objectives of the model presented

- compare and contrast the advantages and disadvantages of the delivery methods used to meet particular objectives

- justify individual approaches for child mental health training

- identify individual strengths by considering participants' own learning and teaching styles.

- apply the principles described to other training situations.

A trainer having the skills above should be able to develop basic training in child mental health and deliver it effectively. Staff involved in delivering training should be able to demonstrate their training skills.

Any training approach needs to be developed with an appreciation of sound educational and training practice principles with adults, which include:

1. Employing active rather than passive learning techniques.

2. Clear and achievable learning objectives, of which the outcome is measurable.

3. Training that is relevant and useful to those receiving it.

4. Using a variety of teaching methods that enable the learning objectives to be effectively met.

5. Encouraging and facilitating trainees to arrive at appropriate solutions rather than just providing information. Trainees may also need to be challenged and encouraged to incorporate reflection in their learning as they often do in their practice.

6. Building on the experience and skills that the trainees already possess.

7. Training should be enjoyable.

8. Awareness of practical limitations such as time, and facilities available.

(based on Reece and Walker 2007)

It is also important to be aware of the diversity of the potential trainees and ensure that the training takes into account different learning styles and abilities. Training staff should be encouraged to have their educational practice observed to ensure that they continue to develop their skills. Being an expert in a subject does not necessarily translate into being an excellent trainer. Co-facilitating workshops can be an excellent way of developing and honing skills as there is an opportunity to learn from colleagues, and to receive and give feedback.

With technological advances, more and more training can now be offered online. However, it is important to be aware that students working alone on a computer (even with interactive programmes) will have a different experience than if they were learning face to face. Online learning gives limited opportunities for students to be challenged. In these situations, it can be helpful for students to learn with peers so that they are able to discuss their learning and hear other perspectives. This is particularly important for learning that focuses on student perspectives and skills.

Trainees are likely to come with different levels of experience, so, at the beginning of training, depending on time frames available, it may be useful just to check out what they are expecting. This does not have to be a detailed exploration of their experience, but a quick show of hands. Unless the training is bespoke, trainers may have had limited opportunity to liaise directly with the potential audience beforehand. Again, email communication may make this more feasible.

Basic child mental health awareness

It is recommended that anyone working with children should have some basic awareness of child mental health. It is likely that many of those working with children will have some experience of mental health, either direct experience or indirectly from less close contexts. In our experience, despite the increasing presence of mental health in the media, it remains a challenging issue for many to consider. Stigma, as we discussed earlier, remains a common barrier for people to be able to be open to and address regarding their own preconceptions and biases. In developing mental health awareness, it is important for trainers to be aware that they may be far more comfortable in this area than their trainees, as they have chosen to work in the area and/or have had time to develop a more positive approach. Trainees need to feel supported and be able to share their views honestly without fear of being judged. When trainees hold stigmatising views about mental health, these should be challenged, but it is important to do this in a sensitive way which seeks to educate rather than chastise. Awareness training therefore needs to include an opportunity for learners to consider their understanding of mental health and where their information has come from and how their perspectives have developed. There can be pressure on trainers to provide information as many learners are more comfortable with concrete knowledge. However, knowledge is contextual and trainers need to ensure they can justify the stance taken without being defensive. Often when the rationale is explained, delegates open up to the training. The outline below is presented as a possible template, but trainers should feel comfortable in developing training collaboratively with the audience, if there is the opportunity to do so.

Specific objectives for mental health awareness workshops

By the end of the training sessions delegates should be able to:

- evaluate their personal views of mental health and illness

- outline a basic understanding of major mental illness

- outline some behaviours that might be indicative of mental health difficulties

- begin to differentiate between mental health problems and common experiences, such as distress

- demonstrate an understanding of their own limitations in terms of their skills

- demonstrate an understanding of their own limitation in terms of their remit

- demonstrate a better understanding of appropriate referral to sources of support.

This approach has been successfully used across a range of different contexts (for example Dogra 2000) and has been applied to mental health training for secondary school staff (Svirzydenka, Aitken and

Dogra 2016). It is best to set aside two to three hours to allow students to discuss, challenge themselves and reflect, but even this short amount of time is often considered too long! The first three outcomes have been used to develop mental health promotion approaches for children and this is discussed in the next chapter.

Objectives for basic child mental health training

In this section, we offer a template for basic training for those for whom mental health awareness is not sufficient. There can be a tendency to expect learners to identify suitable training or build up their own training. The challenge with this approach is that they may focus on specific disorders without having a general framework to fall back on. Making sense of specific disorders without having a basic understanding of the important relevant factors may be more difficult. It would be like starting to read this book from halfway rather than at the beginning. The approach below was developed to support medical student training in child psychiatry (Dogra 1999). Since the original course was developed, modifications have been made to reflect curricula changes. The teaching was supported with specifically made video footage to ensure that students gained a wide exposure to clinical material. Below we offer some potential learning outcomes and how these might be met as a two-day programme. Ideally, training sessions should be staggered to allow students to reflect and therefore build their understanding of the issues between sessions. However, pragmatically, this is not always feasible, especially if courses are not local.

Specific objectives

By the end of the course delegates should be able to:

- define mental health

- evaluate their personal views of mental health and illness

- demonstrate an understanding of their own limitations in terms of their skills

- demonstrate an understanding of their own limitation in terms of their remit

- recognise the diversity of families and evaluate the importance of families to individuals

- recognise that development continues throughout the lifespan and is highlighted in child psychiatry

- describe the following aspects of development – social, emotional, cognitive and moral and also describe family development in the local context

- recognise the multifactorial causation of child psychiatric problems

- demonstrate that psychosocial components are important in childhood problems and recognise that these are not necessarily pathological, and begin to differentiate young people who may have mental health problems and those who may be distressed

- outline some behaviours that might be indicative of mental health difficulties

- observe, describe and apply some of the skills needed to interview children and/or their families

- describe the common psychiatric disorders of childhood

- outline basic treatment/management strategies employed in child psychiatry.

Example programme of a course in basic child mental health

Day one

9.30 – 10.30   Defining mental health and common misconceptions

10.45 – 11.30 Indications for concern

11.30 – 12.30 Case scenarios

Day two

9.30 – 10.30   Child development

10.30 – 11.15 Family development

11.30 – 12.30   Life events that impact on the mental health of young people and aetiology

1.30 – 3.00   Assessment of child psychiatric problems

3.15 – 4.45   Common presentations

Day three

9.30 – 12.30   Overview of treatments, with strategies that can be used in primary care, such as: parenting, behavioural management, relaxation techniques, support and reframing

This type of programme was successfully modified for international contexts (Dogra *et al.* 2005). Again, it is crucial to ensure the principles of effective training are applied and that as much of the learners' experience is incorporated into the programme as possible.

Specialist training

Any professionals regularly working with children who have mental health problems are likely to benefit from more extended training. We suggest some broad learning outcomes below but each session would need specific outcomes. The rationale is to first provide trainees with a sound academic knowledge base of the factors that influence child mental health and enable them to effectively question the basis of their understanding and perspectives and to build on these. The areas covered are:

- setting the context

- child and family development

- the aetiology of child mental health problems

- assessment in child mental health.

The emphasis is on a sound theoretical knowledge of *normal* development and critical analysis of the theories of development.

The second part aims to provide a sound and thorough understanding of key disorders in child mental health and their management. It considers the group of mental health problems that can occur in childhood and adolescence as well as considering specific common disorders/problems and their management. There is an overview of strategies available with an emphasis on planning management with effective resource use. For trainees working in universal services it is important to consider in more detail those strategies that can be applied by non-mental health professionals and those for which specific training is required.

This training approach has a coherent framework and follows the structure of this book. Those working in specialist child mental services should consider this level of training as a minimum standard to be effectively able to carry out their roles.

The broad learning outcomes of the training at this intermediate level are that students should be able to:

- compare and contrast how mental health and illness are understood in different contexts and cultures

- evaluate the impact of sociological and legal factors on how mental health is formulated

- describe child and family development and evaluate the strengths and limitations of the different explanatory theories

- describe and critically evaluate the relevance of biological, psychological and social aetiological factors in child mental health

- describe the different components of an effective child mental health assessment

- reflect on their own assessment skills and those that need further improvement

- describe the presentation of some common child mental health problems

- describe the key principles of commonly used therapies, including behaviour therapy, cognitive therapy, social skills training, family therapy and family work and counselling support

- identify those problems that can be managed in primary care and those that need referral to more specialist services

- apply the learning from the module to their own practice

- critically evaluate their organisation's role in the management of children with multiple needs.

Evaluation

It is important that any training delivered is evaluated. Most often trainees are asked whether the training has been enjoyable and/or useful. Although this information may be useful in describing the acceptability of training and how it is received, it is also important to know how effective training is and whether staff are able to apply the training and are subsequently more able to meet the needs of children with mental health problems. This is more difficult to measure: the core issue is whether the training specifically and measurably improved the delivery of healthcare. There may be multiple perspectives on this, including those of the professionals who undertook to be trained, their managers and colleagues, the families with whom they work, and related agencies. The impact of training on healthcare delivery may also be mitigated by other factors, such as provision of regular supervision, the culture of the organisation within which the professional works, local community approaches, and competing demands on service delivery. Supervision is an important component of support for staff and each organisation needs to ensure that appropriate support is provided to staff to ensure they carry out their roles safely.

References

Dogra, N. (1999) 'The development of an undergraduate course in child psychiatry.' *Medical Teacher 21*, 2, 184–192.

Dogra, N. (2000) 'Mental health awareness training: A pilot programme for university staff.' *The International Journal of Mental Health Promotion 2*, 4, 29–34.

Dogra, N. (2003) 'Training trainers to teach child mental health.' *Journal of Interprofessional Care 17*, 2, 200–201.

Dogra, N., Frake, C., Bretherton, K., Dwivedi, K. and Sharma, I. (2005) 'Training CAMHS professionals in developing countries: An Indian case study.' *Child and Adolescent Mental Health 10*, 2, 74–79.

Reece, I. and Walker S. (2007) *Teaching, Training and Learning: A Practical Guide (5th edition)*. Sunderland: Business Education Publishers.

Svirydzenka, N., Aitken, J. and Dogra, N. (2016) 'Research and partnerships with schools.' *Social Psychiatry and Psychiatric Epidemiology 51*,1203.

CHAPTER 18

Exercise and Case Study Solutions

Chapter 2: Meeting the Mental Health Needs of Young People

Exercise 2.3: Mapping local services

Draw up a list of local resources that you are aware of for addressing the mental health problems of young people, and services for parents to enable them to parent and support young people. To your list add the problem or issue that the resource addresses, and how to contact them.

Specimen Answers

Services	Appropriate problems	Contact details
CAMHS	Overdoses, deliberate self-harm, depression, eating disorders, psychosis, severe anxiety, severe phobias	
School health service	Emotional and behavioural difficulties in school-age children	
Health visitors	Behaviour problems, e.g. sleep, tantrums	
Telephone information services	Help given	Contact details
Young Minds Parent Information Service	Advice to parents on concerns relating to their children's mental health	
Parentline	Advice on parenting; specialises in divorce and separation issues	
Childline	Free helpline for children or young people in trouble or danger	

Chapter 3: Assessing the Mental Health of Young People

Exercise 3.1: Potential difficulties when interviewing young people

When the young person has difficulty in separating from parents

This is usually best managed by reassurance. It is inappropriate to insist on seeing a young child alone unless there are clear indications for doing so. The child can usually be engaged with the parent present, and the relationship built up over time.

When seeing an adolescent, it is useful to give the young person the choice. If, however, the assessment is being hindered by not seeing the young person alone, the professional can set that as a goal. Explain why it is appropriate to see the young person alone; it is usually helpful to frame it in terms of development (i.e. during adolescence young people should begin taking more responsibility for themselves, and part of this is learning to present their perspectives independently from their parents).

When the parent is anxious about the interview

Clarify reasons for anxiety and address these as appropriate; for example, the parent may be anxious that you are going to take their child away, criticise their parenting or give the child permission to do what they want.

When the young person is the one who makes the decisions in the family

It is useful to be clear, consistent and firm about who is in charge. It can be helpful to model appropriate strategies to the parents. Avoid becoming critical or angry with the child. It is useful to employ the strategies described in behaviour therapy (Chapter 14). Also, explain why the parents need to be seen separately and that they too have rights to be heard just as young people do. Courtesy and respect from professionals is due to all members of the family.

When the young person refuses to cooperate

Resist becoming impatient and be flexible in your approach. Try talking about a neutral topic, such as the young person's interests, hobbies or strengths. Acknowledge that the interview might be difficult for the young person and that they might prefer to be elsewhere. Gently try to explore their perceptions, but avoid becoming part of a game where the less the young person cooperates the more you go out of your way to accommodate them. It may seem helpful, but in the long term the young person learns inappropriate ways to engage professionals. Let the young person know why you need their cooperation.

When the young person or their parents are hostile, rude or aggressive

Set clear boundaries and rules. As a professional you do not have to tolerate abuse. Remain calm and firm. If you have any concerns for your safety, terminate the interview and rearrange to see the young person or family with a colleague.

The key principle to managing all difficult scenarios is to remain professional in your manner, which should above all be consistent and firm. There is a need to be flexible in your approach to young people and their families, but make sure that being flexible does not mean there is no consistency in your approach.

Case study: Tim (see page 45)

As a primary care worker what strategies would you employ to engage Tim?

In addition to the strategies outlined in interviewing young people, there is a need to work with other primary care staff to ensure that Tim is getting a consistent message about the importance of referral to CAMHS. Staff should avoid taking Tim on in an open-ended way as it may then be difficult to contain anxieties about him. It is useful to agree to see Tim for a fixed number of sessions to work up to a referral.

Case study: Samuel (see page 50)

How would you respond?

Establish if there are any concerns about what might be discussed and possible outcomes, such as making the situation worse, unclear boundaries to the meeting, potential for violence during or after the meeting. Clarify the purpose of the meeting; offer the option of the parents or individuals being seen on their own at some point in the session.

How to engage with Sam and his father in the session

Asking each member of the family in turn what they are most worried about might engage them more in the session and at the same time add to your understanding of the situation.

Chapter 4: Child and Adolescent Development

Case study: Sunil (see page 73)

What concerns did Sunil have, and what are the related developmental issues?

Sunil was grieving the loss of his grandparents. Their death was sudden and unexpected, so he had no time to prepare – there was no opportunity for anticipatory grieving. He would have a concept of the permanence of death, and the beginnings of an understanding of the beliefs associated with death in his culture. He would have to learn some of these along the way.

He was beginning to learn that death can be associated with taboo. In this instance, this is intimately related to family development, as the family suddenly found itself having to adapt to a new task.

He was also concerned that he may have caused the death of his grandparents. Children of this age can have egocentric views of the world such that they perceive events affecting them or caused by them. Beliefs originating at this age may persist beyond this phase of development, but he was able to address these in counselling.

What is the role of a specialist CAMHS in a presentation like this?

There need not be mental health problems that require direct specialist contact. Simple advice about the appropriate source of counselling would have sufficed, though an assessment was offered and this was able to exclude a serious mental health problem. CAMHS and a primary care mental health worker (PCMHW) can give advice about the developmental aspects of uncomplicated issues like this and determine need for specialist assessment following consultation.

Case study: Alison (see page 77)

What would you do?

Talk with her, and undertake a broad assessment to try to identify if this is just a phase, whether something has happened or whether this is more serious.

What might Alison's lack of interest be related to?

This could be depression, substance misuse, a life event (parental separation, separation from a girl or boyfriend, etc.), peer relationship difficulty, having difficulty with increased educational demands, or developmental and related to issues around trying to develop a sense of self and prioritise what matters to her.

After talking to Alison, you think she is struggling with aspects of her sexuality. What would you do next?

Sensitively say that it appears to you that she is unsure about some thoughts she is having (it is important to leave enough space for her to say that you may have got it wrong as she may not yet be ready to deal with the issues). If she agrees, it will be helpful to create an opportunity to talk further and give her contact details of local resources to help her deal with the issue. If she denies that that is the case, accept that, but then offer to meet with her again as this helps her establish that you are not judging her and are open to her confusion. It may take time for young people to discuss issues relating to sexuality and sexual orientation.

Case study: Julie (see page 81)

Who should next assess Julie?

Initially an assessment should be made of Julie's academic abilities by the school's special educational needs coordinator, and subsequently by an educational psychologist. She needs a developmental assessment by a community paediatrician.

What is the likely diagnosis?

Learning disability (generalised developmental delay) needs to be excluded.

Why do you think Julie's mother sought so many explanations for her difficulties?

She may have difficulty in accepting the developmental difficulties her daughter has and is looking for alternative explanations, particularly ones that may be treatable.

Why do you think Julie had so many non-specific physical ailments?

These ailments kept her off school: she may have realised that she was behind compared with her peers, and she may have been teased. Her parents colluded in keeping her off school, and may have been unable to recognise the significance of the symptoms.

What interventions would you recommend?

Educational assessment to determine whether her needs are best met in a special school or unit. Address parental anxiety about her ability, including the realities of this. Foster a positive approach to identifying and enhancing her skills, which may include activities of daily living that her parents do for her.

Chapter 5: Family Development

Case study: Nigel (see page 90)

What lifecycle issues, both predictable and unpredictable, can you identify and how might they be affecting Nigel and the family?

Nigel is moving towards the transition of leaving home but he is struggling with the dilemma of also wanting to stay at home to support his parents. His mother has recently experienced a transitional stage in her own life cycle: becoming a carer for her father and, to some extent, her husband. She also faces the prospect of her last child leaving home soon.

Nigel's father may be struggling to adjust to his unexpected new circumstances and failing health. The family are having to deal with a range of transitions and Nigel is likely to be feeling overwhelmed by the various issues.

Chapter 6: What Causes Mental Health Problems in Young People?

Case study: Leanne (see page 109)

Consider what Leanne's anxiety might be related to.

On assessment it became clear that Leanne only felt free from symptoms of anxiety when at home with her mother and was worried about leaving her mother in case she became ill again.

Chapter 9: Emotional Problems

Case study: Richard (see page 140)

What should the school nurse also enquire about?

The following should be explored:

- What other worries has Richard got?

- Would he like to talk more about his grandfather and who with?

- How have other members of his family responded to his grandfather's death?

- Has anyone said anything that confirms his worries?

- How is he feeling at the moment? Mostly sad or mostly happy?

- What is his explanation for what is happening?

- Have there been times when Richard has felt down on himself or that life is not worth living or thought of harming/killing himself?

- Has he been bullied?

How should Richard's concern about telling his parents be approached?

Comment on the fact that although he says it's 'silly', he has still been able to talk with the school nurse. Ask him if a friend came to him with similar worries, what his advice would be to his friend. Explore why he would want his parents to know. Explore how they (or other family members) could support him through this. Ideally work towards Richard telling his parents, perhaps with the nurse present if he wishes.

What specific interventions should be made?

Engage him in a trusting relationship – using the skills of listening and reflecting on his comments. If there are thoughts of self-harm, engage local specialist CAMHS. Allow him time to talk through his worries, and identify ways in which Richard can reassure himself.

Case study: Tom (see page 147)

Identify the likely distorted cognitions that Tom may have.

He may:

- be hypervigilant to external cues (events and situations beyond his immediate control) and internal cues (physical features of anxiety and other thoughts of self-doubt) that suggest potential failure, and selectively exclude those that suggest success

- generalise from specific examples – for example, if he makes a common mispronunciation, he may then conclude that he is incompetent at public speaking

- catastrophise – for example, see his physical symptoms as a sign of impending serious illness, or death.

These features may all be enhanced by negative self-talk. These should not be suggested to him, but explored as possibilities.

How would you help him to identify these?

Ask Tom to describe instances when he feels anxious, what was happening before and what he was thinking or what was going through his mind. This may be assisted by keeping a diary of events, thoughts and feelings.

Case study: Jodie (see page 151)

As the school nurse, what further information might you like?

You need to get fuller understanding of Ms Mortimer's concerns as well as Jodie's school and educational history. You also need to establish Jodie's developmental history and a detailed family history.

What would you do next?

You need to discuss the separation with Ms Mortimer and its impact on Jodie, without attributing blame: it may be useful to explain Jodie's behaviour in the context of life events she has experienced. It is important to support Jodie and address the issues around the separation, rather than to see the unhappiness or the learning as the problem. However, it is important that Ms Mortimer's concern about Jodie's learning be addressed. It may also be important to monitor Jodie's progress and if, after the adults have addressed the issues appropriately, Jodie remains unhappy or withdrawn, it would be appropriate to discuss her with a primary mental health worker, if there is one in the area, or with the local CAMHS.

Chapter 10: Behavioural Problems

Case study: Jacob (see page 158)

What should the health visitor do?

Assess and clarify the situation first. Obtain specific examples of the behaviours that Jacob's mother is complaining about and explore what strategies she has used to address these. It may be useful for the health visitor to spend some time with Ms Collins explaining useful strategies for dealing with Jacob's outbursts, such as giving praise for good behaviour and using techniques like time out (see section on behaviour therapy in Chapter 14). Ms Collins would also benefit from putting his behaviour into perspective – she has recently had a very difficult time, and Jacob is possibly reacting to his father leaving. The health visitor could suggest some useful activities to undertake with Jacob, to enable Ms Collins to talk through his worries with him about the absence of his father. Some drawing exercises or play techniques may be useful, and at the same time will help Ms Collins to spend some quality time with her son.

What would you do differently if Jacob's father were still part of the family?

It would be useful to see Jacob's parents together to make sure that they do not undermine each other. It can be difficult to see separated parents together if the relationship is acrimonious, but it can help highlight that, irrespective of their relationship, they both remain his parents and need to work together for his benefit. It may be useful to meet them together with and without Jacob present.

Case study: Jack (see page 170)

What behavioural techniques has Jack's mother unwittingly used that have encouraged the biting?

She has used one of the most potent techniques for encouraging behaviour: intermittent reward; that is, Jack on some occasions receives her approval as she is amused by it (children are keen to seek adult approval, especially that of parents), and on other occasions receives her attention, albeit shouting at him. She also models the behaviour for him.

How effective are the techniques that she has used to discourage the biting?

Shouting, slapping and repeated telling off have only short-term, if any, impact on changing behaviour.

How should this be further assessed?

Use an ABC chart as part of the functional analysis – this will give clear examples to the mother of how Jack's behaviour is shaped. This can be done in school and at home.

What is this assessment likely to demonstrate?

That there are rewards for Jack when he bites other children.

Outline an intervention to reduce the frequency of biting.

The consequences of biting other children need to be clear to Jack and to be consistent. There should be a swift withdrawal of an identified privilege following an incident of biting. Jack could also be rewarded for periods in the day when he has not bitten – say, by use of star chart and praise (i.e. positive attention).

Does Jack's grandmother have a role to play, and if so what?

Her role should be explored. If she dotes on Jack, she may be unable to accept that he behaves in this way. There is potential for members of the extended family (unwittingly) to undermine interventions. If this is the case, she should be involved in the planning, or other means of preventing her from 'blocking' should be explored.

What advice should be given to the school?

The same advice as is given to parents. The school should be able to identify how the behaviour programme fits into school regime. Liaison with an educational psychologist may be needed.

Chapter 11: Neurodevelopmental Disorders

Case study: Oliver (see page 181)

If you were Oliver's teacher, how might
you approach this with the parents?

Validate their concerns and identify the commonalities of concerns at home and school about Oliver's behaviour. Name those features that are related to inattention, impulsivity, and hyperactivity and encourage the parents to seek an assessment of this – it is inappropriate to make a diagnosis at this stage.

Who else might you discuss this with?

The school's Head Teacher and Educational Psychologist, with parental consent.

What would be the most appropriate
service to refer Oliver to?

The local child and adolescent mental health service.

Who might be best placed to make this referral?

Referral for assessment could be made through the family's GP or the school's Educational Psychologist.

How might you be involved in Oliver's
ongoing management?

- Assessment – provision of a school report on Oliver's learning, behaviour, and social interactions; possibly completion of standardised scales about ADHD / behaviour provided by the CAMHS; facilitating any visits in the class room by CAMHS staff / Educational Psychologist.

- Ongoing management – implementation of classroom interventions aimed at facilitating schoolwork in face of ADHD symptomotology (e.g. desk location, structuring time, re-presentation of information and instructions) and addressing complications to ADHD (e.g. provision of socialisation programmes); provision of feedback on the effectiveness of interventions.

Case study: Peter (see page 186)

Peter's parents decide to chat about him with the nurse at their local Health Centre. How should the nurse advise them?
Validate their concerns. Make an initial assessment of development and behaviour, and suggest that they should discuss a referral to a specialist clinic for developmental assessment with their GP.

What form of assessment should be planned and what investigations undertaken?

Ideally a multidisciplinary multiagency assessment comprising a full history from informants (caregivers, preschool teachers), physical and mental state examination, evaluation of functional abilities, observation in multiple settings, and communication and language assessment should be undertaken. Investigations would include: psychometric assessment, physical investigations (Electroencephalogram (EEG), vision and hearing assessments, genetic testing, and possibly metabolic tests).

What is the most likely diagnosis?

Autism needs to be considered as the most likely diagnosis, along with other pervasive developmental disorders. A comprehensive assessment might take several months and indeed some aspects of the developmental assessment would necessarily be postponed. What could be achieved in the interim? An assessment of Peter's current needs and an early educational and supportive intervention package tailored to meet his individual needs does not need to be delayed while awaiting a full assessment.

Chapter 13: Mental Health Disorders

Case study: Tim (see page 204)

What should the management plan include?

A thorough assessment should first be made, including assessment of deliberate self-harm and suicidal ideation. In the first instance, counselling to address issues of self-esteem, social confidence, effective problem solving and managing relationships should be undertaken. If this fails to result in early remission of symptoms, then the biological features suggest that medication is useful, and an SSRI is best prescribed. Cognitive behaviour therapy to address negative cognitions should be undertaken in conjunction with this.

Case study: Simon (see page 215)

Simon's parents come and meet with you to express their concerns. How would you manage this?

Take their concerns seriously and try to see if they can get Simon to see his GP. If there are any concerns about safety, a home visit by the GP may be the only way an assessment is possible.

After some persuasion, Simon agrees to meet with you. What are the key areas that you would need to ask Simon about?

You need to clarify whether he has any change of mood, thoughts of harm to self or others, or suicidal ideation. Check whether he has had any symptoms of psychosis and whether he is using any substances. Also, clarify whether he has had any recent stressful life events.

What roles do the school and the GP have in supporting Simon's rehabilitation?

They may be involved in ensuring he integrates back into school. Both will need to be aware of his illness and to be educated about this and about how to look out for a relapse of symptoms. They can do a lot to support Simon. The school may find it helpful to discuss with Simon whether and how he would like to handle telling his peers. Openness in the school should be encouraged but there needs to be recognition that Simon is very vulnerable and his social skills may be altered by his illness.

What cultural issues might there be?

Most Western societies treat mental illness as a taboo subject. People with mental illness often experience greater stress and less support from the wider family group than in Eastern societies.

Case study: Nasreen (see page 219)

How would you manage the situation?

As a schoolteacher, it may in the first instance be useful to talk to the school nurse or school doctor depending on their availability. If Nasreen's health is in danger, her parents need to be called to the school so the situation can be addressed urgently. Nasreen's view that nothing is wrong should not be accepted unquestioningly. Young people who have anorexia often do not acknowledge that there is a problem.

Can the school use the Mental Health Act to get Nasreen to see a mental health professional?

No. The Mental Health Act has specific legislative purposes and can only be used by specific staff in specific circumstances. Teachers are not permitted to use the Act. The school should ensure that the parents are aware of all the concerns. If they feel the parents are not addressing the concerns, they should discuss the issue with the access social worker in the context of child protection as Nasreen may be at significant risk if she does not receive appropriate help.

What might be the specific cultural issues that need to be considered in this case?

Nasreen is likely to be a Muslim, and it is first important to check this with her. She is also likely to be of Asian origin. There may be issues if her family is traditional, in which case she may have different expectations from those of her parents about her life and how she wants to live it. Wider community issues and expectations may be more relevant. You may need to clarify relevant religious issues. But above all, avoid making assumptions and check out things you are not sure of.

Subject Index

Author Index